KIERKEGAARD SECONDARY LITERATURE

TOME VI: PORTUGUESE, ROMANIAN, RUSSIAN, SLOVAK, SPANISH, AND SWEDISH

Kierkegaard Research: Sources, Reception and Resources
Volume 18, Tome VI

Kierkegaard Research: Sources, Reception and Resources is a publication of the Søren Kierkegaard Research Centre

Kierkegaard Secondary Literature

Tome VI: Portuguese, Romanian, Russian, Slovak, Spanish, and Swedish

Edited by
JON STEWART

Routledge
Taylor & Francis Group
LONDON AND NEW YORK

First published 2017
by Routledge
2 Park Square, Milton Park, Abingdon, Oxon OX14 4RN

and by Routledge
711 Third Avenue, New York, NY 10017

Routledge is an imprint of the Taylor & Francis Group, an informa business

British Library Cataloguing in Publication Data
A catalogue record for this book is available from the British Library

Library of Congress Cataloging in Publication Data
A catalog record for this title has been requested

ISBN: 9781472477781 (hbk)

Typeset in Times New Roman
by Apex CoVantage, LLC

Cover design by Katalin Nun

Printed in the United Kingdom
by Henry Ling Limited

Contents

IV. Secondary Literature in Slovak

V. Secondary Literature in Spanish

VI. Secondary Literature in Swedish

List of Contributors

María J. Binetti, CIAFIC—CONICET ("Consejo Nacional de Investigaciones científicas y técnicas"), Federico Lacroze 2100, C1426CPS, Buenos Aires, Argentina.

Zuzana Blažeková, Trnavská University in Trnava, Hornopotočná 23, 91843 Trnava, Slovakia.

Rodrigo Carqueja de Menezes, Institute of Philosophy and Human Sciences, Rio de Janeiro State University, Rua São Francisco Xavier, 524, Maracanã, Rio de Janeiro, RJ, Brazil.

Joana Cordovil Cardoso, Instituto de Filosofia da Nova, Faculdade de Ciências Sociais e Humanas—Universidade Nova de Lisboa, Av. de Berna, 26–4° piso, 1069-061 Lisbon, Portugal.

Patricia C. Dip, Instituto de Ciencias, Universidad de General Sarmiento, Juan M. Gutierrez 1150, (1613) Los Polvorines, Buenos Aires, Argentina.

Sara Ellen Eckerson, University of Lisbon / IFILNOVA Instituto de Filosofia da Nova—Nova Institute of Philosophy, Faculdade de Ciências Sociais e Humanas—Universidade Nova de Lisboa, Av. de Berna, 26–4° piso, 1069-061 Lisbon, Portugal.

Thiago Costa Faria, Department of Philosophy, Pontifical Catholic University of Rio de Janeiro, Rua Marquês de São Vicente, 225, Gávea, Rio de Janeiro, RJ, Brazil.

Rafael García Pavón, Facultad de Humanidades, Universidad Anáhuac México Norte, Av. Universidad Anáhuac No. 46, Col. Lomas Anahuac, Huixquilucan, Edo. de México, z.p. 52786 Mexico.

Marcio Gimenes de Paula, University of Brasilia, Department of Philosophy, ICC Ala Norte, Campus Darcy Ribeiro, P.O. Box 04661, Brasilia-DF, Brazil, CEP 70910-900.

Arthur Bartholo Gomes, FAFIL—Faculdade de Filosofia, UFG—Universidade Federal de Goiás (Campus II), Goiânia, GO, 74001-970, Brazil.

Alejandro González Contreras, Fakultät der Philosophie, Universität Wien, Universitätsring 1, 1010 Vienna, Austria.

Vasco de Jesus, Unidade I&D, Linguagem, Interpretação e Filosofia, Universidade de Coimbra, Faculdade de Letras, Praça da Porta Férrea, 3004-530 Coimbra, Portugal.

Anders Kraal, Department of Philosophy, University of British Columbia, 1866 Main Mall, Buchanan E370, Vancouver, BC V6T 1Z1, Canada.

Irina Kruchinina, University of Georgia, 131 Joseph E. Brown Hall, The Department of Comparative Literature, Athens, GA 30602, USA.

Darya Loungina, Philosophy Faculty, Lomonosov Moscow State University, GSP-1, Leninskie Gory, Moscow, 119991, Russian Federation.

Matthew T. Nowachek, Marquette University, Department of Philosophy, Coughlin Hall 132, P.O. Box 1881, Milwaukee, WI 53201-1881, USA.

Azucena Palavicini Sánchez, Universidad Nacional Autónoma de México, Faculdad de Filosofía y Letras, Programa de Maestría y Doctorado en Filosofía, Circuito Interior s/n Ciudad Universitaria, Mexico City D.F., 04510, Mexico.

Oscar Parcero Oubiña, Universidade de Santiago de Compostela, Facultade de Filosofía, Praza de Mazarelos, 15782—Santiago de Compostela, Spain.

Guadalupe Pardi, Universidad de Buenos Aires, Facultad de Filosofía y Letras, Puán 480, 1406 Buenos Aires, Argentina.

Milan Petkanič, University of Saints Cyril and Methodius, Faculty of Arts, Department of Philosophy, Námestie J. Herdu 2, 917 01 Trnava, Slovakia.

Humberto Araujo Quaglio de Souza, Universidade Federal de Juiz de Fora, Instituto de Ciências Humanas, Programa de Pós-Graduação em Ciência da Religião, Rua José Lourenço Kelmer, s/n, São Pedro, Juiz de Fora, MG, 36036-900, Brazil.

Fernanda Rojas, Universidad Nacional de Colombia, Facultad de Ciencias Humanas, carrera 45 No. 26-85, Bogotá, Colombia.

Peter Šajda, Institute of Philosophy, Slovak Academy of Sciences, Klemensova 19, 813 64 Bratislava, Slovakia.

Leo Stan, Department of Humanities, York University, 262 Vanier College, 4700 Keele St. Toronto, ON, M3J 1P3, Canada.

Manfred Svensson, Instituto de Filosofía, Universidad de los Andes, Mons. Álvaro del Portillo 12455, Las Condes, Chile.

Juan Evaristo Valls Boix, Departament de Filosofia, Facultat de Filosofia i Ciències de l'Educació, Universitat de València, Avda. Blasco Ibañez, 30, 46010 València, Spain.

List of Abbreviations

Danish Abbreviations

B&A *Breve og Aktstykker vedrørende Søren Kierkegaard*, vols. 1–2, ed. by Niels Thulstrup, Copenhagen: Munksgaard 1953–54.

Bl.art. *S. Kierkegaard's Bladartikler, med Bilag samlede efter Forfatterens Død, udgivne som Supplement til hans øvrige Skrifter*, ed. by Rasmus Nielsen, Copenhagen: C.A. Reitzel 1857.

EP *Af Søren Kierkegaards Efterladte Papirer*, vols. 1–9, ed. by H.P. Barfod and Hermann Gottsched, Copenhagen: C.A. Reitzel 1869–81.

Pap. *Søren Kierkegaards Papirer*, vols. I to XI–3, ed. by Peter Andreas Heiberg, Victor Kuhr and Einer Torsting, Copenhagen: Gyldendalske Boghandel, Nordisk Forlag, 1909–48; second, expanded ed., vols. I to XI–3, by Niels Thulstrup, vols. XII to XIII supplementary volumes, ed. by Niels Thulstrup, vols. XIV to XVI index by Niels Jørgen Cappelørn, Copenhagen: Gyldendal 1968–78.

SKS *Søren Kierkegaards Skrifter*, vols. 1–28, vols. K1–K28, ed. by Niels Jørgen Cappelørn, Joakim Garff, Jette Knudsen, Johnny Kondrup, Alastair McKinnon and Finn Hauberg Mortensen, Copenhagen: Gads Forlag 1997–2013.

SV1 *Samlede Værker*, vols. I–XIV, ed. by A.B. Drachmann, Johan Ludvig Heiberg and H.O. Lange, Copenhagen: Gyldendalske Boghandels Forlag 1901–6.

English Abbreviations

AN *Armed Neutrality*, trans. by Howard V. Hong and Edna H. Hong, Princeton: Princeton University Press 1998.

AR *On Authority and Revelation, The Book on Adler*, trans. by Walter Lowrie, Princeton: Princeton University Press 1955.

ASKB *The Auctioneer's Sales Record of the Library of Søren Kierkegaard*, ed. by H.P. Rohde, Copenhagen: The Royal Library 1967.

BA *The Book on Adler*, trans. by Howard V. Hong and Edna H. Hong, Princeton: Princeton University Press 1998.

C *The Crisis and a Crisis in the Life of an Actress*, trans. by Howard V. Hong and Edna H. Hong, Princeton: Princeton University Press 1997.

CA *The Concept of Anxiety*, trans. by Reidar Thomte in collaboration with Albert B. Anderson, Princeton: Princeton University Press 1980.

CD *Christian Discourses*, trans. by Howard V. Hong and Edna H. Hong, Princeton: Princeton University Press 1997.

CI *The Concept of Irony*, trans. by Howard V. Hong and Edna H. Hong, Princeton: Princeton University Press 1989.

CIC *The Concept of Irony*, trans. with an Introduction and Notes by Lee M. Capel, London: Collins 1966.

COR *The Corsair Affair; Articles Related to the Writings*, trans. by Howard V. Hong and Edna H. Hong, Princeton: Princeton University Press 1982.

CUP1 *Concluding Unscientific Postscript*, vol. 1, trans. by Howard V. Hong and Edna H. Hong, Princeton: Princeton University Press 1982.

CUP2 *Concluding Unscientific Postscript*, vol. 2, trans. by Howard V. Hong and Edna H. Hong, Princeton: Princeton University Press 1982.

CUPH *Concluding Unscientific Postscript*, trans. by Alastair Hannay, Cambridge and New York: Cambridge University Press 2009.

EO1 *Either/Or*, Part I, trans. by Howard V. Hong and Edna H. Hong, Princeton: Princeton University Press 1987.

EO2 *Either/Or*, Part II, trans. by Howard V. Hong and Edna H. Hong, Princeton: Princeton University Press 1987.

EOP *Either/Or*, trans. by Alastair Hannay, Harmondsworth: Penguin Books 1992.

EPW *Early Polemical Writings*, including *From the Papers of One Still Living*; *Articles from Student Days*; *The Battle Between the Old and the New Soap-Cellars*, trans. by Julia Watkin, Princeton: Princeton University Press 1990.

EUD *Eighteen Upbuilding Discourses*, trans. by Howard V. Hong and Edna H. Hong, Princeton: Princeton University Press 1990.

FSE *For Self-Examination*, trans. by Howard V. Hong and Edna H. Hong, Princeton: Princeton University Press 1990.

FT *Fear and Trembling*, trans. by Howard V. Hong and Edna H. Hong, Princeton: Princeton University Press 1983.

FTP *Fear and Trembling*, trans. by Alastair Hannay, Harmondsworth: Penguin Books 1985.

JC *Johannes Climacus, or De omnibus dubitandum est*, trans. by Howard V. Hong and Edna H. Hong, Princeton: Princeton University Press 1985.

JFY *Judge for Yourself!*, trans. by Howard V. Hong and Edna H. Hong, Princeton: Princeton University Press 1990.

JP *Søren Kierkegaard's Journals and Papers*, vols. 1–6, ed. and trans. by Howard V. Hong and Edna H. Hong, assisted by Gregor Malantschuk (vol. 7, Index and Composite Collation), Bloomington and London: Indiana University Press 1967–78.

KAC *Kierkegaard's Attack upon "Christendom," 1854–1855*, trans. by Walter Lowrie, Princeton: Princeton University Press 1944.

KJN *Kierkegaard's Journals and Notebooks*, vols. 1–11, ed. by Niels Jørgen Cappelørn, Alastair Hannay, David Kangas, Bruce H. Kirmmse, George Pattison, Vanessa Rumble, and K. Brian Söderquist, Princeton and Oxford: Princeton University Press 2007ff.

LD *Letters and Documents*, trans. by Henrik Rosenmeier, Princeton: Princeton University Press 1978.

LR *A Literary Review*, trans. by Alastair Hannay, Harmondsworth: Penguin Books 2001.

M *The Moment and Late Writings*, trans. by Howard V. Hong and Edna H. Hong, Princeton: Princeton University Press 1998.

P *Prefaces / Writing Sampler*, trans. by Todd W. Nichol, Princeton: Princeton University Press 1997.

PC *Practice in Christianity*, trans. by Howard V. Hong and Edna H. Hong, Princeton: Princeton University Press 1991.

PF *Philosophical Fragments*, trans. by Howard V. Hong and Edna H. Hong, Princeton: Princeton University Press 1985.

PJ *Papers and Journals: A Selection*, trans. by Alastair Hannay, Harmondsworth: Penguin Books 1996.

PLR *Prefaces: Light Reading for Certain Classes as the Occasion May Require*, trans. by William McDonald, Tallahassee: Florida State University Press 1989.

PLS *Concluding Unscientific Postscript*, trans. by David F. Swenson and Walter Lowrie, Princeton: Princeton University Press 1941.

PV *The Point of View* including *On My Work as an Author*, *The Point of View for My Work as an Author*, and *Armed Neutrality*, trans. by Howard V. Hong and Edna H. Hong, Princeton: Princeton University Press 1998.

PVL *The Point of View for My Work as an Author* including *On My Work as an Author*, trans. by Walter Lowrie, New York and London: Oxford University Press 1939.

R *Repetition*, trans. by Howard V. Hong and Edna H. Hong, Princeton: Princeton University Press 1983.

SBL *Notes of Schelling's Berlin Lectures*, trans. by Howard V. Hong and Edna H. Hong, Princeton: Princeton University Press 1989.

SLW *Stages on Life's Way*, trans. by Howard V. Hong and Edna H. Hong, Princeton: Princeton University Press 1988.

SUD *The Sickness unto Death*, trans. by Howard V. Hong and Edna H. Hong, Princeton: Princeton University Press 1980.

SUDP *The Sickness unto Death*, trans. by Alastair Hannay, London and New York: Penguin Books 1989.

TA *Two Ages: The Age of Revolution and the Present Age. A Literary Review*, trans. by Howard V. Hong and Edna H. Hong, Princeton: Princeton University Press 1978.

TD *Three Discourses on Imagined Occasions*, trans. by Howard V. Hong and Edna H. Hong, Princeton: Princeton University Press 1993.

UD *Upbuilding Discourses in Various Spirits*, trans. by Howard V. Hong and Edna H. Hong, Princeton: Princeton University Press 1993.

WA *Without Authority* including *The Lily in the Field and the Bird of the Air, Two Ethical-Religious Essays, Three Discourses at the Communion on Fridays, An Upbuilding Discourse, Two Discourses at the Communion on*

Fridays, trans. by Howard V. Hong and Edna H. Hong, Princeton: Princeton University Press 1997.

WL *Works of Love*, trans. by Howard V. Hong and Edna H. Hong, Princeton: Princeton University Press 1995.

WS *Writing Sampler*, trans. by Todd W. Nichol, Princeton: Princeton University Press 1997.

I. Secondary Literature in Portuguese

Agustina Bessa-Luís, *Estádios Eróticos Imediatos de Sören Kierkegaard* [Søren Kierkegaard's Immediate Erotic Stages],

Lisbon: Guimarães Editores 1992, 96 pp.

Søren Kierkegaard's Immediate Erotic Stages is a play by the Portuguese author Agustina Bessa-Luís, first published in 1992, and translated into Danish in 1994.[1] It premiered in September 2008 in Oporto (with the director Roberto Merino) and was restaged in Cacilhas in June 2009 (with the director Andresa Soares). It is quite an eccentric piece, whether in the context of Agustina Bessa-Luís' work or in that of Kierkegaard's secondary literature.

Agustina Bessa-Luís (b. 1922) is one of the most prominent and celebrated contemporary Portuguese writers. She has published extensively in a variety of genres, but it is for her work as a novelist that she is more widely known. Some of her novels have been adapted for the cinema by Portuguese filmmakers such as Manoel de Oliveira and João Botelho. Her writing, combining a poetic dimension with a realistic and reflective style, is rich and eloquent and often portrays the mentality and complexity of life and relationships, especially in ancestral families and traditions in northern Portugal. Social and political analysis, often with a focus on matriarchy, a deep reflection on human life, its roots and rhythms, are among her most common themes.

Søren Kierkegaard's Immediate Erotic Stages is one of her four plays. This work has several peculiarities: being a play, it is definitely not the kind of academic study one would expect from its title, and furthermore it is a quite extravagant digression in Agustina Bessa-Luís' literary career, which is mostly devoted to the novel.[2] Deeply moved and impressed by Kierkegaard's life and writings, the author recreates the story of his engagement to Regine Olsen through the narrative plot of "The Seducer's Diary." Since one of the characters in the play is "Sören

---

I am most grateful to Professora Elisabete Sousa for all her kind suggestions, corrections, and contributions to this review.

1 Agustina Bessa-Luís, *Søren Kierkegaards Umiddelbare Erotiske Stadier*, trans. by Jorge Braga, Copenhagen: Forlaget Ørby 1994.

2 Agustina Bessa Luís has written more than 50 novels, 5 plays, and numerous prefaces, articles, and essays.

Kierkegaard," to avoid possible confusion, the character will be referred to either as "Sören Kierkegaard" or simply "Sören" throughout this article, while the philosopher will be referred to only by his family name—Kierkegaard. Also, all the character names will be written in the original Portuguese adaptations (Regina, Luísa, D. João, etc.) made by the author.

There are some references to Kierkegaard and his work in Agustina Bessa Luís' texts, but none is so explicit and relevant. Just as is the case with the choice of drama as genre, so also the theme is not one of her usual ones; she wrote several biographies and fictional biographies, all in the form of novels and all about relevant Portuguese figures, some of which were mystics or artists, which is a strong contrast with a theater play about a foreign figure, be he philosopher or theologian. It is, therefore, very important to notice that Bessa Luís' Sören Kierkegaard is first and foremost an artist and a human being with an extraordinary life.

Every character in the play lives within a complex web, where fiction, myth, and reality are entangled; the dialogues move without warning from quasi-literal translations (most of them excerpts from *Either/Or* and *Fear and Trembling*) to original text by the author, who was probably familiar with Spanish and French translations that circulated in Portuguese intellectual *milieus* from the 1940s onwards, since she is self-taught by intense and extensive reading. Consequently, although her knowledge of literature and philosophy is impressive, she is definitely not an academic—she never seems to be interested in state-of-the-art discussions, and her approach to other artists' lives and works is always, in a broad sense, literary. For her, the task of the literary artist consists in revealing important truths and questions about human nature, not because literature might be useful for that purpose, but because that is precisely its nature. In that sense, one may claim that, in writing *Søren Kierkegaard's Immediate Erotic Stages*, the author is firstly concerned with writing a good literary work. However, this by no means implies that she does not have a reading of Kierkegaard's work. On the contrary, the author herself reminds us, in the brief Foreword, that the play is the result of a "skilled and grave reading"[3] of the philosopher's work.

The action is set in Copenhagen (Acts I and III) and at the Olsen country house in Jutland (Act II), and the plot, as mentioned above, is modeled on "The Seducer's Diary"—the seducer being Sören Kierkegaard himself, who has a terrible plan to prevent Frederik Schlegel's marriage to Regina Olsen. But this narrative of seduction is thickened and enriched with significant contributions coming from the conversations Sören has with the other characters: Frederik, Luísa Heiberg, Paul Möller, the Aunt, and D. João Tenório. D. João Tenório is the usual Portuguese designation for the mythical character Don Juan Tenorio from Tirso de Molina,[4] or to Don Giovanni,[5] and he is the most peculiar character in the play. Just like Luisa, he is

---

[3] Agustina Bessa-Luís, *Estádos Eróticos Imediatos de Sören Kierkegaard*, Lisbon: Guimarães Editores 1992, p. 7.

[4] The 1630 play *El burlador de Sevilla y Convidado de Piedra,* attributed to Tirso de Molina (1571?–1648) is the first known dramatization of the myth of Don Juan.

[5] Mozart's interpretation of the myth of Don Juan, his *opera buffa*, *Il dissoluto punito, ossia il Don Giovanni,* with a *libretto* by Lorenzo Da Ponte, premiered in Prague in 1787.

perfectly aware of what Sören Kierkegaard wrote about him, and he is not very happy about it or about the fact that Sören is himself competing with him for the role of Seducer. The confrontation between the two is the confrontation between seduction through immediacy and sensuality (D. João/D. Giovanni) and seduction through reflection and discourse (Sören/Johannes, the Seducer)—the latter being stronger and ultimately more perfect. Luísa Heiberg is modeled after Johanne Luise Heiberg, the great Danish actress, about whom Kierkegaard wrote extensively.[6] Here, she appears as a kind of old friend who understands Sören's plan and ideas about seduction, even if she does not like or agree with them. It is in the dialogues between the two and with Paul—Poul Martin Møller, the poet and philosopher who was Kierkegaard's professor in Copenhagen and to whom he dedicated *The Concept of Anxiety*[7]—that the reader/spectator becomes aware of the complexity and philosophical meaning of the seduction plan.

All this makes the task of contextualizing the play in the tradition of Kierkegaard research a hard one. Nonetheless, in the first place, it seems clear that Agustina Bessa Luis' approach is a biographical one: not only is the philosopher's life her prime subject-matter, but also this life, with its contradictions, difficulties, and adventures, is presented as the primary source for his work. By carefully transforming Kierkegaard's texts into dialogues in the play, the author is able to suggest that those texts originally sprang from occasions and reflections on his life.

This impulse is set in motion by the famous story of Kierkegaard's engagement with Regine Olsen. Critics have given attention, from the start, to the events surrounding its calling off, on October 11, 1841, and the importance it might have had for the philosopher's work and thought. In the "Historical Introduction" to the Hong translation of *Either/Or*, Regine is taken to be a "special reader," one who should be able to see through the pseudonymous masks: "There was one reader, however, Regine Olsen, whom Kierkegaard wanted to discern him behind the pseudonyms, especially the writer behind the pseudonymous diary, as part of his plan to make it easier for her to part with him."[8] Bessa Luís, then, takes this step a bit further by actually presenting Kierkegaard as the Seducer, Regine as the seduced, and Frederik Schlegel (who eventually married Regine) as Edward, the Seducer's "friend." Moreover, the biographical approach is also manifest in the characters of Paul Martin Möller and Luísa Heiberg. The complexity of the presence and influence of these two figures in Kierkegaard's work has also been carefully examined and discussed,[9]

Kierkegaard considered this to be a work of absolute genius and extensively analyzed it in *Either/Or*, especially in the "The Immediate Erotic Stages or the Musical Erotic" and "Silhouettes."

6 See Kierkegaard's "The First Love" from *Either/Or*, Part One, and "A Crisis and the Crisis in the Life of an Actress."

7 *SKS* 4, 311 / *CA*, 5.

8 *EO1*, xvi.

9 See, for example, Finn Gredal Jensen, "Poul Martin Møller: Kierkegaard and the Confidant of Socrates," in *Kierkegaard and his Danish Contemporaries*, Tome I, *Philosophy, Politics and Social Theory*, ed. by Jon Stewart, Aldershot: Ashgate 2009 (*Kierkegaard Research: Sources, Reception and Resources*, vol. 7), pp. 101–67 and Katalin Nun, "Johanne Luise Heiberg: An Existential Actress," in *Kierkegaard and his Danish Contemporaries*, Tome III,

but in the play their role is basically that of Kierkegaard's confidents thus providing occasion for the public to hear the character's thought.

The novelty of the play lies precisely in its being a play, a dramatic literary work, written to be performed, needing actors and sceneries to become *actual*. Here, as in Kierkegaard's work, the form in communication is at least as important as its content—the real interest lies not only in what is written, but in how it was written. Furthermore, in a play, this form is what really allows the author to show something, to make an idea visible, manifest. And, according to the "Introduction" to the "Erotic Immediate Stages," to create a classic, an artist has to find the perfect match between the idea and its mode of expression through his or her creative individuality.[10] That might be one of the clues to the significance of this work's title. Finding the perfect unity between medium and idea, a unity that the aesthete A claims is brought to life in Mozart's *Don Giovanni*, is certainly one of Agustina Bessa Luís' concerns in giving her "readings" the form of a play. Furthermore, this strategy also brings the author closer to Kierkegaard and his world. Theater was a very important part of his life and work. As a *locus* of social interactions, as a place to see and be seen, the theater represented an opportunity for study, observation, and disguise.

Additionally, the theater was also a subject that Kierkegaard wrote about extensively.[11] By writing a play and by recreating Sören Kierkegaard as its central character, Bessa Luís is able to suggest a new perspective from which to consider the philosopher's life and work. As becomes clear throughout the text, and considering all the connections mentioned above, the author is very familiar with Kierkegaard's writings, and so her choice to create a play instead of a novel reveals, once again, a deep insight into the philosopher's thought that greatly expands and corrects a mere simplistic biographical approach. There is yet another aspect significant to this choice: the concept of repetition. A play needs to be rehearsed—and rehearsing is repeating.[12] This, in turn, brings to light the nature of theater: every performance is the repetition of a repetition.

In the Preface to his *Kierkegaard: A Biography*, Alastair Hannay remarks that theater is much more than entertainment, but rather it is a source of inspiration for reshaping what Kierkegaard gains from introspection.[13] In her *Søren Kierkegaard's Immediate Erotic Stages* Agustina Bessa Luís successfully expressed the same idea in the form of a literary intuition. This is perhaps what brings her so close to an almost intimate connection to Kierkegaard. After all, as she recalls in her short

---

Literature, Drama and Aesthetics, ed. by Jon Stewart, Aldershot: Ashgate 2009 (*Kierkegaard Research: Sources, Reception and Resources*, vol. 7), pp. 189–208.

10 *SKS* 2, 58–66 / *EO1*, 50–9.

11 See, for example, "The Tragic in Ancient Drama Reflected in the Tragic in Modern Drama," "The First Love," both from *Either/Or*, Part One, and "Crisis and a Crisis in the Life of an Actress."

12 In fact, in French, the word used to say "rehearse" is the same as "repetition": *répétition.*

13 Alastair Hannay, *Kierkegaard: A Biography*, New York: Cambridge University Press 2001, p. xii.

Foreword to the work, "Our [hers and Kierkegaard's] understanding is perfect: it does not live on prospects of marriage. It is, like Mozart's music, something so immediate that it is hardly a feeling, but pure art."[14]

Joana Cordovil Cardoso

---

14 Bessa-Luís, *Estádos Eróticos Imediatos de Sören Kierkegaard*, p. 7.

Reviews and Critical Discussions

Peixoto, Isabel, "Agustina em Palco e em Palavras Amigas," *Jornal de Notícias*, October 18, 2008.

Rodrigues, Sofia Isabel, "Obra de Agustina Bessa-Luís em estreia no palco," *Jornal de Notícias*, September 25, 2008.

Ricardo Quadros Gouvêa, *Paixão pelo paradoxo: uma introdução a Kierkegaard* [Passion for Paradox: An Introduction to Kierkegaard],

São Paulo: Editora Novo Século 2000, 317 pp.

The book by Ricardo Quadros Gouvea, *Passion for Paradox*, was published in 2000 in Brazil. Written by a Protestant theologian, it is "an introduction to the study of Søren Kierkegaard and his conception of Christian faith."[1] Works by good theologians about Kierkegaard and his relationship to Christian faith are numerous. Along these lines Silvia Walsh produced her book *Kierkegaard: Thinking Christianly in an Existential Mode.* There, the author says explicitly: "Kierkegaard found in Christianity what gave meaning and purpose to his life. The idea by which he could live or die."[2] Before her, another work in the same direction is that of David Gowens, who is equally emphatic in the purposes of his investigation: "This study should be seen as an attempt to 'think with' Kierkegaard, specifically help an approach to Kierkegaard as a religious thinker. By 'religious thinker' I understand that his thinking is about religion and, at the same time, is itself religious."[3]

Gouvêa starts his undertaking by making an overview of what is conventionally called the Golden Age of Denmark. Here we can clearly see his affinity with the view of Bruce Kirmmse, who produced the classic work *Kierkegaard in Golden Age Denmark.*[4] Obviously, in the context of his book, Gouvêa cannot do the same kind of work as that produced by Kirmmse, but he uses the latter as one of his main pillars for building a very reliable historical framework of the Danish landscape, especially in the first part of his book.

---

1 Ricardo Quadros Gouvêa, *Paixão pelo paradoxo: uma introdução a Kierkegaard*, São Paulo: Editora Novo Século 2000, p. 3.

2 Silvia Walsh, *Kierkegaard: Thinking Christianly in an Existential Mode*, Oxford: Oxford University Press 2009, p. 1.

3 David J. Gouwens, *Kierkegaard as Religious Thinker*, Cambridge: Cambridge University Press 1996, pp. 2–3.

4 Bruce H. Kirmmse, *Kierkegaard in Golden Age Denmark*, Bloomington and Indianapolis: Indiana University Press 1990.

Following the lead of Walter Lowrie,[5] Gouvêa also aims to present something which he refers to as "a very brief life of Kierkegaard."[6] However, he goes beyond Lowrie's classical views and makes use of Kirmmse's *Encounters with Kierkegaard: A Life as Seen by His Contemporaries*.[7] Here, by means of multiple testimonies of people who knew Kierkegaard, Gouvêa builds a picture of Kierkegaard's character, trying to understand it beyond generalizations and within a broader context.

The author then devotes himself to thinking about another problem: the transmission of the legacy and thinking of the Danish author. Relying mainly on Malik's theses,[8] Gouvêa analyzes, notably in a theological framework, the impact of Kierkegaard's views in the works of important theologians of the twentieth century, for example, Karl Barth and Rudolf Bultmann. It is curious to notice, through the panorama constructed by the author, how Kierkegaard ends up receiving, during almost the entire twentieth century, numerous labels that seem unsuitable to his thinking: the founder of Barthian theology, existentialism, and postmodernism.

Finally, Gouvêa reaches the central theme of his work: the elucidation of Kierkegaard as a Christian thinker. Here he provides again a general idea of how Kierkegaard's admirers and opponents built a picture of him in the twentieth century, in other words, the reception of Kierkegaard in a theological context—among liberal, conservative, and other groups. The author here seems to position himself favorably in order to recover the notion of an orthodox Kierkegaard close to the central claims of Christianity. To Gouvêa, as well as to Walsh and Gouwens, Kierkegaard is avowedly Christian, although he comes to Christianity with the use of a complex game consisting of irony as a communicative strategy, and with the use of numerous pseudonyms.

Therefore, in Gouvêa's view, there is a mistake and even a bias in the position of authors like Adorno,[9] who seems not to understand that the fact that Kierkegaard is a Christian does not diminish his philosophy but strengthens it and places him in a select group of thinkers such as St. Augustine, Pascal, and many other paradoxical Christians. Gouvêa points out:

> The reasons for Adorno's and many other's hermeneutic stumbling involve a range of passionately embraced assumptions ranging from simple prejudice against orthodoxy ("it is simply impossible for a thinker who believes in the intrinsic value of the Apostolic Creed to produce such a rich and profound work") to a more subtle inability to admit that the Christian faith has something true.[10]

---

5 Walter Lowrie, *A Short Life of Kierkegaard*, Oxford: Oxford University Press 1938.

6 Gouvêa, *Paixão pelo paradoxo: uma introdução a Kierkegaard*, p. 25.

7 *Encounters with Kierkegaard: A Life as Seen by His Contemporaries*, trans. and ed. by Bruce H. Kirmmse, Princeton: Princeton University Press 1996.

8 Habib Malik, *Receiving Kierkegaard: The Early Impact and Transmission of His Thought*, Washington, D.C.: Catholic University of America Press 1997.

9 Theodor W. Adorno, *Kierkegaard: Konstruktion des Ästhetischen*, Frankfurt am Main: Suhrkamp 1962.

10 Gouvêa, *Paixão pelo paradoxo: uma introdução a Kierkegaard*, p. 114.

Perhaps Gouvêa is right in this criticism, but he is not fully justified when we think that the same Adorno, along with, Horkheimer in *The Dialectic of Enlightenment*, conceives Kierkegaard as a paradoxical Christian. Either it seems that Gouvêa has issued an overly harsh judgment on Adorno, or that, a few years later, the German thinker changed his position. Of course, Adorno is not a theologian or an advocate of Christianity, but he manages to see the paradoxical Christianity of Kierkegaard:

> The old Italian woman who in simple faith lights a candle to San Gennaro to protect her soldier grandson is perhaps closer to the truth than the popes and archdeacons, who—unstained by idolatry—bless the weapons against which San Gennaro is powerless. But to the simple, religion itself becomes a substitute for religion. This fact has been recognized since the earliest days of Christianity, but only the paradoxical Christians, the anti-official philosophers, from Pascal by way of Lessing and Kierkegaard to Barth, made it the cornerstone of their theology.[11]

From this point, we believe that both theology and philosophy are faced with the inevitable Kierkegaardian concept of paradox. Gouvêa uses this concept even in the title of his work and vigorously defends the conception of a theology of the absurd in Kierkegaard. This is not about an irrational absurd, but an absurd in emphatic aspects of Christianity itself, established since the days of Tertullian, that is, a faith that cannot be combined with a systematic kind of knowledge, but a faith that, in itself, has something deeply absurd in it that cannot be reduced to explanations and justifications of a merely rational nature. Such an explanation will be developed by Kierkegaard exhaustively in the course of his work, but, in our view, it is the central point of the *Concluding Unscientific Postscript*, notably in what defines the task of the subjective thinker and the objective thinker, and what brings forth the impossibility of Christianity as a merely historical phenomenon. Gouvêa again enters into discussions quite internal to Protestant theology in order to locate Kierkegaard in debates on Christian issues such as sin, predestination, and Augustinian views.

The author also devotes the final chapters of his book to compose a picture of the Kierkegaardian method of indirect communication. Here his work is in dialogue with numerous researchers and, in our view, reaches a positive advancement, which even surpasses interpretations that do not seem to have understood Kierkegaard's strategy of indirect communication.[12] Such mistakes come from the first interpretations of Kierkegaard in the German context, and Gouvêa dwells so long on Adorno's error that this fact is eventually overlooked by him. Even Walter Lowrie, the classic commentator on Kierkegaard in this context, judged, for example, that the edifying discourses were works authored by Kierkegaard himself and, accordingly, superior to the pseudonymous texts. From this, we believe that Gouvêa also, somehow, seems to believe in Lowrie's thesis, since he divides Kierkegaard's work into veronymic (the works ostensibly written by Kierkegaard) and heteronymic (those written by

---

11 Theodor W. Adorno and Max Horkheimer, *Dialektik der Aufklärung*, Frankfurt am Main: Fischer 1969, p. 188; *Dialectic of Enlightenment*, trans. by John Cumming, New York: Continuum 1982, p. 179.

12 Here Gouvêa is in dialogue with Poole: Roger Poole, *Kierkegaard: The Indirect Communication*, Charlottesville and London: University Press of Virginia 1993.

pseudonyms). Such a division seems problematic and difficult to establish. Gouvea also prefers the use of the term "heteronymic," judging that, like the Portuguese writer Fernando Pessoa, Kierkegaard promotes a game that would overcome the division of pseudonyms. This is a point that deserves to be taken into account and where further investigation can undoubtedly broaden the scope of research.

Gouvêa's book does little to treat the aesthetic part of Kierkegaard, and this is perhaps due to a proper delimitation of the study. Moreover, its final chapter could certainly be expanded, but this too perhaps cannot be demanded of a work, whose focus clearly has a panoramic character. In any case, the final appendices and classifications about the Kierkegaardian *corpus* and on the heteronyms, as well as the references to the reliable literature in English used in the text, are very well organized and can help in further research.

Marcio Gimenes de Paula

Reviews and Critical Discussions

Valls, Álvaro, *Kierkegaard cá entre nós*, São Paulo: Editora Liber Ars 2012, p. 85.
— *O crucificado encontra Dionísio: estudos sobre Kierkegaard e* Nietzsche, São Paulo: Edições Loyola 2013, p. 88.

Ricardo Quadros Gouvêa, *A Palavra e o Silêncio: Kierkegaard e a relação dialética entre a razão e a fé em Temor e Tremor* [The Word and the Silence: Kierkegaard and the Dialectical Relation between Reason and Faith in *Fear and Trembling*],

São Paulo: Fonte Editorial 2009, 440 pp.

The book *A Palavra e o Silêncio* (The Word and the Silence) by Ricardo Quadros Gouvêa was published in 2002 in Brazil. The work aims to present a thorough reading of the theme of faith and reason in an analysis of *Fear and Trembling*. Gouvêa's study presents itself as one of many in which scrupulous exegetical readings of the Kierkegaardian *oeuvre* are developed, which places it in a good philosophical tradition.

Gouvêa knows that Kierkegaard himself recognized *Fear and Trembling* as the main work for which he would become known to posterity.[1] However, for reasons given both by Gouvêa and Lippitt, *Fear and Trembling* seems to have bequeathed upon its author a certain irrationalist reputation, as someone who put faith above reason and, through the story of Abraham, made room for a solitary individual to overcome the universal and the ethical, and would therefore be in favor of irrationalism and arbitrariness. Gouvêa's book presents, at the heart of its discussion, the question about Kierkegaard's position on the relationship between faith and reason, in which the author stands in contrast to irrationalist (or anti-rationalist) readings of the conception of "faith by virtue of the absurd," which Kierkegaard presents as the book's axial thesis. According to Gouvêa, the debate on the radical position of the Danish author still has the task of extirpating the roots of this kind of reading, in order to define the true place of Kierkegaard's position in the theological debate.

This article is dedicated to Halannne Fontenele.

1 Ricardo Quadros Gouvêa, *A Palavra e o Silêncio: Kierkegaard e a relação dialética entre a razão e a fé em Temor e Tremor*, São Paulo: Fonte Editorial 2009, p. 24.

Each chapter of the book is devoted to a part of *Fear and Trembling*, so that the structure of Gouvêa's book is almost identical to Kierkegaard's text, and as such it can be read mainly as an exegetical commentary. The final appendices provide a biography of Kierkegaard and a list of his works with a brief presentation of the entire Kierkegaardian *oeuvre* and the historical situation. The introduction of the text offers a definition of Kierkegaard's project as "a metaphilosophical project, a critique of the *Logos Philosophicus* in which the foundations and even the very possibility of philosophy are at stake."[2] One of Kierkegaard's motivations when writing *Fear and Trembling*, when he found himself between a confrontation with the crisis caused by the end of his engagement to Regine Olsen and the ethical questions posed by Kant and Hegel, is, according to Gouvêa, his perception of the need for a readjustment of philosophical activity "by means of a new metaphilosophy."[3] In the first chapter, and unlike the others, in which textual analysis of *Fear and Trembling* is neatly presented, Gouvêa gives a long history of the text's criticism, in which he analyzes the interpretations of authors such as Brandes, Gouwens, Malantschuk, Buber, and Perkins. From there, Gouvêa acknowledges being influenced by Louis Mackey, Robert Perkins, Merold Westphal, and Robert Merrihew Adams, among other authors who attempt to find theological rationalism in Kierkegaard's position.[4]

In this perspective, Gouvêa's point of view in respect to the debate on irrationalism is configured as eminently theological, even though he proves himself capable of a very well-grounded articulation with philosophy. In the meantime, he shows how some Kierkegaardian scholars ended up stating the irrationalist and subjectivist thesis, and positions himself against them by affirming that theological fundamentalism is ultimately to be identified with liberalism. He also develops his argument about a rational foundation of religion that should work as sufficient evidence for a rational person to have faith, and declares them contrary to orthodoxy in its core.[5] He cites as examples of mistaken interpretations authors such as Buber, Kaufmann, MacIntyre, and Gordon Marino. Gouvêa points out, among the positions of these authors, three ways to charge *Fear and Trembling* with irrationalism: ontologically, epistemologically and ethically. His critical evaluations range from positive or negative assessments; the evaluated authors include David Tracy, Louis Dupré, Vincent McCarthy, Gene Outka, Kaufmann, and MacIntyre, these latter regarding the discussion about moral irrationalism and the charge of blind authoritarianism or of having destroyed the foundations of morality.[6]

Gouvêa presupposes the adoption of hermeneutical assumptions developed by him in another of his works, called *Passion for Paradox*, in which he proposes to unravel the deep meaning of "faith by virtue of the absurd," and the submission of concepts of a more proper philosophical nature, such as anamnesis and reappropriation or repetition (*Gjentagelse*), to the theological frame, by linking them with

2 Ibid., p. 12.
3 Ibid., p. 127.
4 Ibid., p. 50.
5 Ibid., p. 90.
6 Ibid., pp. 34–8.

concepts such as salvation, grace, repentance, and forgiveness. In doing so, he even qualifies *Fear and Trembling* as a philosophical-theological text along Augustinian lines and as "a libel in favor of rationality."[7] The defense of his thesis is done by means of the contrast between appropriative repetition, Platonic reminiscence, and Augustinian illumination, as well as a presentation of how the irrationalist disguise ends by raising reason through its humiliation in the religious absurd, and by showing the exaltation of its reappropriation in its own failure in the realm of faith. Kierkegaard, therefore, defends rationality along the lines of "a *Logos* strengthened by its humiliation and exalted by its reappropriation through a dialectic with the unfathomable, the unusual, the intangible, the unspeakable, in short, a dialectic of Word and Silence."[8]

Gouvêa indeed makes an important point regarding the notion of faith in *Fear and Trembling* as a "critical tool,"[9] from which arises a "metaphilosophical reflection"[10] and a break in Hegel's ethical totality, and that calls into question "the possibility of philosophical activity in general" and "the validity and the direction of the Platonic-Aristotelian tradition as a whole."[11] Along the same lines, Kierkegaard is conceived as a kind of negative theologian for whom faith, as a critical instrument, serves as the primary disposition of a theology, the methods and policies of which have an indelibly negative character, which also determines Kierkegaard's dialectical philosophy. The role of faith in the metaphilosophical context clarifies itself to the extent that it becomes the ultimate resource when there is no other way to "justify philosophical reflection from philosophy itself."[12] It is here that the teleological suspension of the ethical movement of Abraham has its proper sense: at the end of the trial and through the double movement of faith, the *Logos* is "reappropriated as a hermeneutics of reality, with its validity assured and its rationality saved from the danger of the unhappy insanity of theoretical speculation disconnected from reality."[13]

Gouvêa argues, along the lines of John Elrod, that *Fear and Trembling* can be read as an attack on the philosophical project of the nineteenth century of reducing religion to morality, which tries to establish a delimitation of a "realm of ethical decision that is beyond the State, culture, philosophy or theology."[14] Kierkegaard's proposal of a restoration and redemption of rationality by faith seeks to "move beyond the Enlightenment critique of religion, and beyond the Hegelian *Aufhebung* of religion."[15] Thus, the irrational reading of his work commits its major mistakes when it ignores the hermeneutical keys and meta-critical guidelines of the work in the context of the Kierkegaardian *corpus*, such as the method of indirect communication

---

7 Ibid., p. 50.
8 Ibid., p. 51.
9 Ibid., p. 12.
10 Ibid.
11 Ibid.
12 Ibid., p. 242.
13 Ibid.
14 Ibid., p. 250.
15 Ibid., p. 79.

by means of a pseudonym, and, consequently, disregards the structure of the project that lies under the book's surface—although Gouvêa conceives irony as a secondary resource in Kierkegaard, to the extent that it is supplanted by humor. However, the recent attempts to safeguard Kierkegaard's work against the charges of irrationalism are, according to Gouvêa, insufficient, since they are generally tainted by readings too determined by Kantian and/or Hegelian elements, and end up reducing Kierkegaard to the Kantian ethical universalism, or reducing his dialectical operations in the discussion on Abraham's ordeal to the *Aufhebung* or to a Hegelian conception of historicality.[16] Kierkegaard, as Gouvêa tries to show, "does not see religion as dependent or subordinate to ethics. Kierkegaard sees religious faith as an autonomous category....Abraham is out—or beyond—the ethical, with a supra-ethical *telos*";[17] and in this Gouvêa even attacks the modern reconciliation of religion with the ethical as idolatry.

Another point where Gouvêa pretends to stand apart from his predecessors is in the perception of the distinctive element in Kierkegaard's dialectics, and "that what seems to have escaped the attention of the vast majority of its readers and critics,"[18] which is precisely "the establishment and enhancement of the *dialectical tension*."[19] According to him, "Kierkegaard seeks to show the immense power of this tension that never breaks up, but that 'stretches itself to its maximum,' up to its breaking point."[20] This accurate perception, although one could hardly attribute a critical originality to it, is accurate with respect to the dialectic present in the concept of the ordeal, or probation, developed by Kierkegaard in different but analogous ways in both *Fear and Trembling* and *Repetition*. In this sense, the reappropriation of rationality is seen as a restoration of a "homeostatic balance of the human spirit that implies a redefinition of the dialectic between reason and faith."[21] This has as its result, however, a certain detachment in the design of the double movement of faith by virtue of the absurd, which Kierkegaard never gets tired of emphasizing, from a properly dialectical characterization in its tension.

The return—or the repetition—of reason through faith is a common feature in Gouvêa's text, and it is used to express his rejection of irrationalism as a possible reading of Kierkegaard's work. The failure of reason and its humiliation is, in this sense, a condition of possibility for faith, which receives back reason itself, now reborn and baptized in a double movement by virtue of the absurd. The deception perpetrated by the rebel path of reason with regard to faith is pointed out by him as "the noetic effects of sin" or "the *ptomatic* condition (from the Greek *Ptoma*, *ptomatos*—to fall, a fallen object)."[22] Here he refers again to the theological debate and to an opposition to unilateralism common to fundamentalists and liberal

16 Ibid., pp. 44–5.
17 Ibid., p. 156.
18 Ibid., p. 57.
19 Ibid.
20 Ibid.
21 Ibid., p. 61.
22 Ibid., p. 97.

theologians. The possibility that Gouvêa wants to accomplish with the theological key of the debate is, as he says, a "restoration of true rationality through non-fideist faith, true faith through a non-rationalist rationality."[23] Thus, he can assert that "the double movement of faith in virtue of the absurd does not annihilate understanding. On the contrary, it releases it from those elements that restrict it and hinder its full and normal operation...[this is] a necessary step in the process that generates the restoration of the human mind living under the aegis of modernity."[24]

Rationality saved by faith through absurdity does not reduce philosophy to an *ancilla theologiae*, and it remains "rationally possible to believe by virtue of the absurd."[25] Another aspect of his critique of rationalism with respect to faith is given in its dialectical connection with its opposite; rationalism, especially since it does not recognize its own limitations in denying the category of the absurd, denies the very possibility of communication of any rational discourse, and therefore falls by itself on the edge of irrationalism. The paradoxicality of faith does not *per se* imply irrationality,[26] and the dialectical coexistence of paradox and non-paradox is what enables the tension between word and silence, without which both annihilate themselves.[27]

At the end, Gouvêa makes use of resources developed throughout the book in order to criticize postmodernism. He claims that the abandonment of metanarratives that postmodern thinkers propose is a self-contradiction because their starting point is a systemic point of view which is bankrupt and should be abandoned. Compared to the structure of repetition in Kierkegaard, the system must be assumed to appear as reduplicated in the form of a possibility for a double movement by virtue of the absurd; with the paradox there is, therefore, no shutting down of the possibility of the systemic and no "end of history" but a reopening of a renewed possibility.

Arthur Bartholo Gomes

---

23 Ibid., p. 103.
24 Ibid., p. 115.
25 Ibid., p. 204.
26 Ibid., pp. 304–5.
27 Ibid., p. 308.

Reviews and Critical Discussions

Undetermined.

Guiomar de Grammont, *Don Juan, Fausto e o Judeu Errante em Kierkegaard* [Don Juan, Faust and the Wandering Jew in Kierkegaard],

Petropolis: Catedral das Letras Editora 2003, 152 pp.

The book *Don Juan, Fausto e o Judeu Errante em Kierkegaard* (Don Juan, Faust and the Wandering Jew in Kierkegaard), by the author Guiomar de Grammont, was published in Brazil in 2003. The book gained considerable importance with regard to the consolidation of aesthetic studies on Kierkegaard in Brazil, being one of the first dissertations on this topic in this country. Prompted by Alvaro Valls, currently a translator of Kierkegaard for the Portuguese language, Grammont's dissertation became a reference for Brazilian students who were just beginning their studies in the work of the Danish author. Her work recommended itself due to the breadth of her approach, the simplicity of her prose, and the solid grounding in an intense dialogue with renowned international commentators in the field (particularly in the French literature, including names such as Pierre Mesnard, Jean Wahl, and Henri-Bernard Vergote, whose works are for the most part not translated into Portuguese). Grammont, playwright and novelist, received her Master's degree at the Federal University of Minas Gerais, and her Ph.D. in Literature at the University of São Paulo. Today she teaches philosophy of art in Ouro Preto, Minas Gerais.

In her book, Grammont offers a detailed reading of Kierkegaard's work through an aesthetic approach, and her appropriation of the philosophy of the Danish author is quite in keeping with her literary training. She conceives the figures of his thought as conceptual personifications, whose possibilities of interpretation are, in the words of Maria Esther Maciel, "a theater of multiple subjectivities, a game of masks whose purpose is not to hide a real face, but to reveal the drama of a fragmented existence."[1] Grammont proposes to reconstruct Kierkegaard's "architectural"[2] thought through the use of the characters of Don Juan, Faust, and the Wandering Jew, as well as through the way these figures build the relation of the aesthetically

---

1 Maria Esther Maciel, "Preface" to Guiomar de Grammont, *Don Juan, Fausto e o Judeu Errante em Kierkegaard*, Petropolis: Catedral das Letras Editora 2003, p. 13.

2 Grammont, *Don Juan, Fausto e o Judeu Errante em Kierkegaard*, p. 17.

determined subjectivity with its surrounding reality. It should be noted that the design of Kierkegaard's thought, with regard to the spheres or "stages" of existence, acquires, in the sense that she gives to it, an aesthetic tone, which goes beyond superficial hierarchies and emphasizes the relations between the stages of existence in a more uniform way. This allows her to bring into view the aesthetic, as it presents itself in the characters with different personalities and the pseudonyms, such as the reflective seducer and Judge William.

Although Grammont's point of view in her analysis of Kierkegaard's texts is delineated aesthetically, she cannot avoid understanding the limits of the aesthetic sphere for Kierkegaard's task of becoming an individual; the aesthetic stage must, therefore, be understood as a necessary moment of existence that nevertheless points beyond itself. From this perspective, she intends to show the importance of the three figures who embody the distinct aesthetic characters which constitute the main axis of the book. Quoting Kierkegaard, she writes:

> Representing life in its three tendencies, as it were, outside of religion, there are three great ideas (Don Juan, Faust, and the Wandering Jew), and not until these ideas are mediated and embraced in life by the single individual, not until then do the moral and the religious appear. In relation to my position in dogmatics, this is the way I view these three ideas.[3]

Therefore, it can be said that the aim of Grammont's book is characterized by a negative delimitation of the dogmatic point of view attributed to what is usually called the religious sphere, as tends to be the general trend in all aesthetic interpretations of Kierkegaard's work. Grammont's conception of Kierkegaard's indirect communication as a *paideia*, or "a dialectical method for a kind of education of the reader"[4] points to the role that Kierkegaard had arrogated to himself as a maieutic character in the service of Christianity. The role of the "three great ideas" is confirmed, thus, as an ironic feature whose negative movement points to a formative horizon beyond irony itself and which conditions it in the service of the idea, as Kierkegaard likes to say.

The author is correct to note that not only on this point but in general the aesthetic figures that appear in Kierkegaard's work show themselves as personifications of ideas that could be translated into conceptual relations; accordingly, the transition from the sphere of concepts to that of concrete existence requires the implementation of these conceptual relations in a kind of aesthetic "incarnation" of the self, in which the personality of the individual overrides the abstract nature of the concept. So Don Juan, Faust, and the Wandering Jew, to the extent that they are embodied expressions of sensuality, doubt, and despair, respectively, are aesthetic personifications of an insufficient existence that ultimately lacks a meaning of its own, and thus points beyond itself. Grammont sees the key to the possibility of developing this tripartite scheme in Kierkegaard's philosophy in its design and in its use of irony, which is also the resolution and response to the problems posed by Romanticism. Accordingly, the expression of irony as an immanent finality constitutes the fundamental operational

---

3 Ibid., pp. 19–20. *SKS* 27, 134, Papir 140 / *JP* 1, 795.

4 Grammont, *Don Juan, Fausto e o Judeu Errante em Kierkegaard*, p. 18.

nature of Romanticism; and Kierkegaard appropriates irony in the service of the idea beyond its intrinsic negativity, which enables him to develop a "typology that aims to understand the main constitutive elements of man in his internal relations and in his temporal evolution."[5]

The issue of the temporal and historical evolution of the consciousness of the individual is interpreted by Grammont in a way that it makes her cling, maybe excessively, to the aesthetic point of view, particularly because of her concept of the moment. For her, "the aesthete is someone who lives in the moment,"[6] and this concept expresses the relation with the "natural determinations and objective conditions of the world in which it operates."[7] The moment is conceived as "ephemeral" and "evanescent,"[8] as the temporally finite, in that the aesthetic figures, as well as the reader, experience "universal issues such as love, desire, loneliness and death."[9] The moment is pictured here with an aesthetic image of existence as *static*, in which "the aesthete lives suspended in an ineffectiveness, as a paralyzed man facing the dilemma of existence."[10] It is remarkable that this concept of the moment has, in the work of Kierkegaard, a meaning that goes beyond the merely aesthetic and takes on characteristic contours that match the specific sphere of existence in question. In the case of ethics, the moment becomes the condition of the decision and repentance, and, in the case of religion, the moment is when the individual is confronted with eternity by way of the paradox. The aesthetic conception of the moment is, as Kierkegaard would say, life in a "sum of distinct moments, that have no relation to each other."[11] The aesthetic character "does not provide space for retrospective feelings such as repentance: he is a slave of the present time";[12] whereas the moment in its pregnant sense, that is able to establish the religious, constitutes, as shown by Vassili Tsakiri, a "break in the immanence of time."[13] However, the author's aesthetic limits only become an obstacle insofar as her characterization of the religious bypasses the concept of the moment, which in any case is not within the scope of the book. As Grammont herself acknowledges, the conception of the individual in its full meaning should be given in the form of overcoming the aesthetic state itself, in which the mediation of aesthetic ideas in the passage to the ethical becomes indispensable, along with the establishment of religious authenticity.[14]

Thus, the traits of each figure and its representations and meanings within the aesthetic stage are defined: the presentation of Don Juan appears through the prism

---

5 Ibid., p. 19.

6 Ibid., p. 92.

7 Ibid., p. 17.

8 Ibid.

9 Ibid.

10 Ibid., p. 93.

11 *SKS* 2, 85 / *EOI*, 79. Grammont, *Don Juan, Fausto e o Judeu Errante em Kierkegaard*, p. 42.

12 Ibid., p. 42.

13 Vassili Tsakiri, *Kierkegaard: Anxiety, Repetition and Contemporaneity*, New York: Palgrave Macmillan 2006, p. 32.

14 Cf. Grammont, *Don Juan, Fausto e o Judeu Errante em Kierkegaard*, p. 20.

of sensuality and its counterpart, reflective pleasure, which is the idea of "living poetically," so typical of Kierkegaardian irony. Faust, is the one who deeply "desires eternity"[15] but lives plagued by doubt, anxiety, and skepticism derived from this; and the Wandering Jew is the personification of despair, set up as a deep anxiety and the lack of a reference point for the will, in which the idea of wandering is related to an "interchange between repose and movement," and in which despair is depicted as "the sickness of the spirit stuck in itself"[16] and as "the insult to divinity and the indeterminate waiting."[17] Through these poetic and conceptual figures, the aesthetic form of existence shows how the individual appears here as "an artificial life form, referring to a *state* more than a *being*," and "puts himself in the realm of appearances."[18] This shows Kierkegaard's intention to construct these characters as a determination of a "typology of the aesthetic stage,"[19] aimed at understanding the main constituent elements of man in their internal relations and their temporal unfolding.

Finally, the relevance of Grammont's book in the Kierkegaard literature in Portuguese should be pointed out again, particularly with regard to aesthetic studies in Kierkegaard both in philosophy and literature. In order to deepen the discussion on this topic, the approach that the book provides can be fruitful for both fields.

Arthur Bartholo Gomes

---

15 Ibid., p. 45.
16 Ibid., p. 68.
17 Ibid., p. 67.
18 Ibid., p. 70.
19 Ibid., p. 127.

Review and Critical Discussion

Maciel, Maria Esther, "Os Disfarces do Eu: Kierkegaard segundo Guiomar de Grammont," presentation of the book *Don Juan, Fausto e o Judeu Errante em Kierkegaard*, by Guiomar de Grammont, Petrópolis: Catedral das Letras 2003, pp. 13–15.

Alceu Amoroso Lima, *O Existencialismo e Outros Mitos do Nosso Tempo* [Existentialism and Other Myths of Our Time],

Rio de Janeiro: Agir 1956, 329 pp.

The exposition of Kierkegaard's thought is not the main purpose of *Existentialism and Other Myths of Our Time*, even though it is an important point among the arguments defended by Alceu Amoroso Lima. In order to have a better comprehension of this work and its goals, it is relevant to consider the place of its author in Brazilian intellectual life during the twentieth century. In doing so, it is possible to understand why Kierkegaard plays an important role in the text, and why this book's pioneering discussion about him is relevant for the history of the reception of Kierkegaard in Brazil.

Alceu Amoroso Lima was a prolific writer who published hundreds of articles and dozens of books in several fields such as religion, literary criticism, philosophy, and politics, from 1919 until his death in 1983. Born in Rio de Janeiro in 1893, Lima was educated in a secular environment strongly influenced by French culture, and had the education available to the upper classes in that time. His family could even afford some trips to Europe to study French, and in Paris he attended Henri Bergson's lectures. After his graduation in law, Lima worked for a short time as an attorney, but soon turned to writing and teaching, having given lectures in Brazil, France, and the United States. Starting with his first papers, Lima adopted the pseudonym Tristão de Athayde, with which he signed many of his articles, and by which he became famous. Raised in a secular home, Lima converted to Catholicism in 1928, and later he was recognized as an important representative of Catholic thought in Brazil.[1] His writings were influenced by the ideas of Jacques Maritain, a thinker often quoted in *Existentialism and Other Myths of Our Time*.

This book from 1956 is actually a fusion of two previously published texts. The first one, *Myths of Our Time*, was published in 1943, and the second one, *Existentialism*, in 1951. But the first book includes some texts written in 1938, and the author also included articles about existentialism written in 1941 as an appendix. In the 1943 book, Lima calls "myths" some cultural and political conceptions of that time, especially those associated with Nazism, fascism, and communism, such as

---

1 Otto Maria Carpeaux. *Alceu Amoroso Lima*, Rio de Janeiro: Graal 1978.

wealth, race, nation, or class, and he opposes to these notions his own ideas inspired by Christianity.

After the war, Lima expressed criticism about the existentialist philosophical tendencies that became popular during the 1950s, and he started writing about them, emphatically opposing Sartre, whom he called "detestable."[2] Considering that Lima's definition of myth in his previous writing includes an "attribution of an absolute value to a relative reality,"[3] he saw in twentieth-century existentialism a myth that "makes natural existence an absolute value when it is, by nature, a relative reality."[4] So, in 1956 Lima decided to publish his text on existentialism along with the previous book, adding some updating notes. It is in this context of polemic with Sartrean existentialism that Lima discusses Kierkegaard's thought.

From the beginning, Lima makes clear what he means with the term "existentialism" in the title. Influenced by Maritain, Lima claims that the authentic existentialism is the essentialist one of Christian and Thomistic inspiration.[5] The existentialism he opposes is the immanentist, atheist, and "evanecentist" one that denies the reality of essences. Against this existentialism represented mainly by Sartre, Lima presents Kierkegaard, Unamuno, Berdyaev, and Marcel, as the greatest representatives of religious existentialism,[6] mentioning also others such as Jaspers and Lavelle in some passages.

Therefore, the exposition of Kierkegaard's thought in the book is dependent on the author's purpose of refuting anti-essentialist existentialism. Kierkegaard is presented by Lima as "a very healthy reaction" against Hegel.[7] The author's perception of Kierkegaard as an anti-Hegelian thinker is often emphasized in the book, since Hegel, although considered an essentialist, is nevertheless interpreted as a monist, immanentist, and anti-Christian.[8] Lima expresses his approval for this anti-Hegelianism he saw in Kierkegaard, calling it an "admirable crusade."[9] Lima also endorses the image of Kierkegaard as the "founder of existentialism," identifying points of convergence between his thought and twentieth-century existentialism, thus acknowledging some kind of continuity from the Danish thinker to Sartre. However, he clearly accentuates the fundamental divergences between the existentialism he opposes and the religious existentialism represented by Kierkegaard.

For Lima, "Kierkegaard's effort to reinstate faith's place" in philosophy,[10] even though it is laudable, is contrary to his interpretation of the Catholic doctrine of the subject's rational adherence to truths that "exceed but do not contradict reason."[11]

---

2 Alceu Amoroso Lima, *O Existencialismo e Outros Mitos do Nosso Tempo*, Rio de Janeiro: Agir 1956, p. 75.
3 Ibid., p. 9.
4 Ibid.
5 Ibid., pp. 18–19.
6 Ibid., p. 51.
7 Ibid., p. 57.
8 Ibid., p. 127.
9 Ibid., p. 58.
10 Ibid.
11 Ibid.

So, in his interpretation of the Kierkegaardian idea of paradox, Lima sees an appeal to absurdity and to belief against intelligence. Thus, Lima develops an interpretation of Kierkegaard that perceives in his healthy reaction against Hegel the seeds that would paradoxically result in Sartrean existentialism. According to Lima, Hegel professed an essentialist but monist thought, and suppressed the distinction between God, man, and world. Kierkegaard would then be the one who came to restore the pluralism of existence, drawing attention to the substantial distinction between those three concepts. But when Kierkegaard refutes Hegelian essentialism, he does not deny the essence, and does not propose an immanentism. Because of it, Lima considers the development of existentialism, from Kierkegaardian Christianity to Sartrean atheism, as paradoxical. The perception of this paradoxical development is accentuated every time Lima presents atheistic existentialism, with its negation of any ontological foundation of existence, as the promotion of uniformity and indistinctness, in contrast to Kierkegaard's emphasis on distinction and plurality.

In his approach to the reasons why Kierkegaard is considered the founder of existentialism, Lima criticizes the subordination of the abstract to the concrete in Kierkegaard's thought, claiming that this position can lead to a false notion of abstraction, which he regards as an essential element of philosophy. Lima also sees Kierkegaard's ideas concerning the difficulties of communication of existential issues as a harbinger of the vagueness and uncertainty of twentieth-century existentialism. Furthermore, he disapproves of what he sees as a "praise of uncertainty,"[12] a primacy of aesthetics over the proper systematic and coherent way of argumentation in philosophy.

However, Lima clearly distinguishes Christian thought, including Kierkegaard, from the atheistic existentialists when these give primacy to the temporal over the eternal and to contingency over necessity. He sees in these points a fundamental distinction between thinkers like Kierkegaard and twentieth-century existentialists. Kierkegaard is often mentioned in one of the last chapters of the book in which Lima presents the aspects he considers still useful in existentialism in a broader sense. Kierkegaard is thus praised for drawing attention to existence without denying essence, for reinstating the primacy of faith, for drawing attention to the excessive rigidity of philosophical systems and for his emphasis on the individual, in which Lima sees an inspiration for the Christian humanism of Catholic thinkers like Maritain.

In Lima's book, there can certainly be found examples of misunderstandings about Kierkegaard's person and thought. Lima makes some biographical mistakes, such as when he claims that Kierkegaard was the son of a Protestant pastor, or that he was almost unknown until his death.[13] The author also does not make any clear distinction between anxiety and despair in Kierkegaard's thought, even though these themes are only superficially mentioned in the book.

However, it is necessary to notice that Lima's sources about Kierkegaard were much less abundant than those available nowadays in the languages known by the

---

12 Ibid., p. 103.

13 Ibid., p. 56.

author. Lima read Kierkegaard in French translations, and he directly quotes *Philosophical Fragments* (*Miettes philosophiques*) and the *Postscript* (*Post-Scriptum aux Miettes Philosophiques*). Considering the references made in the book, one can see that Lima learned about Kierkegaard from authors such as Jean Wahl (especially the *Études kierkegaardiennes*), Pierre Colin, Otto F. Bollnow, Régis Jolivet, Paul Petit (the French translator of *Philosophical Fragments*), Étienne Gilson, Jean Lacroix, and Theodor Haecker, in addition to Sartre and Maritain. Some of these are, according Alvaro Valls, "relatively reliable French and German interpreters,"[14] but they cannot offer the same comprehension of Kierkegaard's thought provided by the reading of his own works.

Nevertheless, Lima has the merit of being one of the first writers to present Kierkegaard's ideas in Brazil. Among the most popular Brazilian intellectuals of his time, he was surely the first to do so, even though his presentation of Kierkegaardian thought was derivative of his task, as a Catholic thinker, of fighting atheist existentialism.

Humberto Araujo Quaglio de Souza

---

14 Alvaro Valls, *Kierkegaard cá entre nós*, São Paulo: Liber Ars 2012, p. 107.

Review and Critical Discussion

Valls, Álvaro, *Kierkegaard cá entre nós*, São Paulo: Liber Ars 2012, pp. 107–8.

Marcio Gimenes de Paula, *Socratismo e cristianismo em Kierkegaard: o escândalo e a loucura* [Socratism and Christianity in Kierkegaard: Offense and Foolishness],

São Paulo: Annablume 2001, 139 pp.

Marcio Gimenes de Paula is a theologian and was made doctor of philosophy from the Universidade Estadual de Campinas for his thesis *Indivíduo e comunidade na filosofia de Kierkegaard*. He is currently teaching at the Universidade Federal de Brasília in Brazil. This particular book, *Socratismo e cristianismo em Kierkegaard: o escândalo e a loucura* (Socratism and Christianity in Kierkegaard: Offense and Foolishness) was first published in 2001 by Annablume in São Paulo, Brazil, and it is this monograph that granted the author the academic title of bachelor in philosophy.

In this early work, the author makes a case for the similarities and dissimilarities between the figures of Socrates and Christ. De Paula argues for the influence that both Socrates and Christianity had on Kierkegaard's life and highlights the development of the Dane's ideas that took shape in light of his opposition to speculative knowledge and its understanding of a finite being's relation to eternal truth. Trying to come to terms both with Kierkegaard's readings of Xenophon, Plato, and Aristophanes (as presented in *The Concept of Irony*) and with two of his pseudonymous works, *Philosophical Fragments* and *Fear and Trembling*, de Paula's book consists of an analysis of these texts. Maybe due to the fact of this being the author's first approach to Kierkegaard, the book does not engage in polemics nor does it question Kierkegaard's main theses. It remains purely descriptive and avoids being critical. Yet, it proved to be a sound contribution to the ongoing research and debate in Brazil at the time, eventually finding its place among the increasing number of Portuguese-language works devoted to Kierkegaard.

The book comprises a prefatory note written by the renowned Kierkegaard scholar in Brazil, Alvaro Valls, as well as an introductory remark and a concluding section by the author, with three main chapters in between (the first dealing with *The Concept of Irony*, the second focusing on *Philosophical Fragments*, and the third dwelling on *Fear and Trembling*).

In the first chapter, de Paula goes through the three quite different sketches of Socrates drawn in *The Concept of Irony*: those of Xenophon, Plato, and Aristophanes, and tries to devise a fourth one, namely, Kierkegaard's own portrait of

Socrates. In de Paula's opinion, Xenophon's Socrates comes through as an all too common man, indeed, as a harmless man, unworthy of the infamous gadfly epithet. It is de Paula's opinion that this particular Socrates disappears as an individual since he blends all too safely into the crowd. Devoid of passion and closer to being seen as an old man who is tired of living, Xenophon's Socrates seems completely out of character. For de Paula, as for Kierkegaard, there is hardly anything special about him.

Insofar as Plato is concerned, de Paula agrees with Kierkegaard in saying that his is a more reliable portrait of Socrates. This Socrates is fierce, fearless, and resolute, indeed, a force to be reckoned with. Plato's Socrates could not be more different from Xenophon's weakling figure. The true strength of Plato's Socrates is irony—something that in Xenophon's account is almost completely missing. De Paula focuses mainly on the *Apology* and argues for the all-consuming and powerful predatory force of Socratic irony, extending from his defenders to his accusers, encompassing the *polis* itself. In the end, no stone is left unturned. Irony overcomes everything, life and spirit alike—vanquishing even death and leaving nothing but an objective uncertainty in its stead.

Finally, it is de Paula's opinion that while Plato stressed Socrates' ironic earnestness, Aristophanes came to regard it as pure jest. In *The Clouds*, Socrates is depicted as a fake, an esoteric character, who resembles those same Sophists he denounces. If being drawn by Aristophanes' scornful and merciless pen, we were unable to look beyond the caricature, Socrates might even emerge as a great imposter, hiding the emptiness and nothingness of his own thought behind his ironic stance. Nevertheless, de Paula agrees with Kierkegaard when he says that one must come to understand Aristophanes' comic effort as a satire since Socrates does not stand his ground but rather falls prey to irony itself.

In the second chapter, de Paula tackles the *Philosophical Fragments*, a crucial text for the issue of the relation between Platonic philosophy and Christianity—a text that can be interpreted as a kind of intermediary link bridging and filling the gap between *The Concept of Irony* and *Fear and Trembling*. Here, de Paula tends to a recurring question in the whole text: how can one go beyond Socrates—at least, this seems to be implied by de Paula's agreeing with Climacus in thinking Socrates to be an extraordinary, almost insurmountable human being.

Be that as it may, the main focus now is on the categories of the moment, the occasion, decision, contemporaneity, as well as on the relation between master and disciple, time and eternity, the historical and the necessary, the possible and the actual, doubt and belief, freedom and willing, and knowledge and faith. One of the strong points is the close attention paid by de Paula to the question of truth and, most importantly, to the problem of the condition for the possibility of one's relation to (and understanding of) the truth. The themes of forgetfulness and recollection in the Platonic dialogues are put to the test in the light of the categories of the fall, sin, guilt-consciousness, and eternal happiness. There is also mention of the relations between virtue, truth, ignorance, and sin, as well as the concepts of conversion, repentance, and redemption and the acknowledgment of the relation between God and man in their absolute difference. The notion of the paradox resurfaces and is dealt with, together with that of the absurd, as an invaluable category when it comes to understanding the key role of faith and why being offended by the man-God may not be avoided or overcome. Also the insight into man's dependence on God for freedom sets the tone for the discussion of both the validity and the significance of coming into existence and its priority over essence.

In the final chapter, the discussion revolves around the possibility and the meaning of a teleological suspension of the ethical. De Paula addresses the question of the relation between the single individual and the absolute, and presents de silentio's reckoning of Abraham in *Fear and Trembling* as standing higher and above the universal. According to de silentio, either there is faith or Abraham is lost to the world. Abraham is no tragic hero, and there is no way out for him if he is to be tried in the court of ethics. Abraham is either a criminal or a witness to the truth. He either murdered Isaac or his decision to sacrifice his son must be legitimate. De Paula consistently follows de silentio's line of reasoning, considering that in the case of Abraham the temptation would be for him to relapse into the ethical. Also, Abraham cannot speak; he cannot break his silence without coming under the category of the universal. And yet, the possibility of a spiritual trial lurks in his silence. Does not Abraham's loneliness arouse suspicion? Might it not be enclosing reserve? Is Abraham a demonic figure, then? No. Everything was but an ordeal, and Abraham passed the test. He came forward before God and was willing to obey him unconditionally. He had the courage of faith not to say a word to anyone, trusting that God would be merciful. Abraham acted and did so immediately. Not doubt but faith was his point of departure for the double movement that starts with infinite resignation and ends by receiving it all back, his son Isaac and the glory he was promised in the world. De Paula then closes his final chapter by reviewing both Climacus and de silentio's main arguments and categories, setting the figures of Christ and Abraham in contrast to Plato's Socrates with a consideration of the ethical stage and the single individual.

Once having carefully read de Paula's book, someone hoping to find a more daring and challenging view on Kierkegaard's work would have appreciated a thorough discussion of the main categories as well as a proper analysis of a wider set of problems in the context of this book, for example, the issue of indirect communication and its relation to misunderstanding (extending from Socratic irony to Christ's being incognito), the theory of the stages (namely, stressing irony and humor as *confinia*), the difference between ethics in general and the ethical κατ' ἐξοχήν, the meaning of faith as a second immediacy, the key role assigned to moods, the connection between thinking and willing, and Kierkegaard's take on ἀκρασία, and so on. Also, the word "Socratism" is, too say the very least, highly disputable and completely off-putting.

Nevertheless, the overall assessment of this work must be positive. De Paula manages to establish a relation between Socratic irony and Kierkegaard's own conception and understanding of it (pointing to the limits of Socratic irony in Kierkegaard's work and to its methodological and existential implications when interpreted from the Christian point of view). Also, while comparing Socrates with Christ, he comes to see their similarity in the fact that both were extraordinary self-sacrificing individuals in times of decadence, wrongly accused and put to death. But despite these remarkable affinities and the way they stood out as single individuals throughout their lives, they are in death best seen to be infinitely different, in de Paula's opinion. Although Socrates and Christ were both passionate men, Socratic irony and erotic engagement in philosophy have little or nothing in common with Christ's love and his existential task—the one is a seducer of men, and the other their savior; the one standing as a judge of the Athenians, the other the redeemer of all mankind.

Vasco de Jesus

Reviews and Critical Discussions

Undetermined.

Marcio Gimenes de Paula, *Subjetividade e objetividade em Kierkegaard* [Subjectivity and Objectivity in Kierkegaard],

São Paulo: Annablume 2009, 143 pp.

The book *Subjectivity and Objectivity in Kierkegaard*, written by Marcio Gimenes de Paula, is the result of his Master's degree research, concluded in 2002 at the State University of Campinas, Brazil. His Master's dissertation is entitled *Subjectivity and Objectivity in the Debate between Socratism and Christianity in Kierkegaard: An Analysis of the Postscript.* It is substantially the same work issued by the publishing house Annablume in 2009, the purpose of which is to explain the classic and very important split between the concepts of objectivity and subjectivity in the Danish philosopher's thought.

To undertake his investigation the author bases his analysis above all on the *Concluding Unscientific Postscript to 'Philosophical Fragments,'* Kierkegaard's famous work published in 1846 under the pseudonym Johannes Climacus, but which bears the name of Kierkegaard himself as editor. Two important points are highlighted by de Paula with respect to this work. The first is that this book is conclusive in the sense of not opting for science and its abstract systems; the second is that it was originally conceived to mark the end of Kierkegaard's activity as a writer, although this never actually happened. The author explains that *Postscript* deals with two main problems, that is, that of subjectivity and that of inwardness as truth. From these problems, three questions are raised: (1) Is there a possibility of finding a historical origin for eternal consciousness? (2) Is this origin more relevant than a historical perspective? (3) Is there a relationship between eternal happiness and historical knowledge? According to de Paula, the terms we find in the title of this work can, in the Kierkegaardian context, be expressed in the following manner: objectivity is related to the content of Christianity, while subjectivity deals with the conversion of an individual to this religion or, more precisely, to the Christian way of life.

However, de Paula does not rely exclusively on the *Postscript*, but also makes incursions into the philosophies of Lessing and Feuerbach, which, according to the author, had great influence on Kierkegaard with respect to the theme of objectivity and subjectivity. De Paula presents a summary of the historical context in which we can locate the intellectual production of Gotthold Ephraim Lessing, presenting his main philosophical references, namely, the Pietist movement, Deism, Leibniz, Diderot, and Spinoza. The author then discusses important theses in Lessing's thought, such as the history of philosophy as a form of divine pedagogy, the sacred scriptures as aids to reason, man's search for improvement and his desire to overcome death. One of the high points in this delicate investigation of Lessing's philosophy is the analysis of his letter entitled "On the Proof of the Spirit and of Power," in which the concept of prophecy in the Old and New Testament is presented.

De Paula also writes about some important anthropological and philosophical ideas of Ludwig Feuerbach, whose masterpiece is *The Essence of Christianity*. Such ideas are the difference between animal nature and religion, religion as possessing its own logic and being representative of the split of man with himself, miracles as something natural, the essence of man as an object of religion. Further, Feuerbach criticizes both the concept of God as a man as the subjectivist concept of divinity. According to de Paula, Lessing's importance to Kierkegaard is due to the fact that the German thinker pointed out the error in Hegel's systematic philosophy, since the latter had not perceived the problem of subjectivity in the Greeks. As to Feuerbach, his point of agreement with Kierkegaard lies in the fact that both had placed themselves against philosophical theocentrism and against an absolute type of philosophy such as Hegel's.

Beyond the figures of Lessing and Feuerbach, the Socratic figure appears. The author refers to Socrates as a central character for us better to comprehend the concept of subjectivity in Kierkegaard. Socrates had been the first thinker to put forward the problem of inwardness, which would be later developed by Christianity. Further, the Athenian philosopher is, in many aspects, an intellectual and moral model for Kierkegaard, to the point that he is also known as the "Socrates of Christendom." De Paula analyzes the peculiarity of Socrates' thought in the context of the work *The Concept of Irony*, since this concept is extremely important in expressing the point of view of a particular individual and not an abstract idea. In order to execute this analysis, the author follows the critical path used by Kierkegaard in the mentioned work, investigating the means by which Socrates was appropriated by tradition: Xenophon, Aristophanes, Plato, Aristotle, Hegel, and Schleiermacher.

De Paula proceeds with his investigation by reviewing the Kierkegaardian pseudonyms. According to the author, for the pseudonym Johannes Climacus, Socrates would present a systematic philosophy from the point of view of traditional pragmatism. In the case of the pseudonym Anti-Climacus, Socrates would be evaluated starting from his concept of ignorance in comparison to the Christian original sin. In fact, another relevant point analyzed by the author is that Kierkegaard defends faith in the absurd, which is characterized by the manifestation of truth in time—a defense that no Greek, not even Socrates, would have been capable of making. According to de Paula, this issue inevitably leads to a criticism of Hegelian logic, which submits interiority to exteriority and absurdity to conciliation.

Upon concluding this trek through the main ideas of Lessing, Feuerbach, and Socrates, the author turns to Kierkegaard. De Paula then begins to present the Danish philosopher's aesthetic concept. The author explains that Kierkegaardian aesthetics extrapolate the field of the philosophy of art in order to concentrate on the psychological and moral issues of the existing subject. De Paula also presents the Kierkegaardian concept of Christianity through the analysis of some of his pseudonyms, such as Johannes de Silentio, Johannes Climacus, and Anti-Climacus, which relate differently, each in his own way, to the Christian truth. The author concludes that independently from the pseudonyms and their distinct approaches, Kierkegaard's question was always how to "become a Christian."

Subjectivity and Objectivity in Kierkegaard is an interesting book, especially in its forays into the thinking of Lessing and Feuerbach. The author's attempt to show the influence of these German thinkers on Kierkegaard offers us rich material for study. However, due to this and other intellectual forays, the theme of subjectivity such as understood by Kierkegaard himself ends up often in the background, which can be frustrating for the reader interested in delving exclusively into the Kierkegaardian concept. But in no way does de Paula's book become less important for Kierkegaardian studies because of these detours. De Paula was the first Brazilian researcher to dedicate an entire book to the theme of objectivity and subjectivity in Kierkegaard, and, for that reason, his book remains a valid point of support for those who are beginning their Kierkegaardian studies.

Rodrigo Carqueja de Menezes and Thiago Costa Faria

Review and Critical Discussion

Pinho, Marieta Moura de, review in *Horizonte*, vol. 8, no. 16, 2010, pp. 182–4.

Miguel Reale (ed.), *Søren Kierkegaard*

special issue of *Revista Brasileira de Filosofia*, vol. 6, no. 1, 1956 (São Paulo: Instituto Brasileiro de Filosofia), 168 pp.

In honor of the hundredth anniversary of Kierkegaard's death, the Brazilian Institute of Philosophy published, in 1956, a special edition of its journal, in which it brought together eminent names in Brazilian philosophy around the Danish thinker. There are five articles in total, which occupy the first 76 pages of the journal. The rest concerns other topics which are not related to Kierkegaard's works or thought and that, therefore, do not interest us in this review.

"Kierkegaard's Life, Works and Message,"[1] by Luís Washington Vita, is the first essay in this volume and emphasizes Kierkegaard's biography, relating the personal events of his life to the central aspects of his philosophy. At a time in which the Danish thinker was all but unknown in Brazil, the biographical approach had the advantage of making it easier and more attractive to present Kierkegaard to the general public. However, subordinating the interpretation of Kierkegaard's thought to the turbulences of his private life, his melancholy temperament, and even his fragile and misshapen physical constitution, Vita engages in a type of simplistic error, but one which even today is relatively common in Kierkegaardian studies, namely, the "genetic fallacy."[2]

In the second essay, entitled "Kierkegaard and Religious Despair,"[3] Heraldo Barbuy presents to the reader a controversial (so as not to say eccentric or even mistaken) review of *The Sickness unto Death*, based on the French translation of Jean-Jacques Gateau and Knud Ferlov.[4] Although the author calls attention to the fact that the despair that Kierkegaard speaks of does not result from any psychological cause, he does not resist the temptation to excavate the peculiarities of the Danish thinker's life in order to highlight his familiarity with the theme of despair.

---

1 Luís Washington Vita, "Vida, obra e mensagem de Kierkegaard," *Revista Brasileira de Filosofia*, vol. 6, no. 1, 1956 (special issue, *Søren Kierkegaard*), pp. 3–21.

2 See Ricardo Quadros Gouvêa, *Paixão pelo Paradoxo*: *Uma Introdução aos Estudos de Søren Kierkegaard e de Sua Concepção da Fé Cristã*, São Paulo: Editora Novo Século 2000, pp. 55–60.

3 Heraldo Barbuy, "Kierkegaard e o desespero religioso," *Revista Brasileira de Filosofia*, vol. 6, no. 1, 1956 (special issue, *Søren Kierkegaard*), pp. 22–37.

4 Søren Kierkegaard, *Traité du désespoir*. *(La maladie mortelle*), trans. by Jean-Jacques Gateau and Knud Ferlov, Paris: Gallimard 1932.

Barbuy writes: "The consciousness of sin, not only of original sin, but of the particular sin from which he [Kierkegaard] was born, gave him a vivid image of concrete, existential despair,"[5] referring to the fact that Kierkegaard was conceived while his parents were still out of wedlock. Beyond the biographical issues, Barbuy also attributes Kierkegaard's affinity with despair to his Protestant faith: "The absence of the worship of the Mother is one of the Lutheran elements that marks Kierkegaard's religious despair."[6] But the truly controversial point is found in the author's affirmation that Kierkegaard had an idealistic concept of God, according to which he would be identified with the Absolute, but an abstract and absent Absolute.[7] Last but not least, Barbuy accuses Kierkegaard of solipsism.[8] "Everything happens as if Kierkegaard had generalized his own despair,"[9] the essay's author concludes. The greatest merit of this piece was that it summarized the main arguments of *The Sickness unto Death* but not the interpretation of them.

Renato Cirell Czerna is responsible for the third essay, entitled "The Romantic Experience in Kierkegaard and Hegel."[10] The author proposes an analysis of Hegel's and Kierkegaard's reactions to Romanticism, a philosophical movement which both tried, each in his own way, to surpass. According to Czerna, on the one hand, we have "the *Hegelian solution*, which positions itself, deep down, as a dialectical integration in which the Romantic element is, in a certain way, preserved,"[11] and, on the other, "the *religious solution* represented by Kierkegaard, in which the Romantic experience apparently annuls itself in the determination of one of its possibilities."[12] Czerna presents a daring and, to a certain extent, outlandish hypothesis: he alleges that Christianity is a possibility in itself of the development of Romantic conscience and that, in this sense, Kierkegaard, as a Christian author, never stopped being a Romantic.[13] Kierkegaard's "religious solution" to the problematic of Romanticism—a solution which the author insists on opposing to Hegel's "philosophical solution"—would preserve in itself traces of an original Romantic experience, which, according to the author, can be recognized, for example, in the Kierkegaardian concept of faith as a passion which embraces infinity and the Absolute.[14] In attacking the Romantic conscience—so well represented by his aesthetic characters—Kierkegaard was, in truth, trying to criticize himself.[15] With that in mind, we can conclude that for Czerna the religious

5 Barbuy, "Kierkegaard e o desespero religioso," p. 23.

6 Ibid., p. 35.

7 See ibid., pp. 26–7; p. 37.

8 Ibid., p. 36.

9 Ibid., p. 34.

10 Renato Cirell Czerna, "A experiência romântica em Kierkegaard e Hegel," *Revista Brasileira de Filosofia*, vol. 6, no. 1, 1956 (special issue, *Søren Kierkegaard*), pp. 38–58.

11 Ibid., pp. 43–4.

12 Ibid., p. 44.

13 See ibid., p. 55.

14 Ibid., p. 53.

15 See ibid., p. 52; p. 57.

stage is no more than a transmutation or development of the aesthetic stage and that Kierkegaard, therefore, is no more than a kind solipsistic schizophrenic.

In his beautiful essay "Kierkegaard and Current Philosophy,"[16] Efraín Tomás Bó highlights the topicality of Kierkegaard's thought, especially what relates to the treatment he gives of the relationship between existence and reality. The author refers to the *Postscript* to explain the already classic Kierkegaardian opposition between existence and thought, reminding us that the actuality of existence is not reducible to the ideality of thought. But it is with *Philosophical Fragments* that Bó truly occupies himself. He then analyzes the issue contained in this work: the differences between the Socratic and Christian concepts of truth, the relationship between disciple and master, and the importance of the moment for the comprehension of eternity. Briefly, while Socrates defended the view that the disciple already possesses the truth and that the master serves only as an occasion in which he can remember it, Kierkegaard believed that the disciple is stuck in non-truth and that only the master can free him. This master is God, who, out of love, reaches out to man, thus generating the incomprehensible paradox of eternity, which reveals itself through time.

Vicente Ferreira da Silva's essay, "Kierkegaard and the Problem of Subjectivity,"[17] is the last in the series and orbits around the Kierkegaardian maxim "subjectivity is truth." The author highlights the fact that it is not subjectivity from the same mold as Romantic subjectivity, in that the I is responsible for the creation of itself and the surrounding reality. Silva writes: "Deep down, the Romantic will is to Kierkegaard despair, as a forgetting and obfuscation of the finiteness of all existence."[18] According to the author, the subjectivity to which Kierkegaard refers is rooted in Christianity, which emphasizes faith and the personal decision in the relationship of man with truth: in the place of an impersonal relationship with truth, the individual must possess it with passion. Objective knowledge and universal history scorn the subjectivity of the existing subject, making him alienated, distant from himself, as abstract as truth itself, which he contemplates without interest. "Man in our time, generally speaking," Silva writes, "is the man of the masses, the mob, the abstract power of universality and degeneracy of the individual truth."[19] Silva concludes that, according to Kierkegaard, the only way for man to overcome this leveling is to turn passionately to his own subjectivity.

Despite being often superficial and leading to a distorted understanding, these five essays, taken together, witness the effort that the first generation of Brazilian philosophers interested in Kierkegaard's thought had to make in order to penetrate the Kierkegaardian universe. They witness, also, the *status quaestionis* of

---

16 Efraín Tomás Bó, "Kierkegaard y la filosofía actual," *Revista Brasileira de Filosofia*, vol. 6, no. 1, 1956 (special issue, *Søren Kierkegaard*), pp. 59–69.

17 Vicente Ferreira da Silva, "Kierkegaard e o problema da subjetividade," *Revista Brasileira de Filosofia*, vol. 6, no. 1, 1956 (special issue, *Søren Kierkegaard*), pp. 70–6.

18 Ibid., pp. 70–1.

19 Ibid., p. 75.

Kierkegaardian studies in Brazil until the decade of the 1950s and, for that reason, possess great historical value. The task, as one can perceive, was not an easy one nor was it free from error, but it opened, albeit bluntly, the way for future generations to delve even further into Kierkegaard's thought and work.

Rodrigo Carqueja de Menezes and Thiago Costa Faria

Reviews and Critical Discussions

Undetermined.

Elisabete M. de Sousa, *Formas de Arte: a prática crítica de Berlioz, Kierkegaard, Liszt e Schumann* [Forms of Art: The Practical Criticism of Berlioz, Kierkegaard, Liszt and Schumann],

Lisbon: Centro de Filosofia da Universidade de Lisboa 2008, 317 pp.

As the title *Forms of Art* implies, this work refers to the shape, organizational components or physical objects that can be called "art" as well as indirectly referring to ways of making art. On the surface, this perhaps is most strangely applied to Søren Kierkegaard in comparison to Hector Berlioz, Franz Liszt, and Robert Schumann; however, Elisabete M. De Sousa shows that Kierkegaard fits in well with this company. The second half of De Sousa's title broadly encompasses what is the basis of the book's content, namely, a description of the critique these individuals make in their art (and philosophy), both in the writing and practice of crafting their art (composers in their compositions and performances, Kierkegaard in his method of composing philosophy). This study takes us through criticism and other texts authored by those appearing in the title—Hector Berlioz (1803–69), Søren Kierkegaard, Franz Liszt (1811–86), and Robert Schumann (1810–56)—all of whom occupy an interesting place in late Romantic music and the then contemporary philosophical era, where we encounter a shift in compositional techniques and thinking, evolving from the *Sturm und Drang* and early Romantic movement. There is a careful, and often non-intuitive, balance maintained throughout the study, comprised of integrating the different composers' thoughts and ideas about their critical and compositional process with the author's reflections on Kierkegaard's writings.

There are few works in contemporary Kierkegaard scholarship that discuss the problems Kierkegaard raises in the area of philosophy of music while maintaining a bipartite methodology that is both musicologically and philosophically relevant. The importance of this book for Kierkegaard research can be found principally in the first and third chapters. The first chapter focuses primarily on the work of Schumann and his pseudonyms, which De Sousa confronts with Kierkegaard's pseudonymous works; the third chapter emphasizes Kierkegaard's writings on music in *Either/Or*, with reference to recent elaborations on Kierkegaard's work by musicologists.

One of De Sousa's most elegant discussions is found when she makes an insightful comparison between Schumann's pseudonyms in musical criticism and Kierkegaard's pseudonyms in his philosophical writings. She expands on Kierkegaard's *direct* and *indirect* communication, and attempts a reconciliation between the plurality of views found in the whole of the pseudonyms' output. One of the most innovative comparisons between the composer and the philosopher is located in De Sousa's useful metaphor, which supports a parallel in the manner of thought and pseudonymous strategies utilized by both Kierkegaard and Schumann. The metaphor speaks of a pianist playing an advanced keyboard piece where the left hand often invades the space of the right, and vice versa. It is in this "invasion" that sometimes one hand can be considered "helping" the other; in this case it is Schumann who helps give voice to his pseudonyms, when he composes works in their respective names by incorporating compositional ingenuity and "musical opinion." Following this line of thought, we recall Kierkegaard who wrote long, complex philosophical works and attributed them to his pseudonyms as part of his project of *indirect* communication.

In De Sousa's discussion of Kierkegaard's pseudonyms, she respects the pseudonyms as individual and unique authors. Following this, she develops a thesis on Kierkegaard's creation of the pseudonyms as a kind of *rhetorical strategy*.[1] This strategy, in relation to the pseudonyms, is seen as a device to transmit truth in both *direct* and *indirect* communication. The focus, however, is on the method, the difference in style, and the variety of ways in which this is done. In the course of the argument, partially constructed on an enormously important citation from Kierkegaard's autobiographical *On My Work as an Author*, we learn of Kierkegaard's perspective regarding his own creation of the pseudonyms: indirect communication (the voices of the pseudonyms as a unity) *deceives* one in the direction of truth, in contrast to direct communication that is frank in respect to the matters it treats.[2] De Sousa's exhibition of Kierkegaard's argument highlights two aspects that are most relevant to the pseudonyms: (1) they treat themes exposed in works signed by Kierkegaard in a more literary way, from varying points of view, and (2) the reappearance of a pseudonym in a new context often is at odds, or in conflict, with other pseudonyms who appear in the same new context.[3] De Sousa weighs the positions of noted Kierkegaard scholars and concludes that the pseudonyms should be respected, and seen as dialectical in regard to the works published under Kierkegaard's own name, thus maintaining a structure of two series; this leads to a compelling quotation from the book, *From the Papers of One Still Living*, where Kierkegaard considers his *alter* ego and himself, as two souls residing in the same body.[4] The treatment of this intriguing passage serves as an accurate demonstration of De Sousa's claim that the aesthetic views of Kierkegaard's pseudonyms are indispensible for the

---

1 This is discussed in Elisabete M. De Sousa, *Formas de Arte: a prática crítica de Berlioz, Kierkegaard, Liszt e Schumann*, Lisbon: Centro de Filosofia a Universidade de Lisboa 2008, pp. 50ff.

2 Ibid., p. 56. See also *SKS* 13, 13 / *PV*, 7. Citation: " *'Ligefrem Meddelse' er: at bedrage ind i det Sande*." This quotation appears in a Portuguese translation on p. 56 of *Formas de Arte*.

3 See De Sousa, *Formas de Arte*, p. 59.

4 *SKS* 1, 9 / *EPW*, 55. See De Sousa, *Formas de Arte*, p. 70.

understanding of Kierkegaard's religious phase;[5] nevertheless she leaves the door open for more research to be done on this topic.

In De Sousa's third chapter, which is of interest from a musicological perspective, there is an extensive commentary on Kierkegaard's concept of "musical language," a topic often treated by musicologists as a way of integrating Kierkegaard's philosophy into their own treatises (or historical tracings) of the problem.[6] As an example of this, De Sousa juxtaposes the characters of Johannes the Seducer (author of "The Seducer's Diary") and Don Giovanni (as described by A), and shows the difference between them precisely in their use of language, namely, the one can verbalize feelings (Johannes), while the other is purely musical (Don Giovanni). Building on this discussion, De Sousa discusses criticism from musicologists who have found fault with A's/Kierkegaard's chapter on *Don Giovanni* (the flaw being that Kierkegaard has reduced the music of the opera to non-musical concepts). De Sousa constructs her defense of A's discussion of one of Mozart's other operas discussed in "The Immediate Erotic Stages," *Die Zauberflöte* (K. 620, 1791), and comments on the tempo marking of the aria "Alles fühlt der Liebe Freuden" (Act II, scene iii, [n. 13]) as an indication of an erotic pace, feeling, and excitement similar to the "Champagne aria" (marked *accelerando* at the start).[7] Additionally, we are provided with an examination of German Romanticism and philosophical-musical commentary that attributes a religious and sensual aspect to music, shown to be particularly important in Kierkegaard's writings, as well as his writings on Christianity. This study of music in Kierkegaard's writings is further developed when De Sousa enters into the final section of the third chapter where she discusses Franz Liszt and virtuosity. First weighing opinions regarding Liszt as a performer and composer from musicologists and scholars such as Cécile Reynaud, Susan Bernstein, Adrian Williams, and Lawrence Kramer, De Sousa highlights what she argues is most relevant for understanding Liszt as Kierkegaard may have seen and interpreted him. Primarily, she claims that Liszt should be regarded as a demonic, erotic figure, arguing for this based on descriptions from *Either/Or*, Part One and further developing this through commentary on Liszt's virtuosity seen through his compositions, stage presence, and method of interpretation in transcriptions. De Sousa ultimately argues that Liszt influenced Kierkegaard's writing of the "Immediate Erotic Stages." She also proves, presenting considerable evidence, that Kierkegaard attended at least one of Liszt's performances while both were in Berlin between the years of 1841 and 1842. A detailed description of Liszt's *Réminiscences de Don Juan*, his infamous

---

5 See De Sousa, *Formas de Arte*, p. 71.

6 A discussion of musical language in this fashion is elaborated most notably by Carl Dahlhaus in "Musical Logic and Speech Character," in his *The Esthetics of Music*, trans. by Roger Lustig, Chicago: University of Chicago Press 1989, pp. 103–16, specifically pp. 113–15.

7 This is also discussed in Elisabete M. De Sousa, "Wolfgang Amadeus Mozart: The Love for Music and the Music of Love," in *Kierkegaard and the Renaissance and Modern Traditions*, ed. by Jon Stewart, Tome III, *Literature, Drama and Music*, Aldershot: Ashgate 2009 (*Kierkegaard Research: Sources, Reception and Resources*, vol. 5), pp. 137–68.

transcription of Mozart's *Don Giovanni* (K. 527), Liszt's focus on Don Giovanni's aria "Fin Ch'han dal Vino" (popularly known as the "Champagne Aria," Act I, Scene xv, aria 11 in his transcription), along with relevant quotations from Kierkegaard / A, figure among the most convincing evidence.

It is in an act of reconciling two disciplines often at odds with each other that we find De Sousa's work presenting a harmonious balance of Kierkegaard commentary with musicological analysis. She draws particularly interesting conclusions regarding the pseudonyms of both Kierkegaard and Schumann, and Liszt's potential influence on "The Immediate Erotic Stages." Her ability to juggle the methodology of both disciplines is elegantly shown throughout.

Sara Ellen Eckerson

Reviews and Critical Discussions

Undetermined.

Álvaro Luiz Montenegro Valls, *Entre Sócrates e Cristo: ensaios sobre a ironia e o amor em Kierkegaard* [Between Socrates and Christ: Essays on Irony and Love in Kierkegaard],

Porto Alegre: EDIPUCRS 2000, 228 pp.

Between Socrates and Christ is a collection of essays published in the year 2000 by EDIPUCRS. This study is a result of the research that professor Álvaro Luiz Montenegro Valls has been engaging in since 1976. Valls is one of the pioneers and great promoters of Kierkegaardian studies in Brazil. Having learned Danish especially in order better to comprehend the philosopher from Copenhagen, he is, in his own words, a "rare Brazilian bird." The author is responsible for the translation of some of Kierkegaard's most important works, such as *The Concept of Irony*, *Philosophical Fragments*, *The Concept of Anxiety*, and *Works of Love*.

In the first essay, "Between Socrates and Christ," Valls dedicates himself to dealing briefly with Kierkegaard's philosophical career, showing, from the main translations of his works, how his writings were ignored for over 50 years in Brazil. According to Valls, the reasons for which the study of Kierkegaard's work was historically impaired were, on one hand, the lack of a more logical and systematic vision of the work and the pseudonyms and, on the other, difficulties in translation.

In the second essay, "Observations on the Concept of Irony in Socrates, Hegel and Kierkegaard," Valls presents a complicated problematic which involves the concept of irony in Kierkegaard. First of all irony is studied in its Socratic form, in which there was a lot more than a "feigned ignorance" that was a playful critical attitude. After this the author presents irony in its Romantic form, which is criticized by Hegel, since it would lead to a hollow and empty subjectivity. And, finally, we are taken to irony according to Kierkegaard, who disagrees with the Hegelian critique, since irony is not properly hypocrisy (as Hegel believed). For Kierkegaard, irony is the first norm of a truly human life, the first affirmation of subjectivity.

Essays 3 and 4—respectively: "*The Concept of Irony* in Portuguese" and "The translation of *The Concept of Irony* into Spanish: A Speech"—can be presented jointly, since they have a similar structure. Both essays highlight, each in its own way, the importance for Kierkegaard studies of the moment in which translators began to learn Danish and to translate Kierkegaard's works from the original text. The author highlights also the possibility that Kierkegaard, in his dissertation on irony, was himself being ironic, and calls attention to the fact that many experts point to duplicity in this text which deviates from the expected unity.

In "The Irony of The Seducer's Diary," Valls introduces Johannes to us, the seductive character created by Kierkegaard who writes in the pages of his diary that seduction is art and science, and that, for this reason, it demands a method. "The Seducer's Diary" is inserted in the volume of the aesthetic texts of *Either/Or*, in which Mozart's Don Giovanni and Goethe's Faust are also studied. According to Valls, Don Giovanni, Faust, and Johannes constitute three different kinds of seducers and three great aesthetic ideas.

In "Socratic Love: the Kierkegaardian Analysis of its Theory and Practice," Valls begins by explaining the difficulty of presenting an image of the historical Socrates and indicates the works in which Kierkegaard explores the developments and alternatives to Socratic love, namely, *The Concept of Irony*, *Philosophical Fragments*, and *Works of Love*. The author's proposal in this essay is to investigate a certain dimension of the Socratic pragmatism about love, in that it is defined as a search, lack, and need. For Kierkegaard, along with being irresponsible, Socrates is also a seducer. In *Philosophical Fragments*, Socrates is understood by the relationship of symmetry between men and also as someone who is self-contained and does not wish to receive honor, dignity, or money for his teachings. And, finally, in *Works of Love*, Socrates is presented as the one who has anticipated the Christian doctrine of love for one's neighbor, which is analyzed more specifically by Valls in the next essay: "Love thy neighbor, specifically Christian: His exposition in *Works of Love* and the Critique by Adorno."

The purpose of this essay is to understand the relationship between philosophy and theology in Kierkegaard, and, for that, it refers to philosopher Theodor Adorno, who writes about the Kierkegaardian doctrine of love. Adorno perspicaciously perceives two important themes in Kierkegaard: the concept of the essentially Christian (*det Christelige*) and what Valls calls the Pauline sharpening of Christianity. The essay also highlights that the theme of love for one's neighbor discussed by Kierkegaard has many nuances that Adorno did not understand, since this is not Platonic, Freudian, idealized, or "natural" love.

In "On the Duty of Loving," the author offers a brief introduction to the problems which involve the frontiers between ethics and aesthetics, differentiating the duty of loving from other types of duty. Valls then analyzes love according to Ernst Tugendhat, Freud, Kierkegaard, and Kant. According to Valls, only in Kierkegaard do we find the issue of Christian love for one's neighbor in its radicalness, since "The Christian teaching is to love one's neighbor, love all humankind, all men, even the enemy, and not make exceptions, either in preference or in aversion."[1]

In the long essay "Live or like? On the Frontiers of Ethics and Aesthetics," Valls begins by quoting a short dialogue between a Guarani chief/shaman and the famous missionary of the Catholic Church priest Roque Gonzáles, who is today venerated as a saint. Here the author also seeks to show the radicalism and originality of the way

1 Álvaro Luiz Montenegro Valls, *Entre Sócrates e Cristo: ensaios sobre a ironia e o amor em Kierkegaard*, Porto Alegre: EDIPUCRS 2000, p. 123.

in which Kierkegaard interprets Christian love. After visiting two issues concerning Kierkegaardian unlimited love: ethics ("shall it not be an injustice to love anyone?," since not everyone would be worth loving) and aesthetics ("is it not a lack of taste, lack of good taste, to want to love any person?"), Valls concludes this essay by reaffirming that Christian love is, such as Kierkegaard understood it, egalitarian and the enemy of any predilection.

The tenth essay, "Philosophical Fragments," is a presentation of the Brazilian translation of Reichman and Valls of Kierkegaard's book which bears the same name. In it we find a small addendum about the translation of this work. First there is a comment showing the singularity and originality of the pseudonym Johannes Climacus. After this we find the analysis of the problematic of Christianity itself, developed in all its radicalism by Climacus, as follows: "Can a historical point of departure be given for an eternal consciousness; how can such a point of departure be of more than historical interest; can an eternal happiness be built on historical knowledge?"[2] And the answer is given from the question of the moment and the absolute meaning of the historical, in other words, the postulation of what is or should be more than the historical (absolute fact).

In "Follow the Mode or Follow the Model? On a New Religiousness," Valls begins by recounting what it was like to study religion for the people of his generation, who were born in the twentieth century. Upon announcing his return to religious studies in the 1990s, he introduces a new concept of religiousness, which has as its fundamental characteristic the aesthetic aspect, since it helps to compose a profile with good taste: "The new religiousness has an aesthetic accent; it is a lifestyle, and not a moral, ethical or political commitment."[3] Valls concludes, negatively, that this new religiousness expresses a mythical and alienated conversion in opposition to a conversion with true engagement, of renewal and Christianization.

In "Some Thoughts on Reason and Religion in Kierkegaard," Valls proposes to analyze some concepts which undo very common misunderstandings with respect to the relationship Kierkegaard maintained with reason and religion. He first affirms that the Dane, far from being an irrationalist, belongs to the list of great rational philosophers, understanding rationalism, however, as "cerebralism," since "everything he does is very planned, thought out."[4] After this, concerning religion, he says that all those who think Kierkegaard is a preacher make a mistake, often being fooled by the fact that his texts begin with a biblical quotation, since what is presented in them are short texts of pure philosophical thought, considerations, and reasoning.

In the next to last essay Valls analyzes John Paul II's encyclical *Fides e Ratio* (Faith and Reason). From this classic dichotomy, the Pope analyzes the sense of the ontological proof. After all, God is not something we can think; our thoughts are not greater than him, and, in this sense, God is incomprehensible. At the end of the day, the ontological proof assumes a God that we only know in a practical sense, through faith. In Valls' view, Kierkegaard's pseudonym Johannes Climacus has the same

2 *SKS* 4, 213 / *PF*, 1.

3 Valls, *Entre Sócrates e Cristo*, p. 171.

4 Ibid., p. 181.

opinion, since he also affirms that it is not up to the intellect to overcome faith, but, if anything, to beg God for help before attempting its proof. In the last essay, entitled "Annex: Kierkegaard in Adorno," Valls presents us with five numbered texts which focus on the relation between the Danish and the German philosophers.

The fragmented nature of *Between Socrates and Christ*, in which the chapters/essays possess total autonomy among themselves, makes the task of reviewing it challenging. However, it is a gratifying challenge, in that this work offers a vast panorama about two of the main Kierkegaardian themes, irony and love. And it is not without a certain dose of irony that Álvaro Valls presents these essays, which are the fruits of a lifetime dedicated to the study, promotion, and translation of Kierkegaard on Brazilian soil—true fruit, we could say, of his love for the Danish philosopher.

Rodrigo Carqueja de Menezes and Thiago Costa Faria

Reviews and Critical Discussions

Undetermined.

Álvaro Valls, *Kierkegaard cá entre nós* [Kierkegaard, Just Between Us],

São Paulo: Editora Liber Ars 2012, 135 pp.

The book by Álvaro Valls, *Kierkegaard cá entre nós* (Kierkegaard, Just Between Us), was published in 2012 in Brazil. This work consists of a collection of ten essays; the first eight are called "interpretations" and the remaining two represent analyses of Kierkegaard's reception in Brazil (resulting in the expression "just between us"). The author is a renowned translator of Kierkegaard's works into Portuguese, having translated *The Concept of Irony, Philosophical Fragments, The Concept of Anxiety, Works of Love*, and the *Concluding Unscientific Postscript.* Moreover, he has also produced numerous books and articles in the field of Kierkegaard studies.

I think there is a singularity in the work under examination: the essays, regardless of their academic rigor, were produced with the utmost freedom that the various contexts of production and public afforded the writer. Thus, all of them may be read separately from one another. This type of collection is certainly not new with respect to its philosophical reflections or in the context of Kierkegaardian studies; similar kinds of work have been produced by authors such as Evans and Pattison.[1]

In the first essay there is an analysis of the translator's hermeneutic work, and Valls discusses the theme of translation in philosophy. One of his assertions deserves our consideration:

> we would like to characterize our activity as "lending our Brazilian speech to a foreign author." And if, for some good reasons, it was necessary to translate *The Concept of Irony* in a form literal enough, seeking maximum accuracy in regard to the original meaning of the thought of the author of the dissertation from 1841, there would have to be another strategy to translate the *Philosophical Fragments* from 1844.[2]

In other words, a good translator's duty is not only to strictly observe what would be faithfulness to the originals, but also to develop a communicative strategy,

---

1 George Pattison, *Kierkegaard and the Quest for Unambiguous Life: Between Romanticism and Modernism: Selected Essays*, Oxford: Oxford University Press 2013; C. Stephen Evans, *Kierkegaard on Faith and the Self: Collected Essays*, Waco: Baylor University Press 2006.

2 Álvaro Valls, *Kierkegaard cá entre nós*, São Paulo: Editora Liber Ars 2012, p. 21.

seeking correspondence in his native language, to make the text attractive and meaningful to his countrymen.

"The Absolute Fact" is the title of the second essay, where the discussion about the absolute comes out as a central issue in the philosophy of religion. Here, through elucidation of the theories of Johannes Climacus, the pseudonymous author of *Philosophical Fragments*, our author wanders through traditional themes of philosophy with lightness and rigor at the same time. Valls points out, however, that these issues are extremely complex and depend, strictly speaking, on intensive research in the writings of Leibniz and Lessing, who strongly influenced Kierkegaard by the time he wrote *Philosophical Fragments.* The question about to what degree Christianity is (or is not) something historical seems to be at the heart of the presented arguments. Valls points out: "if what in fact really happened is just history, it has value only historically, it does not have in itself any absolute value."[3] In an extremely provocative way, this thesis is, in fact, an anticipation of the position that will be detailed in the *Concluding Unscientific Postscript,* where Kierkegaard treats Christianity in detail as a historical phenomenon and, at the same time, discusses the relationship between Christianity and subjectivity. Henriksen has already addressed this fact about Christianity's historicity in his book *The Reconstruction of Religion: Lessing, Kierkegaard and Nietzsche.* There, after an analysis of Lessing's text, "On the Demonstration in Spirit and Strength," the author points to the important relationship between faith, history, and subject: "Consequently, for Lessing, mere historical facts cannot move the subject to hold a truth that is independent of history. The faith of the subject thus becomes detached from the history from which faith takes its point of departure."[4]

The Danish intellectual Poul Martin Møller is the object of the third essay. It is in fact not just an essay but also an exercise in translation and an explanation of aesthetic themes. Valls presents here information about Møller as a thinker, teacher, and friend, to whom Kierkegaard devoted *The Concept of Anxiety*, although the approach lacks the great richness of detail that one finds, for example, in Gredal Jensen's work.[5] The topic is important to the extent that it draws attention to a major contemporary who is generally very little known outside Denmark.

The unlikely dialogue between Freud and Kierkegaard is the theme of the fourth essay. The Danish author can be read with much interest through the eyes of psychoanalysis and psychology, and themes such as anxiety and despair are not foreign to his vocabulary. In this sense, Valls points out what Kierkegaard, along with Fichte, called a theory of the *self* and how it seems to anticipate some important

---

3 Ibid., p. 26.

4 Jan-Olav Henriksen, *The Reconstruction of Religion: Lessing, Kierkegaard and Nietzsche*, Grand Rapids: Eerdmans 2001, p. 39.

5 Finn Gredal Jensen, "Poul Martin Møller: Kierkegaard and the Confidant of Socrates," in *Kierkegaard and his Danish Contemporaries*, Tome I, *Philosophy, Politics and Social Theory*, ed. by Jon Stewart, Aldershot: Ashgate 2009 (*Kierkegaard Research: Sources, Reception and Resources*, vol. 7), pp. 101–68.

aspects of Freudian theory, yet, at the same time, he points out the crucial differences between the two authors. As Valls himself emphasizes:

> We realized immediately that Kierkegaard belongs to a generation prior to Charles Darwin, and we don't expect from Kierkegaard things that only Freud did. We accept the claim that he has a profound influence on psychology and philosophy of existence, and try to show what kinds of nuances are there, what kinds of discoveries, and what are his intentions. We should see that at some points the approaches [of Kierkegaard and Freud] are very similar, and there are rich points of overlap here and there, but there are also, shall we say, different intentions.[6]

The aesthetics in Kierkegaard's work, and the understanding of the author as an art critic, is the subject of the fifth chapter. By analyzing Kierkegaard's book review of *Two Ages*, Valls shows us a perhaps less-explored dimension of the author. As in the essay on Poul Martin Møller, Valls does not seem to excel here with respect to depth or detail of analysis, but since this is still a little-explored theme in the Brazilian context, the text has the great merit of provoking and instigating interest. Katalin Nun also explores this important topic of Kierkegaard's aesthetic in a more detailed way.[7]

The next two essays deal with *Works of Love* ("Love and Christhood in *Works of Love*" and "The Work of Love that Consists in Remembering the Dead"). Valls addresses here the theme of the typically Christian duty to love, and analyzes what it would mean to remember the dead if we seek to understand things in the way of the Gospels, that is, why does the love for a dead seem to be the best kind of love. Taking advantage of the Kierkegaardian discourse, which claims that someone's love for the dead is the most sincere kind of love that could exist since there is no interest or any possible reward, Valls argues for the hypothesis that the author was himself posing as "dead" to Regine Olsen, when his ex-fiancée was newly married to another man. He seems to make the argument to Regine that she should give him a love, that is, the work of love that is to remember a deceased person, and she ought never to forget him. Thus, the Kierkegaardian text presents itself here with an extremely exciting multiplicity of meaning since it can be something deeply theological and religious but, at the same time, also have a loving and ironic character. In the words of Valls: "For if faith is the certainty of victory, death and time are no longer the last word, and the deadest of the dead still has a future ahead and can then seamlessly dream of the day when, 'at last,' he will be reunited with all of his best loves."[8] Valls then enters into a dialogue with authors known for their

---

6 Valls, *Kierkegaard cá entre nós*, p. 48.

7 Katalin Nun, "Thomasine Gyllembourg: Kierkegaard's Appreciation of the Everyday Stories and *Two Ages*," in *Kierkegaard and his Danish Contemporaries*, Tome III, *Literature, Drama and Aesthetics*, ed. by Jon Stewart, Aldershot: Ashgate 2009 (*Kierkegaard Research: Sources, Reception and Resources*, vol. 7), pp. 151–67.

8 Valls, *Kierkegaard cá entre nós*, p. 93.

interpretations of *Works of Love*, such as Evans and Ferreira.[9] An equally exciting interpretation that assesses the subject of *Works of Love* with an interesting look at the theme of post-Hegelianism is that of the Argentine researcher Patrícia Dip. In her book *Teoría y práxis en las obras del amor* (Theory and Praxis in *Works of Love*) the typical themes of nineteenth-century German philosophy are explored, and in this way she can determine what is typical in Kierkegaard's philosophy and how it differs from the philosophies of Feuerbach and Marx, for example.[10]

Finally, the last two texts deal with the reception of *The Concept of Anxiety* "just between us" and also questions from the current (Brazilian) reception about how we "must" read Kierkegaard today. Notably, the final text is, in a sense, an autobiographical confession of the author and shows his tribute to a leading researcher of Kierkegaard's work: the French scholar Henri-Bernard Vergote, from whom Valls takes his interpretative view and the theoretical position that Kierkegaard's work is irony from the beginning to the end of his production.[11]

Marcio Gimenes de Paula
Translated by Arthur Bartholo Gomes

---

9 C. Stephen Evans, *Kierkegaard's Ethic of Love: Divine Commands and Moral Obligations*, Oxford: Oxford University Press 2006; Jamie M. Ferreira, *Love's Grateful Striving: A Commentary on Kierkegaard's Works of Love*, Oxford: Oxford University Press 2001.

10 Patricia Carina Dip, *Teoría y praxis en las Obras del amor*, Buenos Aires: Editorial Gorla 2010, pp. 19–20.

11 We refer here especially to the monumental work of Henri-Bernard Vergote, *Sens et Répétition*, vols. 1–2, Paris: Cerf/Orante 1982.

Reviews and Critical Discussions

Undetermined.

Álvaro Valls,
O crucificado encontra Dionísio: estudos sobre Kierkegaard e Nietzsche [The Crucified Meets Dionysus: Studies on Kierkegaard and Nietzsche],

São Paulo: Edições Loyola 2013, 188 pp.

The book by Álvaro Valls, *O crucificado encontra Dionísio: estudos sobre Kierkegaard e Nietzsche* (The Crucified Meets Dionysus: Studies on Kierkegaard and Nietzsche) was published in Brazil in 2013. This publication marked a significant date: the bicentenary of the birth of the Danish author. The book is the result of many years of work by the author and collects, in its twelve chapters, thirteen essays on Kierkegaard and Nietzsche. The author makes it clear that he is not an expert on Nietzsche but rather an interested reader attentive to the comparison of his thought with that of the Danish thinker.

"Ironia e Melancolia" (Irony and Melancholy) is the first essay in the collection. Here, the author creates a dialogue between Brazilian writers such as Machado de Assis, Gregorio de Mattos, and Moacyr Scliar, with Kierkegaard's views on topics such as melancholy. It is a very curious dialogue, the purpose of which is to go through the coldness of Denmark and arrive at the tropics, making contact with Brazilian authors such as Paulo Prado and Mario de Andrade. Prado, author of the provocative work *Sobre a Tristeza Brasileira* (Essays on Brazilian Sadness), begins his reflection in a tone that seems to put melancholy close to the tropics in a way that is more than we are usually aware of:

> In a radiant land lives a sad people. This melancholy was bequeathed to them by the discoverers who revealed it to the world and populated it. The splendid dynamism of this rude people obeyed two great impulses that dominate every psychology of discovery, and which were never generators of joy: the ambition for gold and the free and unbridled sensuality that the Renaissance resurrected as a cult.[1]

A fruitful approach to Kierkegaard could be established from this point, leaving aside the relationship with Brazilian thought. The theme of melancholy and modernity can also be found in a sociological perspective in an intriguing work by Harvie Ferguson, called *Melancholy and the Critique of Modernity*. According to the author,

---

1 Paulo Prado, *Ensaio sobre a tristeza brasileira*, São Paulo: Ibrasa 1981, p. 17.

"the notion of melancholy was adapted to describe all that is peculiar in the modern world....Melancholia is a modern Prometheus."[2] Here there is a clear relation to aspects of modern life, such as observation, the *flaneur*, and one recalls Baudelaire's theses on *spleen.* In the twentieth century, one can find these topics in many other authors who knew Baudelaire as well as Walter Benjamin, and also in the classic work of Julia Kristeva.[3] Valls surely makes an advance with respect to Kierkegaard's contributions to the view about the formation of Brazilian national identity, but he could have gone further in Kierkegaard's relationship with modernity and in the research of authors who are as important for this set of issues.

The following text, called "Sócrates oscilando entre Kierkegaard e Nietzsche" (Socrates Oscillating between Kierkegaard and Nietzsche) is a curious interpretation of the Athenian thinker through the lens of Nietzsche. Indeed, this is also an interpretation of the concept of Socratic irony and how it became central to the Kierkegaardian *oeuvre.* It is actually an attempt to show in nuance the multiple faces of Socrates in the works of the Danish author, comparing it with the Nietzschean way of understanding these nuances. If Nietzsche seems to comprehend Socrates as the creator of dialectics and a denier of life, and if Kierkegaard sees in Socrates the origin of irony and seeks to take up this position, it could then be said that Valls' text seems to address exactly this confrontation. Strictly speaking, the view that seeks to understand Nietzsche's Socrates in a more proper way is old and seems to come from the writings of Kaufmann.[4]

The next essay, "Ironia socrática e Ironia kierkegaardiana" (Socratic Irony and Kierkegaardian Irony), delves into this question a little further. Valls follows here the view of Vergote,[5] for whom the work of Kierkegaard began and ended in irony. The convergence of Kierkegaard's and Nietzsche's views or the debate over its meaning in the nineteenth century has already been addressed in a very meaningful work by Angier called *Either Kierkegaard or Nietzsche.*[6] Here, there is a discussion about the notion of subjectivity in both authors, which strengthens the discussion of the figure of Socrates in Kierkegaard as much as in Nietzsche. Angier's discussion turns out to be very thought-provoking due to a more intense treatment of the moral discussion.

The text "Heiberg e Brandes, críticos contemporâneos de Kierkegaard e Nietzsche" (Heiberg and Brandes: Contemporary Critics of Kierkegaard and Nietzsche) investigates two authors, one who was important to Danish Hegelianism (Heiberg), and the other for the cultural dissemination of Kierkegaard's work in Europe (Brandes). Both were students of aesthetic issues, which makes the comparison useful. Brandes was even a personal friend of Nietzsche, with whom he exchanged numerous

---

2 Harvey Ferguson, *Melancholy and the Critique of Modernity*, London: Routledge 1995, p. xiii.

3 Júlia Kristeva, *Soleil noir, dépression et mélancolie*, Paris: Gallimard 1987.

4 Walter Kaufmann, *Nietzsche: Philosopher, Psychologist, Antichrist*, Princeton: Princeton University Press 1974.

5 Henri-Bernard Vergote, *Sens et Répétition: essai sur l'ironie kierkegaardienne*, vols. 1–2, Paris: Cerf/Orante 1982.

6 Tom P.S. Angier, *Either Kierkegaard or Nietzsche*, Aldershot: Ashgate 2006.

letters and, in one, recommended that he read a deep Danish psychologist: Søren Kierkegaard. This was unfortunately impossible for Nietzsche due to his illness, and, it seems, we have only this record about it. The Danish critic and cosmopolitan thinker Georg Brandes is one of the most intriguing figures of the nineteenth and twentieth centuries. His extensive work, whose influence surpassed Denmark's borders and went even beyond Europe, comprises several volumes. One of its merits was perhaps to insert Danish philosophy into the most important intellectual debates of the period. Brandes' writings contain polemical and literary works, and biographies. A distinctive feature of his polemical writings is that they are marked by the central themes of the nineteenth century, especially in the German context. One of the main traits of his thought is atheism. With this point of view in mind, Brandes builds his vision of Kierkegaard, seeing him as an ally in the defense of his views. Heiberg, in turn, is presented here more as a man of the arts than as a Hegel scholar. It could be said the work would have profited remarkably, had it investigated the clues provided by Habib Malik concerning Brandes' interpretation of Kierkegaard and his relationship with his contemporary Heiberg.[7]

"A ética dos discursos kierkegaardianos" (The Ethics of the Kierkegaardian Discourses) is the title of the fifth essay of Valls' work. In it, the author, strongly influenced by the interpretation of Henri-Bernard Vergote, begins with the question of how to read Kierkegaard's work, understanding it as irony from beginning to end. This approach serves also to emphasize what Vergote calls the second Kierkegaardian route,[8] where the Danish author seems to ally himself with those who, some might assume, would be his opponents, such as Feuerbach and other critics of Christianity. However, these authors actually become allies in the critique of Christianity and in an attempt to articulate a new concept: Christhood, or the typically Christian. This second route also has a connection with what is called "second ethics," that is, the typically Christian ethics in contrast to Greek ethics of the good and the beautiful. The discussion is deepened even more when it takes into account *Works of Love* in the next essay called "Estética, ética e religião nos discursos de 1847" (Aesthetics, Ethics and Religion in the Discourses of 1847).

The ethical discussion is also the theme of the seventh chapter, "O amor dos poetas e o que se torna dever" (The Love of the Poets and that which becomes Duty). Here, in a very Kierkegaardian mood, Valls points out, based on two central works (*Fear and Trembling* and *Works of Love*), what an ethical duty to love implies and where it differs from Kantian rational duty. The dialogue with the views of the German thinker are also valid in virtue of the gaps left open by him, possible clues for an investigation of greater scope. Evans points out, with extreme shrewdness in one of his works, that the clue to a rapprochement between Kierkegaard and Kant can lie in a further investigation of the philosophical views of the nineteenth century: "The tendency of theology from Kant to Hegel, and even in the liberal Protestantism of the nineteenth century as a whole was to reduce genuine faith to ethics. Jesus

---

7 Habib Malik, *Receiving Kierkegaard: The Early Impact and Transmission of his Thought*, Washington, D.C.: Catholic University of America Press 1997, pp. 183–90.

8 Vergote, *Sens et Répétition: essai sur l'ironie kierkegaardienne*, vol. 2, pp. 245–307.

was seen more as a profound ethics teacher and less as a divine savior."[9] Evans also seems right when he claims that "for Kant, individuals are subject to moral duties simply because, as human beings, they are rational."[10] This seems to contrast sharply with Kierkegaard, who believed that the certainty of our duty to love can rest only in God, who, being immutable, provides a guarantee to men, and rationality cannot provide its own foundation, as Kant argued. Of course, there is room both in Kierkegaard and Kant for free agency, although that might run counter to God or reason. In the same way, the next text, "O Elogio do amor desinteressado" (In Praise of Selfless Love), deepens the analysis of the same theme by examining *Works of Love.*

Nietzsche reappears in the next essay, "Sobre a saúde e a doença" (About Health and Disease). This is a discussion that seeks to rescue a function often neglected by philosophy: healing, care, and concern with issues of life and death. Such a discussion also fits well with contemporary debates on bioethics, including Michel Foucault's works. The next two chapters, "Temor, Medo e Angústia I e II" (Fear, Dread and Anxiety I and II), explore a theme quite dear to Kierkegaardian studies. Based on a reading of *The Concept of Anxiety*, the author seeks to juxtapose important ethical concepts in Kierkegaard and Nietzsche to one another, by means of inserting these topics into the discussions presented by Danish literature. The work *The Concept of Anxiety* will be, not fortuitously, recalled in the final essay, which has the title "Enfim, ler o Conceito de Angústia" (Anyway, Reading *The Concept of Anxiety*). As Marino claims, this is one of the most difficult books by Kierkegaard.[11] Its Introduction, for example, makes an attempt to describe dizziness, and it could be taken as merely playing with profound themes and concepts. Kierkegaard's text has all the elements of a farce. His ethical intuition, which follows the Socratic path, is to distinguish what is known from what is unknown.

The last essay in Valls' book, "Um leitor de Nietzsche avant la letter" (A Reader of Nietzsche *avant la lettre*), is perhaps the most provocative in this work. In it, the author presents us with a Kierkegaard, who, perhaps, would have been "Nietzschean" even before Nietzsche, and makes use of much of his criticism, notably the criticism of Christianity. There is here a similarity to the central view of Karl Löwith that regards Nietzsche and Kierkegaard as post-Hegelian authors and critics of Christianity as well.[12]

Marcio Gimenes de Paula
Translated by Arthur Bartholo Gomes

---

9 C. Stephen Evans, *Kierkegaard's Ethic of Love*, Oxford: Oxford University Press 2004, p. 83.

10 Ibid., p. 69.

11 Gordon Marino, "Anxiety in *The Concept of Anxiety*," in *The Cambridge Companion to Kierkegaard*, ed. by Alastair Hannay and Gordon Marino, Cambridge: Cambridge University Press 1998, pp. 308–28.

12 Karl Löwith, *Von Hegel zu Nietzsche. Der revolutionäre Bruch im Denken des Neunzehnten Jahrhunderts*, Hamburg: Meiner 1978.

Review and Critical Discussion

Paula, Marcio Gimenes, review in *Revista de Filosofia Moderna e Contemporânea da Universidade de Brasília*, vol. 2, no. 1, 2014, pp. 177–9.

II. Secondary Literature in Romanian

Mădălina Diaconu, *Pe marginea abisului. Søren Kierkegaard și nihilismul secolului al XIX-lea* [On the Edge of the Abyss: Søren Kierkegaard and Nineteenth-Century Nihilism],

Bucharest: Editura Științifică 1996, 238 pp.

A fairly voluminous amount of scholarship documents Kierkegaard's distinct insights into the nihilistic crux of modernity by virtue of the latter's anti-spiritual proclivities. Yet, not so much attention has been paid to the nihilist latencies of Kierkegaard's thought itself, including its religious side. Mădălina Diaconu's volume tries to fill this gap and does it quite convincingly by first unfolding a series of nihilistic characteristics in Kierkegaard's early works and in a more controversial fashion, by unearthing the incipient nihilism of Kierkegaard's personality and religion. The book unfolds in five sequences. It first delimits the conceptual ambit of nihilism and offers a short history of its nineteenth-century Romantic and post-Romantic expressions. Next, it draws a nuanced tableau of the theme at hand. Diaconu views nihilism as having multiple causes. The main ones are an existentialist view of reflexivity, the self's misrelation to or refusal of, alterity, a distorted understanding of freedom, and a disastrous reaction to limit situations. In the third part—which is the richest—Diaconu discovers traces of the nihilist constellation in Kierkegaard's *The Concept of Irony*, *Either/Or*, Part One, *Repetition*, *Fear and Trembling*, *The Concept of Anxiety*, and *The Sickness unto Death*. The fourth part is more speculative and deals with the allegedly latent nihilism in both Kierkegaard's biography and theology. The volume ends with an applied analysis of three, specifically nihilistic, motifs—namely, nothingness, the shadow, and the marionette—without substantial reference to Kierkegaard.

On the Edge of the Abyss fruitfully brings Kierkegaard into dialogue with the early Romantic nihilism of the genius (or the exception), the disabused nihilism cultivated by the late Romantics, and to a much lesser extent the active, violent nihilism of the Russian anarchists. While signs of Romantic nihilism are clearly present in *The Concept of Irony* and *Either/Or*, Part One, the active form is more insidious but can be uncontroversially illustrated by Kierkegaard's reflections on the demonic. To be more specific, Diaconu equates the nihilist self with "a perverted inwardness,"[1] that is to say, with a dysfunctional or corrupted relationality between the opposing, constitutive elements of human nature. The core of Diaconu's argument is that the nihilistic stance originates either in the hedonistic playfulness and ironic subjectivism of aesthetic existence; or in spiritual demonism, which almost irreparably vitiates humankind's relations to transcendence.

Diaconu develops three kinds of nihilism in Kierkegaard's pseudonymous works: the aesthetic, the ironic, and the demonic. The coordinates of the aesthetic nihilism—which, interestingly enough, constitute a possible prolegomenon to the authentically ethico-religious existence—are inferred from the opening section of *Either/Or*, Part One, the "Diapsalmata." Diaconu notes that on its dark side, aestheticism entails, besides a traumatic break with immediacy, "the individual's extrication from both ordinary existence and the unproblematic harmony with the world, compelling one to return to and discover one's selfhood."[2] Thus, the turmoil and tribulations of the aesthete can be interpreted as "the call of [true] selfhood requiring actualization,"[3] a call that succeeds the experience of pure immediacy and precedes the leap into the ethical or religious sphere. Diaconu's thesis states that the aesthetic self is haunted by nihilism because of its chaotic inwardness, detached hedonism, morally and socially disengaged individualism, emotional instability, inner contradictions, boredom, despair, and depression. Thus, aesthetic existence—as depicted not only in the "Diapsalmata" but also in *Repetition*[4]—harbors a nihilistic potential because it is "immoral from an ethical viewpoint, existentially inauthentic, and religiously sinful."[5] In a critical vein, one should note Diaconu's omission that the aesthetic writer A is more often than not ironic in his confessions, and that he also can be quite humorous in his dismissive attitudes.

Concerning ironic nihilism, Diaconu claims that it issues from the infinite and absolute negativity of irony (with its rigid detachment from exteriority); from the ironist's cynical interiority, given his misuse of freedom which allows him to isolate himself from others and treat them degradingly; from irony's sublimation of reality into imaginary possibilities; and finally, from the rejection of the divine alterity which posited the ironist's self.

Still, for Diaconu, Kierkegaard seems to get to the crux of the nihilistic phenomenon in his multifaceted discussion of the demonic. The first echoes in this sense come from *The Concept of Anxiety*, where anxiety appears as a possible hindrance to spiritual becoming whenever it confronts the self with the void of its freedom and with its burdensome infinite responsibility. But the nihilistic charge is the most potent in what Kierkegaard calls the anxiety before the good. Diaconu holds that the latter

---

1 Mădălina Diaconu, *Pe marginea abisului. Søren Kierkegaard şi nihilismul secolului al XIX-lea*, Bucharest: Editura Ştiinţifică 1996, pp. 65–70. All translations are mine.

2 Ibid., p. 160.

3 Ibid.

4 In *Repetition*, Diaconu highlights the melancholy solipsism of the exceptional individual whose nihilistic *Weltanschauung* results from "a futile effort to make the leap into the ethical and to realize the reconciliation with the universal" (ibid., p. 103).

5 Ibid., p. 91.

is the most destructive because it arises when the individual has already discovered one's true, transcendently given self. Subsequently, the individual "refuses to accept any dependence on the divine, while seeing oneself as fully autonomous, and absurdly trying to ground the world from an absolute position."[6] Even more nihilistic is the defiant enclosing reserve of the demonic with the ensuing refusal to open itself to any kind of alterity. From *The Sickness unto Death* Diaconu obtains additional confirmations that the nihilist is driven by a perverted will which keeps him at bay from spiritual authenticity. In this particular volume the author identifies and carefully develops the "passive nihilism"[7] of the despair of weakness in tandem with the scornful and more assertive negativism of the demonic personality.

The most debatable hypothesis of the book is that Kierkegaard was, not only a theorizer of nihilism *avant la lettre*, but also an idiosyncratic, albeit never full or deliberate, nihilist in his own right. Diaconu holds that signs of this possibility can be clearly detected in Kierkegaard's private life as well as in his public authorial output. To begin with the second, Diaconu contends that there exists a deeply embedded negativity in Kierkegaard's thought, pervading each and every stage of existence, including the religious. Thus, apart from aestheticism, the ethical also opens a nihilistic vista via its inevitable failures in the confrontation with guilt, repentance, and the religious exception.[8] Furthermore, Diaconu conjectures that religion itself is not entirely void of nihilistic undertones. She relies on the fact that Kierkegaard's spiritual self-realization is purportedly predicated on the individual's "isolation from the world, the narcissistic introspection inherent in the process of self-becoming, irrationalism, epistemological skepticism or subjectivism, the presence of suffering in the religious sphere, and the permanence of anxiety and despair."[9] Next, Diaconu realizes that, on the one hand, Kierkegaard conceives the divine alterity in radical terms; namely, his "God is *das ganz Andere*, incomprehensible because paradoxical, and reveals himself only through miracles or the Holy Ghost."[10] On the other hand, Kierkegaard diminishes God's difference "inasmuch as faith runs the risk of instituting an object about which one cannot know whether it exists or not, and thus what ultimately counts is not the object of faith (that is, the divine otherness) but rather the relation to it (i.e., the passion of interiority)."[11] To further illustrate her point, Diaconu invokes the figure of Abraham with whom the nihilist shares a fundamental feature: both are self-withdrawing exceptions who consider themselves entitled to suspend moral principles and ethical teleology. When faced with an ordeal, the demonic exception practices a deliberate self-enclosing while rejecting both the good and God's help. In contrast, Abraham does seem justified

---

6 Ibid., p. 161.

7 Ibid., p. 141.

8 Diaconu derives this thesis from Kierkegaard's delineation of the ethical from *Fear and Trembling*, *Repetition*, and *Stages on Life's Way*. Unfortunately, she leaves aside the auspicious connotations of religious ethics from *Works of Love*.

9 Diaconu, *Pe marginea abisului*, p. 197.

10 Ibid., p. 203.

11 Ibid., p. 203.

before God but solely by virtue of the absurd. From here Diaconu infers that "Kierkegaard's idea of the [religiously] justified exception, of a teleological suspension of morality, and of an absurdist faith contains an incipient nihilism which could lead to monstrous moral acts."[12] To phrase it briefly, the nihilistic danger of Kierkegaard's religiosity is that after having overcome the existential-spiritual insufficiencies of aestheticism and ethics, the person is called to a type of faith that remains inaccessible. As Diaconu puts it, "the individual seems condemned to persist in a painful suspension between all the stages given that, after having forsaken the world, one cannot reach even God."[13]

As to the nihilistic traits of Kierkegaard's own personality, Diaconu enumerates his split neurotic nature, the flight from himself as a result of self-alienation, his proverbial melancholy, his intense disillusioned reflexivity, his solitude and suicidal propensities, his incapacity to assume the marital role, a quasi ahistorical detachment from his contemporaries, and so on. However, Diaconu hesitates to classify Kierkegaard as a classic nihilist and prefers to stress his ambivalence towards the subject.[14] Contra Diaconu, we should remember that many of the above-mentioned attributes have been long dismissed as part of the Kierkegaard myth. Others remain pertinent, but we cannot say for sure whether they are necessarily conducive to a nihilistic world-view. Moreover, Diaconu ignores other aspects of Kierkegaard's personality which might temper her stark judgments: for instance, Kierkegaard's humor, generosity, and even playfulness, not to mention his eagerness to communicate with anybody on the streets of Copenhagen, be they strangers or acquaintances, merchants or intellectuals, poor or privileged. It may be that Kierkegaard was a melancholy neurotic, and yet, it is his seemingly endless sufferings that occasioned an incredible literary production. Further, Kierkegaard might have displayed an abnormal inclination toward self-punishment,[15] but he also warned against the morbid appropriation of repentance, which he openly qualified as demonic.

Two different factors lay at the root of almost all the misunderstandings of this volume. The first is Diaconu's avoidance of Kierkegaard's entire edifying authorship and an arbitrary selection of the pseudonymous works. Secondly, her approach rests mainly on secondary sources, the most prominent of which are Helmuth Vetter, Hermann Deuser, Wilfried Greve, George J. Stack, Michael Theunissen, Jean Wahl, Karl Löwith, and Hubertus Tellenbach. Had she dealt more directly and holistically with Kierkegaard's *oeuvre*, Diaconu could have realized that there are significant affinities and even overlaps between all spheres of existence;[16] that the image of

---

12 Ibid., p. 155.

13 Ibid., p. 195.

14 On this issue, Diaconu may run into a self-contradiction. She wants to argue that nihilism is a positive phenomenon only insofar as it can help one find God. At the same time, she insists that Kierkegaard's religiosity is negative at its core. Moreover, if the latter point is the case, then Kierkegaard's attitude towards nihilism was not as ambiguous as Diaconu seems to suggest.

15 Diaconu, *Pe marginea abisului*, p. 177.

16 For the opposite view, see ibid., p. 102; p. 203.

Kierkegaard's Christianity as unattainable is directly contradicted by the sanguine depiction of it in *Works of Love* and *Upbuilding Discourses in Various Spirits*; that the only way out of despair is essentially Christian and not Judaic;[17] that Abraham is presented more like an ideal and for this very reason Kierkegaard clearly opposed any reenactment of Isaac's sacrifice; that Kierkegaard's religious thought also has a cataphatic component which dialectically counterbalances its negative side; that Kierkegaard affirmed the traditional Christian dogma to a greater extent than is usually admitted; that he displayed a subtle combination of rigor and lenience when trying to communicate the severity or loftiness of the Christian religion; and that solipsism and acosmic fideism are labels which do not capture the spirit of Kierkegaard's religiosity.

Nonetheless, *On the Edge of the Abyss* constitutes a cornerstone in the Romanian reception of Kierkegaard's thought. Equally noteworthy is that initially the volume was the graduation thesis for the author's bachelor of letters degree. Furthermore, upon publication it constituted an immense gift to all Romanian philosophy readers, deprived as they were of any contact with Kierkegaard ever since the communist takeover in 1945.

Leo Stan

[17] Contrast with ibid., p. 143.

Review and Critical Discussion

Irina, Nicolae, "Romania: A Survey of Kierkegaard's Reception, Translation, and Research," in *Kierkegaard's International Reception*, Tome II, *Southern, Central and Eastern Europe*, ed. by Jon Stewart, Aldershot: Ashgate 2009 (*Kierkegaard Research: Sources, Reception and Resources*, vol. 8), pp. 301–16; see pp. 306–7.

Grigore Popa, *Existență și adevăr la Sören Kierkegaard* [Existence and Truth in Søren Kierkegaard's Thought],

Sibiu: Tiparul Tipografiei Arhidiecezane 1940, 354 pp.

Grigore Popa (1910–94) was first and foremost a historian of philosophy. He received his doctorate in 1939 and was a promising academic. However, immediately after World War II, he was dismissed on political grounds from his assistant lecturer post and imprisoned. After his release, his authorial output consisted only of translations and scattered newspaper articles. In addition to being a scholar of philosophy, he was a poet and an open advocate of Eastern Orthodox Christianity. The two main figures who influenced his philosophical outlook are the prominent philosopher, poet, and dramatist, Lucian Blaga (1895–1961) and Popa's mentor, Dumitru D. Roşca (1895–1980), a philosopher and historian of philosophy. Blaga introduced Popa to historicism, the philosophy of life (particularly, Bergson), and German culture. More importantly, Blaga offered Popa a complex theory of spirit, where the ultimate horizon of existence is an anonymous transcendent entity called "the mystery," whose interaction with humankind gives the latter the highest meaning and existential plenitude in life. Through his main work, *Existența tragică*,[1] Roşca mediated Popa's introduction to existentialism, on which he wrote an entire book.[2]

These details are absolutely vital for understanding the intellectual context and spiritual amplitude of *Existence and Truth*. Without exaggeration, the book can be safely considered the first and most reliable introduction to Kierkegaard's thought in the Romanian republic of letters. It uses the German and French translations that were available to the public between 1909 and 1937, while at the same time engaging with a significant part of the extant European literature on Kierkegaard. Indeed, given the time of its publication, Popa's study displays incredibly few gaps or misunderstandings. Among the book's debatable aspects are its style and structure. More often than not, the author intersperses his discourse with lyrical and

---

[1] Dumitru D. Roşca, *Existența tragică* [The Tragic Existence], Bucharest: Fundația pentru Literatură şi Artă "Regele Carol II" 1934.

[2] Grigore Popa, *Existențialismul* [Existentialism], Sibiu: Institutul de arte grafice "Dacia Traiană" S.A. 1943.

quite nebulous declarations, which undermine the theoretical quality of his analyses. Also, especially in his espousal of Kierkegaard's religion, Popa is unnecessarily repetitive and even sermonic, while his lax organization of the material can easily confound the reader.

Existence and Truth is divided into three parts. The first is entitled "The Dialectic of Life" and conveys the spiritual anthropology that buttresses the entire volume. Popa claims that humans generally feel an irrepressible need to surmount the multiple limitations and insufficiencies of their worldly existence. Popa identifies this need with the longing for God—that is, for both inner completeness and transcendent meaningfulness—and, not unlike Lucian Blaga, he holds that it can be fulfilled by both religion and the high achievements of culture, that is, by the quest for truth, beauty, goodness, and faith. Thus, the essence of humanity "goes beyond the sensible and finds fulfillment only in the proximity of the divine."[3] Again under the influence of Blaga, Popa adds that communing with transcendence entails our participation in "the ultimate horizons of the cosmic order."[4] In a soteriological vein, he states that our "appetite for the divine"[5] is endless as well as antagonistic since religious faith is contingent on the individual's "permanent struggle with the immediate surroundings upon which he wants to impose his desires and the laws of his soul."[6] Therefore, "while aware of our dramatic initial condition and of the evil powers that ceaselessly stalk us, we keep struggling to bring heaven into the world."[7]

An integral element of "the tragic beauty"[8] of our life is that it abounds in irrevocable paradoxes. Existence, for Popa, is structured around "the unity and discord of contradictions."[9] Furthermore, Popa holds that "the paradox mediates the communication with the concrete multiplicity of the finite and with the transcendence of the infinite, both of which are sheer offense to reason."[10] So, even if it does not entirely take away reason's prerogatives and applicability, the paradox does indicate "the existence of a world which is rebutted by the geometrical logic of the universal."[11]

Returning to the soteriological horizon, Popa notes that human nature oscillates between sinfulness—which increases suffering, while further alienating us from the sacred—and godly grace (which allows eternity to enter finitude and transfigure it). Thus, throughout the entire book, Popa repeatedly insists on the dialectical duality between sinful immanence and merciful transcendence, between the good news of salvation and the numerous dangers of evil, all against the backdrop of a ceaseless nostalgia for our holy origins.

---

3 Grigore Popa, *Existență și adevăr la Sören Kierkegaard*, 2nd ed., Cluj: Dacia 1998, p. 46. All references are to this second edition. All translations are mine.

4 Ibid., p. 27.

5 Ibid., p. 46.

6 Ibid., p. 46.

7 Ibid., p. 31.

8 Ibid., p. 36.

9 Ibid.

10 Ibid., p. 38.

11 Ibid., p. 37.

In Popa's eyes, Kierkegaard confirms in a particular way each and every element of this world-view. With that in mind, in the second part, while starting from Kierkegaard's biography, Popa initiates a philosophical, existential, and hermeneutic journey that traverses the three stages of existence (with all the intermediary passageways), and describes the "dialectical function of time"[12] in light of the opposition between a salvifically impotent worldliness and the all-powerful divinity.

In Popa's hands, Kierkegaard's philosophical portrait is nuanced and mindful of multiple angles. After insightfully observing that the unity of his thought is "symphonic, whereas his dialectic is contrapuntal,"[13] Popa characterizes Kierkegaard as "the poet of the aesthetic stage, the moralist of the ethical stage, and the lyrical dialectician of the religious stage."[14] The more problematic side of this part lies in the alleged isolationist acosmism of religiosity. Popa overstresses the solitude of Kierkegaard's believer before a radically different deity, so much so that he parallels the category of the single individual with the Nietzschean *Übermensch*.[15] Additional support for this conjecture is found in Climacus' insistence on the personal appropriation of truth, which assigns exteriority and objectivity a secondary role in spiritual matters. The conclusion will be that, for Kierkegaard, the ultimate meaningfulness of life stems solely from religion, wherein primacy belongs to the unique person and individualization is synonymous with self-denial, martyrdom, and the redemptive imitation of Christ.

In the third part, the author goes to great lengths to lay out the exclusively religious coordinates of Kierkegaard's thought. Starting from the premise—abundantly documented in the previous two parts—that the crux of human existence is spiritual, and that truth must be fully and even self-sacrificially assumed, Popa reconstitutes Kierkegaard's Christianity along the lines of disquieted interiority, passion, volition, meta-rational paradoxes, and indirectness. Christianity targets primarily the particular self because in the latter's world we deal with "decisions, supreme tensions, and concrete personal relations, full of commitment and passion."[16] Spirit, inwardness, and passion are all interrelated because the individual, by virtue of her higher call, is infinitely concerned with eternal happiness.

In the remainder of the book, Popa tackles (somewhat erratically) a host of other religious motifs. To recall the most important, he elaborates the qualitative dialectic of personal passion and objective uncertainty. In detailing the existential challenges and theoretical intricacies of the subjective appropriation of truth, the author successfully brings to the fore the dramatic, onerous, albeit always edifying, path to the eternal. The upbuilding side of this path is given by the necessity of witnessing to the truth of the suffering exemplar—an attitude which implies humility, simplicity, self-abnegating acts, a comprehensive catharsis but also perennial tribulations. A significant part is dedicated to the reciprocity between the existential commitment to the truth and paradoxicalness, the dialectic interaction of which bespeaks the

---

12 Ibid., pp. 105–17.

13 Ibid., p. 78.

14 Ibid., p. 79.

15 See ibid., pp. 92–5.

16 Ibid., p. 188.

ongoing tension and vividness of faith. While clarifying that the true object of faith is not a more or less abstract doctrine but rather the concrete reality of the teacher-redeemer, Popa adroitly points to the vigor of the exemplar and his high demands on the follower. In the same perspective, Popa succeeds in showing how emphatically and masterfully Kierkegaard struggled against the saccharine sentimentalizing, speculative dilution, and utilitarian perversion of the absolute truth.

Certainly, *Existence and Truth* is marked by a few striking points of lack of clarity or unresolved tensions. One of them concerns the acosmic undertones of Kierkegaard's soteriology. As stated above, Popa excessively focuses on the isolation, solitude, individualism, and unworldliness inherent in the human pursuit of God and salvation.[17] Whenever he admits the role nature's beauty and the openness towards others play in the individual's endeavors to draw closer to God, he does so only in passing and mainly for rhetorical purposes.[18] Additionally, the book lacks any reference to *Works of Love*, in particular to the indispensability of human otherness in aiming for salvation. Even more, when referring to Kierkegaard's meditations on the biblical theme of the lilies in the field and the birds of the air, Popa retains only the importance of invisibility,[19] without mentioning the open celebration of the visible present, not only in the above-mentioned discourses, but also in *Fear and Trembling*.

The next debatable issue regards the dialectical encounter between temporality and the eternal. An initial ambiguity stems from Popa's insistence on the almost constitutive link between futurity and the eternal. However, when speaking of becoming contemporary with the God-man via imitation, Popa recognizes that the central temporal dimension of religious existence is the present.[20] Furthermore, in the same context Popa observes that in Kierkegaard's fideism history appears transfigured by fideistic engagements.[21] And yet, when dealing with the clash between eternal bliss and earthly sufferings, Popa acknowledges their infinite qualitative difference.[22]

A similar tension can be found in Popa's minute analysis of faith's relation to reason. The author is careful enough to point out that Kierkegaard's religiosity does not eliminate the place and role of rationality due to its justified superrationalism.[23] Simultaneously, whenever confronted with the multilayered contradictoriness and absurdity of religion, Popa tends to imply that the latter is much more irrational than expected.[24] Critical comments can also be made concerning the import of grace in the attainment and preservation of faith. Popa is very clear when warning that God's unmediated assistance is absolutely indispensable in the decision to believe and follow Christ,[25] but at the same time he asserts that, once attained, faith "takes away

17 See ibid., p. 184; p. 204; p. 210; p. 236.
18 See in this sense ibid., pp. 227–8; p. 238.
19 Ibid., pp. 242–4.
20 Compare and contrast in this sense, ibid., pp. 107–8; p. 246; p. 249 with p. 221, p. 248.
21 Ibid., p. 247; p. 250.
22 Ibid., p. 241.
23 Ibid., p. 114 note 35.
24 See, for example, ibid., p. 187; p. 195; p. 203.
25 Ibid., p. 218; p. 240; pp. 257–8.

any possibility of offense and sin."[26] Finally, one could object to Popa's too sharp distinction between the three spheres of existence;[27] to his contradictory statements on time's priority vis-à-vis the eternal[28] or on repentance's effect on sin;[29] and to his misleading understanding of the two movements of faith from *Fear and Trembling*.[30] Yet, despite all of these problems, the book can be commended for its holistic approach—which never loses sight of the particulars—not to mention its expansion of Kierkegaard's impact beyond the borders of Western Europe.

Leo Stan

[26] Ibid., p. 252.

[27] See ibid., p. 55; p. 119 and contrast with p. 131 where Popa alludes to the ethical's coexistence with the aesthetic and the religious.

[28] See ibid., p. 112; p. 117; p. 172 note 87.

[29] Contrast ibid., p. 157; p. 160.

[30] Ibid., p. 255.

Reviews and Critical Discussions

Diaconu, Mădălina, "Die Kierkegaard-Rezeption in Rumänien," *Revue roumaine de philosophie*, vol. 45, nos. 1–2, 2001, pp. 149–64.
Irina, Nicolae, "Romania: A Survey of Kierkegaard's Reception, Translation, and Research," in *Kierkegaard's International Reception*, Tome II, *Southern, Central and Eastern Europe*, ed. by Jon Stewart, Aldershot: Ashgate 2009 (*Kierkegaard Research: Sources, Reception and Resources*, vol. 8), pp. 301–16; see pp. 304–5.
Micu, Constantin, review in *Meşterul Manole*, vol. 3, nos. 5–6, 1941, pp. 27–8.

III. Secondary Literature in Russian

Piama Pavlovna Gaidenko, *Трагедия эстетизма. О миросозерцании Серена Киркегора* [The Tragedy of Aestheticism: On the World-View of Søren Kierkegaard],

Moscow: Iskysstvo 1970, 207 pp.

Piama Pavlovna Gidenko (b. 1934) is a Soviet Russian philosopher and historian of philosophy. She has published a number of books dedicated to the works and philosophy of freedom of Fichte, Kierkegaard, Vladimir Soloviev, and Heidegger. A special focus of her academic research has been the relation between philosophy and science. The reason for the strong interest in Kierkegaard's works and personality in the twentieth century is an overarching question Gidenko approaches in her monograph *The Tragedy of Aestheticism: On the World-View of Søren Kierkegaard.*[1]

Gidenko reads Kierkegaard as a dialogue of the author with himself in order to identify the problems and grasp the actual content of what is at issue, rather than to find an explanation. Her dialectical approach is presented in contrast with existentialist, Freudian, Protestant, and Catholic interpretations, which build Kierkegaard's existential concepts into existing philosophical systems.

Kierkegaard's main argument, according to Gidenko, is that the truth is not what one knows, but what one can either be or not be, and that the objectivization of the truth is one of the reasons for the spiritual crisis of the epoch. Kierkegaard compares the state of a speculative philosopher as an impartial objective scientist with one of a suicide, who withdraws himself out of his finite nature in order to grasp the infinite. In order to show the frailty of the systematic holism, Gidenko refers to a passage in the Gospels that Kierkegaard uses in *Either/Or*,[2] *Four Upbuilding Discourses* (from 1843),[3] and *The Point of View for My Work as an Author*,[4] namely, "What good is it for someone to gain the whole world, yet forfeit their soul?"[5] Following the French

---

1 Piama Pavlovna Gaidenko, *Трагедия эстетизма. О миросозерцании Серена Киркегора* [The Tragedy of Aestheticism: On the World-View of Søren Kierkegaard], Moscow: Iskysstvo 1970 (2nd ed., Moscow: Respublika 1997; 3rd ed., Moscow: LKI 2010).

2 *SKS* 3, 172, 210 / *EO2*, 176, 220.

3 *SKS* 5, 141 / *EUD*, 138.

4 *SKS* 16, 12 / *PV*, 24.

5 Matthew 16:26.

philosopher Jean Wahl and his book *Kierkegaardian Studies*,[6] she emphasizes the homogeneity of Kierkegaard—the philosopher—and Kierkegaard—a single individual—whose philosophy serves not to gain possession of the truth but to help one become true to oneself. Gidenko juxtaposes Kierkegaard to the philosophy of rational conceptualization, developed in the post-Cartesian time, and approaches him as a "private thinker,"[7] rather than a philosopher. Kierkegaard denies the possibility of being a single individual and a universal medium simultaneously, and Gidenko describes fascist leaders as being an example of such a perverted transformation: in the nineteenth and especially the twentieth century, the Marxist concept of "communal essence," having been applied to the spiritual sphere of life, turned individuals into bureaucrats, or demagogues, whose care for the communal well-being became their means of subsistence or wealth.

Making another attempt to reconcile the truth's subjective character and its objective credibility, the twentieth-century existentialists only multiplied the former. Shestov addresses faith in the absurd, without leaving his philosophical work for the sake of absolute intimacy with God, and this makes the content of his philosophy contradict its form; Karl Jaspers, trying to deal with the impossibility of combining existentialism and the subjective philosophy's universality, or communal validity, replaces the latter with the concept of "existential communication." Using examples from *Three Upbuilding Discourses* (from 1843), Gidenko places the origin of this paradox where Kierkegaard tries to mark a borderline between the madness of those pursuing the subjective or objective truth.

Gaidenko suggests that the twentieth-century capitalist and mass media society reflect the mind described by Kierkegaard as passively succumbing to objective truth, which has been mechanically imposed upon it by the ideologues. She shows that consumer society, the birth of which Kierkegaard predicted in his critique of objectivity, is comic and lunatic. Gidenko also uses a dialectical trope and juxtaposes his concept of freedom with Hegel's philosophy of a man in history.

Kierkegaard's emphasis on the inward life made Gidenko look for the keys to his philosophy in his intimate spiritual, albeit not purely personal, life, as it had been suggested for instance by August Vetter in his book *Frömmigkeit als Leidenschaft. Eine Deutung*.[8] She claims that these very personal concerns that Kierkegaard put at the center of his philosophy were what made his works so popular in the epoch of impersonal slogans and propaganda, which turned the different concepts of truth into the manipulating mottos.

Gidenko inevitably addresses the facts of Kierkegaard's biography in order to approach the central theme of the monograph, namely, the problem of the correlation between the aesthetic and the ethical. Gidenko's methodology balances between and synthesizes all possible systematic ways of interpreting Kierkegaard, starting with the biographical, existentialist, psychoanalytical (Erich Przywara and his concept of Kierkegaard's "unconscious Catholicism"), historical, historico-genetical

---

6 Jean Wahl, *Études kierkegaardiennes*, Paris: F. Aubier 1938.

7 Gaidenko, *Трагедия эстетизма. О миросозерцании Серена Киркегора*, p. 19.

8 Ibid., p. 32.

(Niels Thulstrup), and the scientific and philosophical (namely, dialectical and comparative) approaches.

The monograph focuses on the analysis of the maze of pseudonyms that Kierkegaard creates in order to hide and at the same time manifest his intimate self through making himself absolutely incomprehensible. Gidenko supports the idea of Kierkegaard's indirect communication as the only way to talk about the ambiguous nature of key concepts. Kierkegaard does not juxtapose different ways of understanding the truth, but rather focuses on being in truth. Thus the works of Kierkegaard become not a dialogue but an existential drama, where not only particular characters, but whole works, play the crucial roles. Kierkegaard's forms of indirect communication as the very essence and value of his philosophy are investigated by Gidenko in terms of Kierkegaard's interest in Romanticism with its tendency to break through human limitations; she also explores Kierkegaard's interest in the concept of irony, in the context of which he creates an ungraspable image of Socrates. Gidenko connects Kierkegaard with Immanuel Kant's transcendental aestheticism, Friedrich Schiller's ideas about moral delight, and Friedrich Schelling's philosophy of art as the target of the ethical education. She places him between the real and the ideal, between cognition and creation, and regards him as a vehicle of the imagination as a myth-creating force. Gidenko shows how Kierkegaard, following Fichte's idea of transition from the direct relation with the world into the realm of ethics, makes it through the leap, or act of choice, which transforms the nihilistic, ironic freedom of Socrates into a positive, "co-creative" freedom, which prevails in the Romantic cult of longing and melancholy. Gidenko finishes her analysis by building on Kierkegaard's concept of the "demonic" aesthetic in her discussion of the history of music and tragedy, Dostoevsky's depiction of beauty and spirituality, and the demonism of faith, which, according to Kant, would be considered as sinful preference of the individual to the communal. Following Kierkegaard's poetics, Gidenko paradoxically (or rather ironically) returns to the discussion of irony as an absurd faith in Abraham's "cruel and fearful God-the ironist."[9]

Irina Kruchinina

---

9 Ibid., p. 202.

Reviews and Critical Discussions

Kostelanitz, Boris, *Драма и действие: Лекции по теории драмы* [Drama and Action: Lectures on the Theory of Drama], ed. by Vadim Maximov, Moscow: Sovpadeniye 2007, pp. 279–81.

Makolkin, Anna, "Russian, Stalinist and Soviet Re-readings of Kierkegaard: Lev Shestov and Piama Gaidenko," *Canadian Slavonic Papers*, vol. 44, nos. 1–2, 2002, pp. 79–96.

Sergey Alexandrovich Isaev, *Философско-эстетическое учение С. Кьеркегора (критический анализ)* [The Philosophico-Aesthetic Teaching of S. Kierkegaard (A Critical Analysis)],

Moscow 1982, 149 pp.

A graduate of the Faculty of Philosophy of Moscow State University, Sergey Isaev (1951–2000) made his way into philosophy as a scholar with interests that remained practically unchanged throughout his life. Isaev's dissertation, *The Philosophico-Aesthetic Teaching of S. Kierkegaard (A Critical Analysis)* became a foundation for his further research, the scope of which had been already outlined in 1976–79, during his Ph.D. courses. This work was unfortunately never published as a book but is available as a manuscript in the Russian State Library. After his dissertation, the range of Isaev's interests included (1) the possibility of communicating religious truth; (2) the connection between religious content and aesthetics, and specifically the possibility of translating the divine revelation into textual form, and, in particular, into the form of belles-lettres, which was of fundamental importance for European culture; (3) the connection of the Creator and the Artist; the equating of religious creativity with artistic creativity; the idea of Revelation as some kind of drama embodied in a piece of art; and (4) the avant-garde in theater and literature and its themes.

Later, Samuel Beckett's *Waiting for Godot* and Antonin Artaud's plays, which were translated by Isaev, would become classics of Russian theater translation. For twelve years and up until his death, Sergey Isaev held the post of rector of the Russian Academy of Theater Arts (GITIS), and his administrative activities are thought to have led to his death (according to one of the versions, he fell victim to the conflict that had broken out about the academy building having great historical value).

Kierkegaard had already excited Isaev's interest during his time as student, and the aroused interest led to a new kind of theologian, an actor theologian. But such a phenomenon was not easily tolerated in the Soviet Union. In order to understand the way in which Kierkegaard was received and identified by official Soviet philosophical discourse, be it as a fervent idealist, obscurant and, furthermore, antagonist of Hegel's dialectics (as Kierkegaard was seen in light of predominant materialistic ideology), it is necessary to call to mind some circumstances. By the end of the 1970s, the Soviet history of Western philosophy appeared as an extraordinarily miserable phenomenon. The quick-tempered Stalinist prosecutors of "bourgeois" philosophy seemed to have fallen into the past. Nevertheless, the efforts of a free and substantive reception of philosophy that emerged in the years of the Khrushchev thaw (one of them being the brilliant *Tragedy of Aestheticism* by Piama Gaidenko issued in 1970)[1] were also fading away under a suffocating stagnation. Timelessness seemed to last forever. Implemented at philosophical faculties, the practice of systematical analysis of philosophical studies for the sake of clarifying their "fitness" for particular purposes of Marxist interpretation of philosophy was becoming the flesh and blood of "ideological front line functionaries." Unfortunately, this practice was also absorbed by Sergey Isaev. Unlike Genet, Beckett, and his other later interests, Isaev's Kierkegaard always bore the imprint of this restricted, utilitarian approach.

The practice of embedding a thinker in the procrustean bed of Marxism had adverse effects for the late Soviet translation schools as well. The need to set forth modern philosophical studies with inadequate language was changing them beyond recognition. This gave birth to the sad prejudice that a true philosopher articulated his thoughts in a tensile and obscure manner. The strange irony of it is that Isaev's translation of Kierkegaard—unlike those of Beckett and other no less complicated authors—fell victim to this very approach.

But this would not happen until the 1990s, when Isaev and his wife started publishing their translations from the Danish. Still, Isaev's articles and thesis work (written with a reliance on Hirsch's translations) always presented Kierkegaard as a fairly clear writer, whose range of problems, in general, was not difficult to comprehend. I may add that to defend a thesis in the 1970s meant, first of all, to demonstrate skills of classifying philosophical trends as those belonging to "materialism" or "idealism." Further classification implied linking those trends to a certain rubric or a thinker to a certain school. Then it was necessary to prove that the subject matter of the thesis expressed this movement to a full extent. In light of the fact that a thesis about a reactionary and anti-Hegelian such as Kierkegaard stood very little chance of being admitted for a defense, it becomes clear why Isaev played according to all the rules. Chapter titles such as "The History of Religious Teachings," "Protestantism," and "Aesthetics" were neutral enough to ensure a successful "introduction" of Kierkegaard's theology to Moscow University.

Isaev expatiates upon Kierkegaard with maximum distance and without any emotions so as to remove any suspicion that he is sympathetic towards Kierkegaard's thought. The thesis also contains a short biography of Kierkegaard, which notes the drama of his relation with certain family members such as his brother Peter Christian and his father. Isaev's attempt to attribute Kierkegaard's philosophical method, beyond being a result of an authorial neurotic temperament (as seen in biographical pieces on Kierkegaard in the 1950s), to that of his particular reaction to Hegel's absolute idealism, on the one hand, and Pietistic and Romantic theology, on the other hand, was a major step forward in the context of Kierkegaard studies.

---

1 Пиама Гайденко [Piama Gaidenko], *Трагедия эстетизма. О миросозерцании Серена Киркегора* [The Tragedy of Aestheticism: On the World-View of Søren Kierkegaard], Moscow: Iskusstvo 1970.

For Isaev, Kierkegaard's effort to advocate the purity of *Christentum* in contrast to *Christenhed*, addressed the misdirection of Lutheran theology, Pietism, the Romanticism of Schleiermacher and speculative idealism, all of which seemed united in supporting the latter. This is where Kierkegaard's uprootedness in tradition and his innovation come from, as well as his intensive search for a new approach to Christianity that made him develop his own method—the method of indirect communication. Isaev's primary focus was always on the so-called "left-hand writings," with his thesis being no exception.

Isaev thoroughly studied this subject; it is worth mentioning that he articulated the most adequate and reasonable solution for understanding the relation between the pseudonymous works and the signed works which had confused previous Soviet Kierkegaard studies. While Piama Gaidenko was sure that Kierkegaard's pseudonyms were a guise for his own various egos, which betrayed the extent to which Kierkegaard wrote with a fragmented conscious, Isaev insists that with the beginning of *Either/Or* Kierkegaard already was a religious thinker "who had overcome the 'ironical' existential stage....The integrating component of all works of the Danish philosopher was religious pathos."[2] Thus, for Isaev, all of Kierkegaard's writings, even the pseudonymous works, serve the task of orienting the reader toward the religious stage.

However, it was much more complicated to explain to members of the dissertation committee, most of whom could barely have had an idea of the character of Protestant dogmatics and hermeneutics, why the communication problem was of such significance for Kierkegaard's religiosity. Isaev preferred to stick to the following pattern: since Kierkegaard's religiosity excludes social dimensions and uniquely interprets the idea of the neighbor, his catechizing pathos implies an addressee of a special kind. This "neighbor" must be outlined not as an anonymous social or political person, but as *der Einzelne*—whose uniqueness is embraced in his mere existence.

Although Isaev used the term "existence," he understood it to a large degree in a Sartrean sense which was popular in the Soviet Union at that time; a proper Kierkegaardian notion of existence was not Isaev's aim. Thus for Isaev, existence is human reality, for which absence of "substance" and "essence" is typical, and which is determined by "ignorance," and to a lesser degree, "knowledge." While Sartre's existentialism was determined by his atheism, Kierkegaard interpreted human existence in relation to God, that is, the God relation serves as the ground for human existence, specifically religious existence.

But due to Sartre's popularity in the USSR, Isaev had an opportunity to develop his own view of Kierkegaard. Kierkegaard's religiosity implies not actual (natural) truths, but existential ones that evade objectification. That is why direct exhortation must give place to an indirect one: "The direct form of the message...excludes the

---

2 Сергей Исаев [Sergey Isaev], *Философско-эстетическое учение С. Кьеркегора (критический анализ)* [The Philosophico-Aesthetic Teaching of S. Kierkegaard (A Critical Analysis)], Moscow 1982, p. 26.

main requirement existentialism sets forth for the method of message, which is: its author must not 'cease to be an existing individual.'"[3]

To meet this condition, it was necessary to invent a literary form that would preserve the author's own, genuine, attitude to the truth. In other words, the form must prevent the author from being objective. "In Kierkegaard's work, this function is performed, in part, by pseudonyms."[4] But this function goes, as stated earlier, beyond the pseudonymous writings. "Kierkegaard saw the purpose of his books as leading the reader to genuinely embrace the Christian truth. However, the trouble is that in his works he appealed, first of all, to people who were 'systematically' well-read, who had adopted the Christianity 'externally.' From this, according to Kierkegaard, it follows that 'to communicate...is the most beautiful triumph of resigned inwardness.'"[5]

For this purpose, his works are sophisticated to the maximum possible extent. They are aphoristic, allusive, and full of paradoxes and ambiguities; they are overloaded with never-ending comparisons, references, and digressions. Finally, Kierkegaard's books have no end. Hence, it turns out that although Kierkegaard's works recall well-known Christian truths, "a reader can hardly recognize what he himself has done with it long ago."[6]

Although it contains an abundance of quotations that reveal the author's desire not to say anything beyond what one can find in Kierkegaard's works, Isaev's dissertation does not look like a bare synopsis. It projected the overall feeling that he wanted to break the tether of what was read and that he had his own vision. Nevertheless, publications of the perestroika and post-perestroika period emphasize this strange peculiarity of Isaevian scholarship: he always only outlined the theme but never dared to disclose the essence of the problem to the full extent.

In the 1990s, Isaev linked the problem of indirect communication to the peculiarities of Protestant (and, wider, modern) exegesis. In this way, he found an explanation for many facets of the avant-garde movement that were unclear to him, in particular, for the correlation between the "author" and the "text." Believing that Protestant dogmatics offered the correct way to comprehend the New Testament as well as to protect both the essence of God and the freedom of the individual, Isaev concluded that the entire creative thought of the modern age bears the impress of God's silence and impenetrability. In the inaccessibility of God and the impossibility of comprehending him Isaev would see the origin of the "open text" phenomenon (to use

---

3 Ibid., p. 31. With reference to the *Concluding Unscientific Postscript* Isaev quotes the German translation: Søren Kierkegaard, *Gesammelte Werke und Tagebücher,* vols. 1–28, trans. and ed. by Emanuel Hirsch, Düsseldorf and Cologne: Diederichs 1953–71, vol. 16 (1), p. 66.

4 Исаев [Isaev], *Философско-эстетическое учение С. Кьеркегора (критический анализ)* [The Philosophico-Aesthetic Teaching of S. Kierkegaard (A Critical Analysis)], p. 32.

5 Ibid., p. 38. Isaev quotes Kierkegaard, *Gesammelte Werke und Tagebücher,* vol. 16 (1), p. 271.

6 Исаев [Isaev], *Философско-эстетическое учение С. Кьеркегора (критический анализ)* [The Philosophico-Aesthetic Teaching of S. Kierkegaard (A Critical Analysis)], p. 46. Isaev quotes Kierkegaard, *Gesammelte Werke und Tagebücher,* vol. 16 (1), p. 273.

Umberto Eco's locution)—the endless text of modern literature open to being interpreted and in line with the rules of indirect communication. The avant-garde, which was initiated by the activity of Kierkegaard as a writer, will continue creating work, whose reader will deal not with a holistic view, but rather with the targeted effect that will preserve his internal freedom, his capability to co-create, and his right to risk.

Darya Loungina

Reviews and Critical Discussions

Undetermined.

Valery Podoroga, *Метафизика ландшафта. Коммуникативные стратегии в философской культуре XIX–XX вв* [Metaphysics of the Landscape: Communicative Strategies in the Philosophical Culture of the Nineteenth and Twentieth Centuries],

Moscow: Nauka 1993, 319 pp.

The chapter "Abraham in the Land of Moriah: Søren Kierkegaard" makes up the first section of this three-part monograph written by Valery Podoroga (b. 1946). This book (published under the title *Metaphysics of the Landscape: Communicative Strategies in the Philosophical Culture of the 19th–20th Centuries* and devoted to Kierkegaard, Nietzsche, and Heidegger) has become an outstanding event in the history of the Russian Kierkegaard reception, primarily due to the philosophical influence of its renowned author. *Metaphysics of the Landscape* was published in 1993, when the post-Soviet academic environment manifested not merely a willingness to extend the school-level introduction to Kierkegaard that started as early as the 1960s during the Khrushchev Thaw,[1] but also the ambition to establish a genuine philosophical

1 Among the most notable articles of the 1960s were the following: Татьяна Гайдукова [Tatyana Gaidukova], "Эстетическое существование в философии Кьеркегора" ["The Aesthetic Mode of Existence in Kierkegaard's Philosophy"] in *Из истории зарубежной философии XIX–XX веков* [From the History of Foreign Philosophy of the 19th–20th Centuries], Moscow: Izdatel'stvo Moskovskogo Gosudarstvennogo Universiteta 1967; Владимир Карпушин [Vladimir Karpushin], "Серен Киркегор—предшественник экзистенциальной антропологии" ["Søren Kierkegaard as a Forerunner of the Existentialistic Humanism"], *Вопросы философии* [Issues of Philosophy], no. 12, Moscow 1967, pp. 103–13]; Татьяна Гайдукова [Tatyana Gaidukova], "Проблема выбора в философии Кьеркегора" ["The Problem of Choice in Kierkegaard's Philosophy"], *Вестник МГУ* [Moscow State University Bulletin], no. 6, series 8, Moscow 1969, pp. 32–44]; and an article of an influential Soviet historian of philosophy Valentin Asmus: Валентин Асмус [Valentin Asmus] "Лев Шестов и Кьеркегор (Об отношении Л. Шестова к зачинателю западноевропейского экзистенциализма)" [Lev Shestov and Kierkegaard (On L. Shestov's Attitude towards the Pioneer of European Existentialism)]," *Научные доклады высшей*

dialogue with the thinker. The first who dared to proceed with the tradition of direct conversation with Kierkegaard in the USSR was Podoroga's colleague from the academic Institute of Philosophy, Piama Pavlovna Gaidenko (b. 1934).[2] Unlike the famous work of Lev Shestov,[3] her book, *The Tragedy of Aestheticism*, did not seek to incorporate the study of Kierkegaard into another system of coordinates, alien to his views, but was conceived as an attempt at a debate in the spirit of Dostoevsky's "Legend of the Grand Inquisitor." But, bringing the aesthete to the court of morals, Gaidenko was trying to see aestheticism in a wider perspective than that available to the opponent of the aesthetician, Judge William. Gaidenko revealed how features of "demonic" Abraham were present in the everlasting egocentrism of contemporary Europeans, and how inhuman grimaces of totalitarian regimes of the twentieth century could be glimpsed beneath his suspension of the ethical.

Podoroga's Abraham did not have anything in common with the character constructed by the political and religious criticism of modern aestheticism. On the contrary, right from the start he rejected the opportunity of any ideological polemics with the philosopher; in the beginning he confined himself to hints, while by the end of the book he openly stated the foundations of his position:

> Development-in-the-faith is far from the question: *what* is faith? The question, the answer to which threatens to be focus on the *what* does not bring us closer to understanding faith. Shestov does not see Kierkegaard as the communication strategist, oeconomus,[4] cartographer, and disciple of Lessing and Spinoza; rather, Shestov is searching for "direct" answers and constantly confusing development-in-the-faith with the developed idea of it. But Kierkegaard did not give helpful advice and did not answer questions with strong emphasis on the "what" and probably would be surprised by such questions, which run counter to his philosophical writings, which include the main answer to the question *How faith can be performed, not understood.*[5]

It is Podoroga's belief that all Kierkegaard's activity as a writer can be conceived as searching for fundamentally anti-speculative types of writing—writing capable not of abstract speculation about God but of "creating the place, where God

---

школы. Философские науки [Scientific Reports of the Higher Schools. Philosophy Disciplines], no. 4, Moscow 1972, pp. 72–80].

2 Пиама Гайденко [Piama Gaidenko], *Трагедия эстетизма. О миросозерцании Серена Киркегора* [The Tragedy of Aestheticism: On the World-View of Søren Kierkegaard], Moscow: Iskusstvo 1970.

3 Лев Шестов [Lev Shestov], *Киргегард и экзистенциальная философия (Глас вопиющего в пустыне)* [Kierkegaard and the Existential Philosophy (Vox clamantis in deserto)], Paris: Sovremenniye Zapiski, Dom Knigi 1939.

4 Oeconomus is understood by Podoroga as a house builder and land surveyor in a figurative sense—as a creator and treasurer of the landscape of thought.

5 Валерий Подорога [Valery Podoroga], *Метафизика ландшафта. Коммуникативные стратегии в философской культуре XIX–XX вв* [Metaphysics of the Landscape: Communicative Strategies in the Philosophical Culture of the Nineteenth and Twentieth Centuries], Moscow: Nauka 1993, p. 139.

would descend to."[6] This place (landscape) is understood by Podoroga literally, while the chapter "Exordium" from *Fear and Trembling* is chosen by him as the *opus* that is best suited to demonstrate this technique of Kierkegaard: to exclude any possibility of reflexive, sympathetic, or any other normative attitude toward Abraham.

Contrary to the academic tradition of interpreting *Fear and Trembling*, Podoroga asserts that Abraham's deed cannot be made the subject matter of ideological discourse just because it cannot be imagined or objectified in the image. But it is the contrary that is required from the reader! In order to stop seeing Abraham at a distance—that is, properly speaking, seeing him on his way to God on Mount Moriah—and to perceive this ascent solely as the demand to go this way together with him, Kierkegaard, according to Podoroga, develops a special strategy. His only and main purpose was not to show something to the eye, but to change the eye's optics, so that the reader's perception would be deprived of its capacity for critical evaluation—as this is done (at least sometimes) by Kierkegaard's marionette pseudonyms.[7] The ability of the narrator Johannes de silentio in the chapter "Exordium" to coincide with Abraham physiologically and corporally must be transferred to the reader as well. For "the intrinsic shock experienced by the reader proceeds not from Abraham's deed, but from it being impossible to assimilate this deed ethically and reflexively. It is the incomprehension of Abraham's heroic deed that opens for the reader a way to his own self."[8]

Podoroga's proposition would have been unsubstantiated, if it had not been supported by references to Kierkegaard's reflections on the nature of writing. Based on extracts from the journals, where Kierkegaard presents writing not as a detached or abstract operation, but as a corporal one,[9] Podoroga refers reading to the same type of operations. He substantiates this in the following way:

> when reading Kierkegaard, we read only to the extent to which we surrender ourselves to the rhythm of his philosophical writing, and not due to us having the divine right to halt

---

6 Podoroga quotes the well-known words of Kierkegaard: "Mein Aufgabe: Platz zu schaffen, daß Gott kommen kann." He quotes from Søren Kierkegaard, *Die Tagebücher 1834–1855*, trans. by Theodor Haecker, Munich: Kösel-Verlag 1953, p. 639.

7 By introducing this image, Podoroga meaningfully selects Heinrich von Kleist, author of a famous essay, "Über das Marionettentheater" (1810), as his predecessor and does not provide any references to Martin Thust's "Das Marionettentheater Soren Kierkegaards" (in *Zeitwende*, no. 1, Munich 1925, pp. 18–38).

8 Подорога [Podoroga], *Метафизика ландшафта* [Metaphysics of the Landscape], p. 134.

9 In the first instance, Kierkegaard, *Die Tagebucher 1834–1855*, pp. 270–1; p. 273; p. 454 et al. Words of Kierkegaard from *The Sickness unto Death* serve Podoroga's additional reasoning for corporal representation of any creative (including religious) act: "Personality is a synthesis of possibility and necessity. The condition of its survival is therefore analogous to breathing (respiration), which is an in- and an a-spiration. The self of the determinist cannot breathe, for it is impossible to breathe necessity alone, which taken pure and simple suffocates the human self. The fatalist is in despair—he has lost God, and therefore himself as well;

> the process of reading and bring the verdict: "This means this, and the other means that...." The reading process is regulated not by us, but by a joint corporal rhythm, which both reading and writing fall in line with. Sense is a corporal rhythm.[10]

Kierkegaard is not abstract, his writing and punctuation express his corporal status, his irregular breathing; he communicates the pulsed, irregular breath of Abraham. For, according to Kierkegaard, if faith is natural to the human body, the same corporal concordance must be conveyed to such, at first sight, reflexive action as writing.

It should be noted that the origin of this idea about Kierkegaard's writing strategy is rooted, mainly, in post-structuralist theories of the twentieth century. Among the most highly recognizable is one of the basic propositions of Roland Barthes' semiotics consisting of the idea that the writing may be read not as *oeuvre* but as *texte*. However, to make this quality of the text the aim in itself, depriving it of historical, personal, and other references is not a goal in itself, in Podoroga's understanding. To read not the work but the text means to perceive the thought which is not "about something" but which is in itself "something." For to think means to express oneself, just as to believe, to think, means to breathe.

According to Podoroga, Kierkegaard was thoroughly persuaded that a thought existed only as the thought to be *expressed*,[11] and that is why it is more correct to consider his maieutic manner of philosophizing not as an implicit technique, which is external to the thought, but as what already inheres in the effect the reader is exposed to. Podoroga is persuaded, "Kierkegaard's writing produces the reality. Life is moving in the space of writing, and this space *is* the space of *Innerlichkeit*."[12]

Another of Podoroga's conceptual sources is Jacques Derrida's deconstruction. As is known, deconstruction was intended to return the initial significance to the philosophical text and remove from it the borrowed strata (layers) of interpretation. Just like any tradition, historical philosophical analysis seeks to arrogate to itself even the most impertinent, the most "deviant" text. And this happens due to the effort of interpretation that establishes priority of one of many possible ways

---

for if he has no God, neither has he a self. But the fatalist has no God—or, what is the same thing, his god is necessity. Inasmuch as for God all things are possible, it may be said that this is what God is, namely, one for whom all things are possible. The worship of the fatalist is therefore at its maximum an exclamation, and essentially it is dumbness, dumb submission, he is unable to pray. So to pray is to breathe, and possibility is for the self what oxygen is for breathing." (Podoroga's source is Søren Kierkegaard, *Krankheit zum Tode* in Kierkegaard, *Gesammelte Werke*, vols. 1–32, trans. by Emmanuel Hirsch, Düsseldorf and Cologne: Diederichs 1950–74, vols. 24–5, p. 37).

10 Подорога [Podoroga], *Метафизика ландшафта* [Metaphysics of the Landscape], p. 44.

11 This thesis was developed in Podoroga's next book *Expression and Sense*: *Выражение и смысл. Ландшафтные миры философии: Сёрен Киркегор, Фридрих Ницше, Мартин Хайдеггер, Марсель Пруст, Франц Кафка* [Expression and Sense. The Landscape Worlds of Philosophy: Søren Kierkegaard, Friedrich Nietzsche, Martin Heidegger, Marcel Proust, Franz Kafka], Moscow: Ad marginem 1995.

12 Подорога [Podoroga], *Метафизика ландшафта* [Metaphysics of the Landscape], p. 121.

of reading over all others. Podoroga suggests reading Kierkegaard's texts from the point of view of the genealogy of introduced notions. Let us determine the historical continuity of reading by ascertaining the dates when the main works were created and by looking at all secondary supporting materials (diary notes, magazine publications, correspondence). We will also have to include these works in a historically determined context and, in the first place, to define Kierkegaard's relations, as a religious thinker, with official church dogmatics. In the second place, we will have to explore the implicit and explicit contradictions of his position in relation to assumptions of famous philosophers of his time—authors of complete systems (Hegel, etc.). But in this case what has been written by Kierkegaard appears to have been transferred from the plane of existential deed (faith as event) to the plane of the history of ideas.

But the Kierkegaard who appears in *Metaphysics of the Landscape* sets an entirely different aim—to free the read text from the predominance of interpretation, so that the unequal layers will open up, so that reading would not take the form of a linear and continuous process entirely directed by the reader, but, on the contrary, so that it would show itself in the fullness of its ruptures and omissions, in its various changeable distances that manipulate the reader and make him forget himself. Podoroga's Kierkegaard appears as a maestro of such manipulation that has proved that not only belles-lettres (through imagination) but also philosophical writing are capable of affecting the reader.

Darya Loungina

Reviews and Critical Discussions

Ivanov, Alexander, review in *Новый мир* [New World], no. 7, 1994, pp. 201–2.
Petrovskaya, Yelena, review in *Логос* [Logos], no. 5, 1994, pp. 258–62.

IV. Secondary Literature in Slovak

Andrej Démuth (ed.), *Postskriptum ku Kierkegaardovi* [A Postscript to Kierkegaard],

Pusté Úľany: Schola Philosophica 2006, 140 pp.

A Postscript to Kierkegaard was published by Schola Philosophica in 2006. It is an anniversary volume containing a collection of papers related to the life and work of Søren Kierkegaard. This compendium is a result of the cycle of lectures organized on the occasion of the 150th anniversary of Kierkegaard's death by the Schola Philosophica association, together with The Department of Philosophy at the Philosophical Faculty of Trnava University and The Slovak Philosophical Association at the Slovak Academy of Sciences. Andrej Démuth, the editor of the volume, formulates his main intention as follows: "The intention of the project was to provide a broader background for a closer understanding of Kierkegaard's legacy and to enable a deeper penetration into the context of his thinking."[1] The compendium was reviewed by Slavomír Gálik in the academic quarterly *Ostium*, a peer-reviewed open-access journal in 2006[2] and also by Roman Králik in the Czech *Philosophical Journal* in 2007.[3]

A Postscript to Kierkegaard consists of 15 papers. One of the methodological ideas was to present a variety of papers from well-known Slovak and Czech Kierkegaard experts together with young philosophers passionate about Kierkegaard. The *Postscript* also has another ambition: to be a handbook for students interested in Kierkegaard.

The first, introductory paper is written by Renáta Kišoňová. "Søren Kierkegaard: *Curriculum vitae et vitae opus*" offers a brief outline of Kierkegaard's biography and a chronological overview of his basic works. The second text, written by Roman Králik, provides a survey of Kierkegaard's worldwide reception and influence. This paper acquaints us with the most important lines of Kierkegaard studies in Denmark, Germany, the USA, Australia, Canada, and Japan.

---

1 Andrej Démuth (ed.), *Postskriptum ku Kierkegaardovi*, Pusté Úľany: Schola Philosophica 2006, p. 9.

2 Slavomír Gálik, "O jednom P.S." [About One P.S.], *Ostium*, vol. 1, nos. 2–3, 2006 (on-line journal).

3 Roman Králik, "Postskriptum ku Kierkegaardovi" [A Postscript to Kierkegaard], *Filosofický časopis*, vol. 55, no. 1, 2007, pp. 148–50.

The paper "Concerning Some Literary Aspects of Kierkegaard's Work" provides a broader background for an understanding of Kierkegaard's literary style. It highlights Kierkegaard's attempt at "seducing" people into the truth through his literary style instead of simply presenting objective truths along the lines of Hegel. The author, Milan Žitný, is a prominent Slovak translator and historian of literature. Thanks to his analysis of Danish language and history, we acquire an access to the cultural climate, which might have had an impact on Kierkegaard's thinking. Milan Žitný presents the context of the origin and influence of Kierkegaard's literary work on European ideas. He tries to uncover Kierkegaard's relation to his contemporaries: his literary, musical, and philosophical sources and the influence of Scandinavian folk tales.

František Sirovič contributes a study called "The Historical-Speculative Bases of Kierkegaard's Anti-Hegelianism." This paper explores the reasons behind Kierkegaard's attempt to separate Christianity and Hegelianism once and for all in the context of Kierkegaard's dialogue with German Romanticism and Hegelianism. František Sirovič presents Kierkegaard's theological inspirations from Franz von Baader, Frederich Schleiermacher, I.H. Fichte, and especially Schelling and Trendelenburg. This fertile comparison leads to the clarification of Kierkegaard's affiliation with realism and empiricism.

The focus of the fifth paper is methodological. Václauf Umlauf introduces to us "The Sympathetic Kierkegaard." Due to the difficulties in interpreting Kierkegaard's authorship, he criticizes an attempt to read Kierkegaard's works objectively, only with respect to the dogmatic point of view to literary work and style. The author offers us an alternative based on a sympathetic hermeneutical interpretation of Kierkegaard's works which takes into account Kierkegaard's preference for indirect communication.

The next contribution, "A Strasbourg Goose in Copenhagen: An Outline of the Concept of Irony in Søren Kierkegaard's Work," is written by Peter Šajda. The author clarifies the circumstances of the origin, structure, and content of Kierkegaard's Master's thesis. His analysis concentrates on Kierkegaard's understanding of irony, his relation to Socrates, and irony in the totality of his work. The conclusion of this text points to the irony of Kierkegaard's personal life.

Anton Vydra provides us with an analysis of Kierkegaard's concept of the moment. In "Søren Kierkegaard's Moment" the author underlines not only the importance of this concept for the creation of Kierkegaard's philosophical ideas, but also the importance of the moment in Kierkegaard's inward personal mission. The text focuses especially on *Philosophical Fragments* and *The Moment* and, from this perspective, points out the meaning of this concept for Kierkegaard.

The paper "The Concept of Passion in Kierkegaard's Critique of the Present Age" is a study focusing on Kierkegaard's well-known concept of passion. On the basis of the dichotomy of "The Present Age" and "The Age of Revolution," the author, Milan Petkanič, sees the essence of Kierkegaardian passion in the existential interest in one's own existence.

"Who's the Single Individual?" is the main question for both Kierkegaard and Martin Vydra, the author of the ninth paper. On the basis of the difference between the single individual and the crowd, the author shows that Kierkegaard's single individual is always situated in a concrete time and place. This concreteness is not defined just with characterizations of his body, but primarily with his exclusiveness in relation to infinity and similar exclusiveness in relation to other people.

Andrej Démuth, in his paper "Kierkegaard's Fear, Trembling and the Concept of Anxiety," examines these concepts from a philosophical-psychological point of view within the framework of Kierkegaard's *The Concept of Anxiety* and *Fear and Trembling*. The author aims to point out that fear and trembling do not have just a theological meaning but are also a door to one's own existence, a door to the realization of the earnestness of individual existence, and to the responsibility for its realization vis-à-vis infinity.

Michal Žitňanský, the author of the study "Quiet and Silence in the Context of Kierkegaard's Work," analyzes the phenomenon of quiet and silence in the frame of three biblical stories (the sacrifice of Isaac, Jephthah, and Sarah) and reflects on reasons for silence and on Kierkegaard's metaphorical communication. He shows that pseudonymous silence is not just the author's personal interest, but it is a reaction to the inexpressibility of existence and the incommunicability of the people who carry their burden face to face with God.

"The Seducer's Diary and Kierkegaard's Relation to a Woman," written by Renáta Kišoňová, presents us with an interesting insight into Kierkegaard's understanding of the woman—from a woman's point of view. The text highlights the importance of the notions of temptation, enjoyment, the aesthetic way of life, and desire, which are also connected to Kierkegaard's autobiographical motifs.

The next paper is entitled "The Ethical in Kierkegaard," and the author is Ladislav Tkáčik. Based on the comparison of the aesthetic and ethical stages of life, the author shows that, for Kierkegaard, the ethical stage is characterized by, first, the dialectical motion of separation from the finite, then, the motion of negation of the finite by infinity, and finally the motion to the finite, that is, the motion of the separation and retrieval of the world. In conclusion, Tkáčik contemplates whether the religious stage of life must necessarily suspend the ethical stage.

The fourteenth study is written by the prominent Czech translator and author, Marie Mikulová Thulstrupová. In her text "Kierkegaard and the Church of his Era," she invites us to a deeper understanding of Kierkegaard's theological position and his relation to the official church and its representatives in his era.

The concluding paper is written by Roman Králik. "The Problem called Kierkegaard or Kierkegaard as a Religious Author" points to the theological dimension of Kierkegaard's thinking. He shows us that Kierkegaard's faith is not established on the confirmation of any philosophical or dogmatic opinion, but rather on the passion of the original Christianity.

A Postscript to Kierkegaard represents a good mosaic of studies for philosophers interested in Kierkegaard's thought. The variety of problems addressed in the abovementioned papers provides us with a broader background for understanding Kierkegaard's concepts, which are put into the historical, cultural, religious, biographical, and philosophical framework of his times. The literary style of the volume is comprehensible; therefore, *A Postscript to Kierkegaard* is accessible not only to philosophers and theologians, but it can be of interest for a broader readership as well.

Zuzana Blažeková

Reviews and Critical Discussions

Gálik, Slavomír, "O jednom P.S." [About One P.S.], *Ostium*, vol. 1, nos. 2–3, 2006 (on-line journal).

Králik, Roman, review in *Filosofický časopis*, vol. 55, no. 1, 2007, pp. 148–50.

Milan Petkanič, *Filozofia vášne Sørena Kierkegaarda* [Søren Kierkegaard's Philosophy of Passion],

Cracow: Towarzystwo Słowaków w Polsce 2010, 202 pp.

In the last ten years Slovakia has experienced something of a "Kierkegaard renaissance."[1] This has been due to several factors, whose synergy has caused Kierkegaard to became firmly rooted in the Slovak philosophical discourse. First, the translations of *Fear and Trembling* (2005) and *Either/Or* (2007) by Milan Žitný have attracted the attention of the broad literary public.[2] Second, Kierkegaard became a frequent topic in the most prestigious Slovak philosophical journal *Filozofia*. Third, several conferences on Kierkegaard have been organized at the universities in Zvolen, Trnava, and Nitra. Fourth, a number of anthologies and collective volumes about Kierkegaard have been published, most importantly the series *Acta Kierkegaardiana*. And fifth, half a dozen Slovak authors have published single-author monographs on Kierkegaard. Slovak Kierkegaard studies have evolved in a close contact with the international Kierkegaard community.

Milan Petkanič has been an important voice in the Slovak discourse about Kierkegaard, and his monograph *Søren Kierkegaard's Philosophy of Passion* has contributed to its liveliness.[3] The book is an enlarged version of Petkanič's dissertation, which he defended at the Philosophical Faculty of the Comenius University in Bratislava in 2007. The title of the monograph suggests a focus on Kierkegaard's philosophy of passion, but the book is by no means a narrow specialist study. On the contrary, it offers a comprehensive portrait of Kierkegaard's thought: through the prism of the concept of passion Petkanič gradually elucidates the overall structure

1 This term was initially used to describe the dynamic discourse about Kierkegaard in the Germanophone world during the interwar period.

2 Žitný's translation of *Either/Or* was awarded the highest prize of the Literary Foundation for a scholarly translation, the Matej Bel Award.

3 For Petkanič's most recent reflections on Kierkegaard's philosophy of passion, see his articles in the *Kierkegaard Studies Yearbook* and *Filozofia*: Milan Petkanič, "Passion as a Will to Existence in Kierkegaard," *Kierkegaard Studies Yearbook*, 2013, pp. 325–41; Milan Petkanič, "Kierkegaard: O vášni ako vôli k existencii" [Kierkegaard: On Passion as a Will to Existence], *Filozofia*, vol. 68, no. 1, 2013, pp. 62–74; Milan Petkanič, "K pojmu voľby seba samého v Kierkegaardovom diele Buď-alebo" [On Kierkegaard's Concept of Self-Choice in *Either/Or*], *Filozofia*, vol. 69, no. 5, 2014, pp. 388–98.

of Kierkegaard's philosophy. He describes this approach as "the method of gradual immersion."[4] His inquiry begins with an analysis of Kierkegaard's critique of the passionless present age, continues with a detailed study of the problem of existence, and culminates in the presentation of Christian faith as the highest passion of subjectivity. The concept of passion is a leitmotif that connects the different chapters.

The extensive aspect of Petkanič's reflections serves two main purposes. First, it introduces the reader to the complex structure of Kierkegaard's *oeuvre* and provides an overview of its different perspectives and its broad variety of genres. Petkanič pays special attention to the *Concluding Unscientific Postscript* and *A Literary Review*, but he discusses important themes from other works, too. Thus the reader is familiarized with philosophical issues that Kierkegaard treats in different parts of his authorship. Second, while Petkanič focuses on the theme of passion, his reflections are not limited to anthropology and theory of subjectivity. He examines the impact of the notion of passion on Kierkegaard's theory of intersubjectivity, social philosophy, and philosophy of religion, which enables the reader to venture beyond the issues of affectivity and authenticity of action and explore Kierkegaard's theory of relationality and critique of modernity or his view of the limits of rationality.

The first part of Petkanič's monograph, entitled "Passion and the Age," takes its point of departure from Kierkegaard's juxtaposition of an age full of passionate enthusiasm (the age of revolution) and an age characterized by passionlessness (the present age). In this juxtaposition, adopted from *A Literary Review*, Petkanič focuses mainly on the present age. He paints a detailed picture of an age dominated by excessive reflection, which has abolished the principle of contradiction (either/or) and thus has rendered qualitative differences ambiguous. The main consequence of the spread of ambiguity is the lack of will to commitment and lack of passion. Abnormal reflection leads to indecision and gives rise to a number of superficial forms of communication. These are promptly used by the press, which is the main agent of leveling. People in the present age "fear the reflection of others more than God and death"[5] and regard the opinion of the public as the highest authority. Petkanič connects the notions of "the public" and "the crowd" and explores their characteristics. After a critical assessment of the passionless, leveled age, he goes on to identify Kierkegaard's concepts which can be seen as antidotes to the problems of the present age: inwardness, the single individual, existence. He notes that "Kierkegaard sees the very origin of the negative process of leveling of modernity in the absence of religious inwardness."[6] Being skeptical about collective solutions to the problem of leveling, Kierkegaard sees hope in the single individual who is transformed by the pressure of leveling: "Yet by means of it every individual, each one separately, may in turn be religiously educated, in the highest sense may be helped to acquire the essentiality of the religious by means of the *examen rigorosum* of leveling."[7] Thus,

---

4 Milan Petkanič, *Filozofia vášne Sørena Kierkegaarda*, Cracow: Towarzystwo Słowaków w Polsce 2010, p. 10.

5 Ibid., p. 27.

6 Ibid.

7 *SKS* 8, 84 / *TA*, 87.

Petkanič proceeds to deal in more depth with the theme of the single individual and his or her existence.

The second part, entitled "Passion and Existence," concentrates on the self-formation of the individual, on the processes of becoming and the choice of oneself. Petkanič highlights Kierkegaard's definition of the self as a dynamic synthesis which is in a permanent tension and represents a challenge of responsibility: one is called to develop his or her givens and capacities in a balanced and holistic way. In this connection Petkanič makes the important claim that Kierkegaard uses a series of fundamental terms—such as subject, the self, the (single) individual, and existence—in a two-fold way:

> Kierkegaard works with two different senses of the concept of subject, just as he does in the case of the concepts of the individual and the self (and as we shall later see, also in the case of existence). In order to become a subject in the other, narrower sense of the word (it is in fact in an eminent or ideal sense), one needs first and foremost passion—the involvement of his or her whole personality; thus to be a subject in the narrower sense of this word means to exist with passion.[8]

The role of passion in self-formation is succinctly described at the end of the chapter: "without essential passion no one can become a whole human, nor can one become him- or herself."[9] Petkanič treats the issue of passion both with respect to self-relation and relation to others. He connects this treatment to topics that proved to be important in the later debates about Kierkegaard's thought. These include the issues of authenticity and inauthenticity of existence, the individual's exposure to despair and anxiety, or the popular existentialist category of decision. An important line of thought is the consideration of the relation between passion and subjective truth. This line is most intensely present in this part, but it pervades the whole book. Petkanič emphasizes the fact that passion is the measure and criterion of subjective truth, while maintaining that subjective truth is always linked to "objective uncertainty."[10] It is precisely this uncertainty that awakens passion and stimulates its intensity.[11] Kierkegaard's theory of the single individual, subjectivity, and existence is also explained with a reference to the historical-philosophical context of its origin: it is seen as a criticism of abstract objectivist philosophies. The climax of this chapter is Petkanič's presentation of the subjective passionate thinker.

The focus of the third part, called "Passion and Faith," is made clear in the opening statement: "A full unfolding of the problem of passion in Kierkegaard can only be achieved through an analysis of his conception of faith."[12] In this part different lines of thought from previous chapters come together: the religious dimension of Kierkegaard's theory of the self, the commitment of an accepting and corrective love for one's neighbor, and the challenge of a relation to a transcendence that manifests

8 Petkanič, *Filozofia vášne Sørena Kierkegaarda*, p. 57.

9 Ibid., p. 86.

10 Ibid., pp. 68–76.

11 Ibid., pp. 75–6.

12 Ibid., p. 87.

itself, yet remains ungraspable. Drawing on the pseudonymous works *Fear and Trembling* and *Practice in Christianity*, as well as on Kierkegaard's *Nachlass*, Petkanič examines the possibilities of appropriation and realization of faith. He discusses the related motifs of infinite resignation, leap, offense, and imitation. Constantly emphasizing the existential nature of faith, he elaborates on the necessary connection between an individual expression of faith and *pathos* (*passio*), which is a term that denotes both passion and suffering. Faith is based on an individual "passionate 'either/or,'" which means that the opposite of faith is not the rejection of God but religious indifferentism.[13]

The concluding part of the book shows that Petkanič is concerned not only with a conceptual reconstruction of Kierkegaard's thought-project but also with its relevance for our contemporary situation. He asks about "the place of passion in the world of today" and examines why "Kierkegaard's challenge to passionately take hold of one's own existence" still matters.[14] When reflecting on the spread of apathy, indifference, lack of commitment, and slackness of faith in modernity and postmodernity Petkanič highlights the synergy of Kierkegaard's ideas with the critical insights of Friedrich Nietzsche, Fyodor Dostoevsky, José Ortega y Gasset, Aldous Huxley, Gilles Lipovetsky, and Viktor Frankl. Petkanič presents his own poignant diagnosis of the present age, which targets both the individual and society.

Although—as it is obvious from the preceding lines—Petkanič's monograph is inspirational and enriching reading, this review would be incomplete without a few critical remarks. One of the objections that can be addressed to the author concerns the absence of a clearer distinction between Kierkegaard and his pseudonyms. To be sure, Petkanič is aware of the philosophical differences between Kierkegaard and his pseudonyms and even explicitly mentions them, but in some arguments Kierkegaard is amalgamated with the fictitious authors. Such amalgamation is more legitimate in some cases than others.

When treating Kierkegaard's relation to Hegel and German idealism, it would be beneficial if Petkanič took into account to a greater extent the recent international scholarship which has more accurately identified the targets of Kierkegaard's criticisms. What was previously seen as Kierkegaard's "polemic with Hegel" has been transformed into Kierkegaard's polemic with a broader array of often lesser-known thinkers.

The last objection is more of a matter of opinion and personal interpretation of Kierkegaard's philosophy. It concerns Kierkegaard's conception of the choice of oneself. Petkanič's analyses,[15] in my opinion, overemphasize the formal aspect of this choice (inwardness, passion, involvement) and downplay the aspect concerning content. The priority of *how* over *what* is undoubtedly present in some of Kierkegaard's works, as Petkanič rightly claims. However, the Anti-Climacan works *The Sickness unto Death* and *Practice in Christianity*, as well as numerous journal entries show an unambiguous emphasis on the content of the choice of oneself. It is

13 Ibid., p. 124.
14 Ibid., p. 142.
15 See, for example, ibid., pp. 59–60.

exactly this moment of content that makes Kierkegaard's doctrine incompatible with some existentialist "Kierkegaardisms" of the twentieth century.

A great advantage of Petkanič's monograph on Kierkegaard's philosophy of passion is that it is written with passion. It is clear that the author reads Kierkegaard in an engaged way, exploring both the depths and breadths of his thought, and does not remain only at the level of objective findings. Therefore this book can be recommended to all those who want to encounter Kierkegaard in a way which he himself wished for: as thinking individual readers who search for an answer to the question of the authenticity of their own existence.

Peter Šajda

Reviews and Critical Discussions

Čikel, Marek, "Knižné novinky z regiónu," *Knihovník*, no. 1, 2011, p. 20.
Drobná, Darina, "Viac než vášeň," *Ostium*, vol. 7, no. 3, 2011 (on-line journal).
Madarová, Dana, "Vášeň v novom svete," *Extra Plus*, vol. 11, October, 2011, p. 42.
Olšovský, Jiří, review in *Filosofický časopis*, vol. 60, no. 6, 2012, pp. 956–7.
Šajda, Peter, review in *Filozofia*, vol. 67, no. 3, 2012, pp. 262–4.

Peter Šajda, *Buberov spor s Kierkegaardom: O vzťahu náboženstva k etike a politike* [Buber's Polemic with Kierkegaard: On the Relation of Religion to Ethics and Politics],

Bratislava: Kalligram 2013, 222 pp.

Martin Buber's relationship to Søren Kierkegaard is particularly interesting for its ambivalence. On the one hand, Buber highlights Kierkegaard's emphasis on *the person*, in which he sees a significant contribution to founding his own dialogical philosophy, but, on the other hand, he accuses him of acosmism (absence of essential intersubjectivity), which Buber sees as in principle contradictory to dialogical thinking. Buber's ambivalent relationship to Kierkegaard is examined in detail by the Slovak author Peter Šajda in his first monograph, *Buberov spor s Kierkegaardom: O vzťahu náboženstva k etike a politike* (Buber's Polemic with Kierkegaard: On the Relation of Religion to Ethics and Politics), which was issued by the prestigious Slovak publishing house Kalligram in late 2013. In his monograph, Šajda made good use of his long-term study of the *corpus* of both thinkers' works. Some partial results of his study that focused on Buber's critical reception of Kierkegaard were successively published in erudite articles at home as well as abroad,[1] and the conclusions of these articles are ultimately reflected also in his monograph.

The central theme of Šajda's book is Buber's coping with Kierkegaard's and his own acosmism. At the outset, it should be noted that this is not a book

I would like to thank Carson Webb for his kind help with proofreading my text.

[1] Peter Šajda, "Martin Buber: 'No One Can so Refute Kierkegaard as Kierkegaard Himself,'" in *Kierkegaard and Existentialism*, ed. by Jon Stewart, Aldershot: Ashgate 2011 (*Kierkegaard Research: Sources, Reception and Resources*, vol. 9), pp. 33–61; Peter Šajda, "A Jewish, a Catholic and a Neo-Marxist Critique of Kierkegaard's Philosophy of Religion," *Kierkegaard Studies Yearbook*, 2012, pp. 303–21; Peter Šajda, "Problém náboženského akozmizmu: Buberova filozoficko-politická kritika Kierkagaarda," in *Náboženstvo a nihilizmus*, ed. by Martin Muránsky, Bratislava: Filozofický ústav SAV 2010, pp. 44–57; Peter Šajda, "Kierkegaardov príspevok k Buberovej filozofii židovstva, teórii vlastenectva a teórii politických skupín," *Filozofia*, vol. 68, no. 1, 2013, pp. 5–16; Peter Šajda, "Náčrt kritiky Kierkegaardovho konceptu lásky v diele M. Bubera, T. W. Adorna a K. E. Løgstrupa," *Filozofia*, vol. 58, no. 7, 2003, pp. 484–93.

primarily about Kierkegaard, but about Buber and his own intellectual development. The book concerns Kierkegaard only indirectly, since he is here perceived only through Buber's optics. However, this does not mean that it is of no interest to the enthusiastic Kierkegaardian. On the contrary, the book is a historical testimony to how Kierkegaard's existential philosophy stood at the birth of dialogical philosophy.

With regard to structure, the book consists of five main chapters and a conclusion, while the first chapter is in fact a lengthy introduction. In addition to an extensive bibliography and a register of names, the conclusion is followed by an important supplement with a complete list of citations and paraphrases of Kierkegaard's thoughts in the German editions of Buber's writings, which the author leaves in the original German for the sake of preserving the authenticity of the text.

The first chapter defines the objectives and methodology of work. At the very start the author emphasizes that his intention is not to write a comparative study that will try to map the affinities and differences between the two thinkers. His goal may sound a little more modest: "I will examine Buber's gradual discovery of, and coping with, the legacy of Kierkegaard's thought, and the result will be the narrative of Buber's thought seen through the reflection of Kierkegaard's philosophy."[2] Thus, the primary intention of the author is a detailed description of the history of one philosophical dispute, or more precisely, a detailed description of Buber's philosophical coping with Kierkegaard's thought. The confrontation of the two authors is thus asymmetrical and one-sided. In this dispute Kierkegaard is, figuratively speaking, silent (and so it is questionable whether the term "polemic" in the title of the book is not a bit misleading). This is why the author does not provide any imaginary responses by Kierkegaard to Buber's objections, as commentators in comparative studies usually do "when they are constructing a reverse criticism of Buber from the perspective of Kierkegaard's philosophy."[3] In any case, the book is full of useful information, and in this sense it is more reconstructive than constructive. In fact, Šajda's book is not an attempt at his own original interpretation of the ideas of both authors, but rather at the most faithful historical description of the development of Buber's philosophical reception of Kierkegaard's ideas. To this purpose the chosen methodology is appropriate, as the author himself states: the book is based on "the method of source-work research (*Quellenforschung*), which aims to offer the most precise and comprehensive picture of Buber's reception of Kierkegaard's thought."[4]

In the second chapter of the book the author gives us insight into the historico-philosophical context of Buber's dispute with Kierkegaard. Thus he surveys here the German-speaking world's gradual awareness of Kierkegaard, as well as Buber's early familiarization with Kierkegaard and the scope of his overall knowledge of Kierkegaard's works. This chapter is particularly rich in factual information. Among other things, here we learn that Buber was first acquainted with Kierkegaard already during his youth in 1897 while studying at universities in Vienna and Leipzig, and

---

2 Peter Šajda, *Buberov spor s Kierkegaardom: O vzťahu náboženstva k etike a politike*, Bratislava: Kalligram 2013, pp. 13–14.

3 Ibid., p. 15.

4 Ibid., p. 21.

therefore far earlier than other thinkers in Germany who sparked discussions about Kierkegaard after World War I.[5] Šajda comes to that date by deduction from one of Buber's remarks included in his little-known 1912 article "A.M. and Constantin Brunner," where Buber confesses that Kierkegaard had influenced his own thinking for fifteen years.[6] The author also acquaints us with other facts that delineate the breadth of Buber's knowledge of Kierkegaard, as well as the frequency of his references to this thinker. In Buber's writings there are more than fifty references to Kierkegaard's works (of which four-fifths are references to his short essay "The Single Individual") and twenty-four quotations from his journals, according to Šajda's research. Besides "The Single Individual" and journals, Buber quotes from four more of Kierkegaard's writings; the second most-cited work is *Fear and Trembling*, while Buber quotes from the other three only occasionally.[7] As Šajda remarks, throughout the *corpus* of Buber's works and his correspondence we do not find a single reference to Kierkegaard's *Works of Love*, which is the key to understanding Kierkegaard's conception of the relationship between religion and ethics. These facts clearly underline the selectivity and inconsistency of Buber's reading and interpretation of Kierkegaard.

The subject matter of the third, crucial, and most extensive chapter of the book is Buber's criticism of Kierkegaard's "religious acosmism." The author reveals and explores the writings in which Buber makes his most explicit references to Kierkegaard's work, that is, *The Question to the Single One* (*Die Frage an den Einzelnen*, 1936), *What is Man?* (*Das Problem des Menschen*, 1943), *Love of God and Love of Neighbor* (*Gottesliebe und Nächstenliebe*, 1945), *On the Suspension of the Ethical* (*Von einer Suspension des Ethischen*, 1952), as well as in the central work of Buber's dialogical philosophy, *I and Thou* (*Ich und Du*, 1923), where, however, those references are present only implicitly. The largest space is here naturally devoted to *The Question to the Single One*, which contains the majority of Buber's references to Kierkegaard and which Šajda therefore characterizes as Buber's "most comprehensive study of Kierkegaard."[8] Šajda first examines Buber's positive reception of Kierkegaard in this work. Here he points out that Buber values Kierkegaard's category of the single individual as "particularly topical and necessary for the ideological discourse of the 1930s."[9] According to Buber, Kierkegaard integrated into the category of the single individual two very important concepts for dialogic philosophy: *relationship* and *person*. Perhaps the most accurate evaluation of Kierkegaard's positive significance for Buber after his own "dialogical turn" can be nevertheless found in his letter to Hans Trüb from 1935,[10] where "he refers to Kierkegaard as the thinker who most significantly thematized the issue of personation in modern philosophy."[11]

5 See ibid., p. 43.
6 See ibid., p. 44.
7 See ibid., pp. 60–3.
8 Ibid., p. 74.
9 Ibid., p. 75.
10 Ibid., p. 51.
11 See ibid., p. 52.

With regard to Buber's negative reception of Kierkegaard's category of the single individual, Šajda highlights Buber's repeated citation from Kierkegaard's essay "The Single Individual": "everyone should be careful about becoming involved with 'the others,' [and] essentially should speak only with God and with himself."[12] This statement, as the author remarks, is for Buber "a symbol of the problematic nature of Kierkegaard's entire philosophy."[13] Buber believes that precisely this statement convicts Kierkegaard of religious acosmism. The roots of this acosmism, Buber assumes, lie in Kierkegaard's concept of the individual's exclusive relationship to God, which, Buber argues, lacks a dimension of inclusivity and therefore excludes any essential relationship to others. The consequence is the conflict between religion and ethics—the religious suspension of ethics.

Šajda devotes the fourth chapter to reactions to Buber's interpretation of Kierkegaard. The author identifies three basic groups of this "reception of reception." To the first and most numerous group he assigns those studies "which focus on the revision of Buber's criticism and corrections of his image of Kierkegaard."[14] As Šajda points out, the critical-corrective analyses of Buber's image of Kierkegaard are in substantial agreement that Buber's reading of Kierkegaard is selective and inconsistent. For the representative studies of this group, Šajda closely expounds essays by Jacob L. Halevi, Robert L. Perkins, Pia Søltoft, and Shmuel Hugo Bergman. Into the second and least numerous group Šajda places those authors who basically agree with Buber's critical reception of Kierkegaard or even further radicalize it. This group includes essays by Jewish authors like Haim Gordon, Tilman Beyrich, and Emil Fackenheim. Into the third group Šajda incorporates those studies that "map affinities between Kierkegaard's and Buber's thinking."[15] In this group Šajda recounts essays by Robert L. Perkins (again), John W. Petras, Michael Oppenheim, and Wanda Warren Berry.

In the final, fifth chapter the author familiarizes Slovak readers with the largely unknown pre-dialogical Buber. In accordance with Buber commentators Paul Mendes-Flohr and Maurice Friedman, Šajda dates this period from the beginning of Buber's work until 1916, that is, until the year in which Buber began revising his own vision of the individual and society due to his conflict with Gustav Landauer. However, as Šajda argues at the end of this chapter, Buber's turn to dialogical thinking was not made solely on the basis of critical impulses from Landauer, but also by virtue of his own long-time reflection on the Jewish spiritual tradition, whose peak he saw in Hasidism, which "carried out a fundamental transformation from pathos to ethos; thereby it became the prototype of Buber's own thought transformation."[16] In this chapter Šajda reveals several elements of religious acosmism in Buber's pre-dialogical thinking. In the period before his dialogical turn Buber focused primarily on the inner world of the individual, on his subjective experience (*das Erlebnis*).

---

[12] *SKS* 16, 86 / *PV*, 106.

[13] Šajda, *Buberov spor s Kierkegaardom: O vzťahu náboženstva k etike a politike*, p. 79.

[14] Ibid., p. 127.

[15] Ibid., p. 144.

[16] Ibid., p. 185.

Initially, the subject of his philosophical interest was mysticism, or more specifically the inner life of a mystic and the notion of an acosmic psychologico-metaphysical community (*Ecstatic Confessions* (*Ekstatische Konfessionen*), 1909). Later, against the background of World War I and under the strong influence of this historical event, in essays "Movement" ("Bewegung," 1915) and "Watchword" ("Die Losung," 1916), Buber elaborates his own vision of a pathic-kinetic community of soldiers united not by a common purpose but by a subjective experience of passion. However, as Šajda further shows, in both mentioned cases it is characteristic for Buber's idea of society in his pre-dialogical period that it lacks an essential relationship and ethical commitment to the particular other and the community. Despite this chapter's wealth of information on Buber's pre-dialogical thinking, it lacks explicit references to Buber's confrontation with Kierkegaard. This chapter thus only indirectly corresponds to the main theme of the book and can therefore be regarded rather as complementary. This minor deficiency is noticeable particularly when Šajda presents Buber's concept of pathic-kinetic community, which bears a number of features reminiscent of Kierkegaard's positive vision of the passionate spirit of (revolutionary) society in the third part of *A Literary Review of Two Ages*. The reader thus remains with the unanswered question of to what extent (if at all) Kierkegaard and his above-mentioned work were influential for Buber's idea of the pathic-kinetic community.

If I had to name the attributes that most adequately characterize Šajda's book, I would say "precision" and "comprehensiveness." One could hardly find a more precise and comprehensive work in the field of the history of philosophy in the Slovak world. It is therefore no coincidence that both official reviewers of the book, František Novosád and Jana Tomašovičová, excerpts of whose reviews appear on the back cover, highlight these very qualities. On page after page, the author evinces his profound dedication to the theme, his wide knowledge of the sources, and his highly scholarly style. That this is the first monograph published in Slovakia devoted to the thought of Martin Buber further highlights the significance of this publication. Šajda's book is undoubtedly a valuable contribution to research in the history of modern philosophy. Despite the aforementioned fact that his book is not primarily dedicated to exploring Kierkegaard's work, it has also from this point of view its indisputable importance, since it may be confidently classified among those books that help us determine the place and significance of Kierkegaard in the history of thought. I believe Šajda's book would be suitable for translation into one of the world languages in order to become accessible to a wider, international readership, which might appreciate even more the author's diligent, painstaking work in the field of historico-philosophical research.

Milan Petkanič

Reviews and Critical Discussions

Majerník, Jozef, "Skutky lásky," *Ostium*, vol. 10, 2014, no. 2 (on-line journal).
Tomašovičová, Jana, "O ľudskom spoločenstve," *Týždeň*, no. 4, 2014, p. 53.
Petkanič, Milan, review in *Filozofia*, vol. 70, 2015, no. 4, pp. 323–7.
Zigo, Milan, review in *Slovenské pohľady*, no. 5, 2015, pp. 131–4.

František Sirovič, *Søren A. Kierkegaard: Filozoficko-kritická analýza diela* [Søren A. Kierkegaard: A Philosophical-Critical Analysis of His Authorship],

Nitra: Spoločnosť Božieho Slova 2004, 200 pp.

František Sirovič's study *Søren A. Kierkegaard: A Philosophical-Critical Analysis of His Authorship* was published by the Society of the Divine Word in 2004. The author of this monograph was a well-known Slovak philosopher and theologian. In view of the political situation in Slovakia after 1989, philosophers have been primarily interested in social and political philosophy, and there has been little genuine interest in existentialist philosophy. The uniqueness of the book lies in the fact that it is the first monograph published in Slovakia which is dedicated entirely to Kierkegaard's life and work. The author emphasizes a need to return to Kierkegaard in the twentieth and twenty-first centuries. He writes:

> Kierkegaard plays an important role in reconsidering human reality in the 20th century. To study Kierkegaard's thoughts about an existing individual, who finds himself in different levels of relationships and acts in the world, is an important part of the self-education of the contemporary human. Kierkegaard can help us to become more sensitive to freedom, to interpret various human problems and to find the living God.[1]

The book was reviewed by Karol Bošmanský in the weekly *The Catholic Newspaper* in 2004.[2]

Søren A. Kierkegaard: A Philosophical-Critical Analysis of his Authorship consists of a Preface, an Introduction, ten chapters, a concluding summary, and a bibliography. František Sirovič describes his main aim as follows: "The aim of this study is to acquaint the reader with the content of Kierkegaard's thinking. The analysis and

---

1 František Sirovič, *Søren A. Kierkegaard: Filozoficko-kritická analýza diela*, Nitra: Spoločnosť Božieho Slova 2004, p. 7.

2 Karol Bošmanský, "Náhľad na svet a na človeka. František Sirovič: Søren A. Kierkegaard: filozoficko-kritická analýza diela" [A View of the World and of the Human. František Sirovič: Søren A. Kierkegaard: a Philosophical-Critical Analysis of his Works], *Katolícke noviny*, no. 31, 2004, p. 20.

critical evaluation will be from the philosophical point of view."[3] The author considers Kierkegaard neither as a philosopher nor as a theologian. He always perceives him as a religious thinker. Despite this fact, František Sirovič has a methodological ambition to criticize Kierkegaard only from the philosophical perspective (even though Sirovič himself was both a philosopher and a theologian).

The author is convinced that although Kierkegaard is very inspirational in formulating and pointing to the core problems connected with human beings, he is unable to solve them. Sirovič sees a complication in understanding Kierkegaard's authorship; namely, he finds two dichotomies in Kierkegaard's works. The first is the dichotomy between intention and fact. Sirovič states: "Kierkegaard neglected an adequate use of philosophical and theological resources for solving his problems. This could lead to atheistic consequences."[4] The second is the dichotomy between mind and heart. It is a conflict between the outer philosophical cover and the inner religious core. Kierkegaard used dialectics. That is why, according to Sirovič, Kierkegaard's solutions to problems are ambiguous and open to various interpretations. In this respect it can be said that Sirovič's work reveals more about his own philosophical-theological views on the human being's search for God than about Kierkegaard's thoughts.

The author begins his book with a detailed biography of Kierkegaard. Sirovič describes him from four different viewpoints. He introduces Kierkegaard as a son, Kierkegaard in love, Kierkegaard as a polemical author, and finally Kierkegaard as a witness of the truth. Sirovič tries to connect the consequences of Kierkegaard's life events with his publications, taking into account the historical, cultural, and political conditions of Kierkegaard's times.

The book is primarily concerned with Kierkegaard's philosophy of life stages. The author also tries to provide a comparison between Kierkegaard and Hegel, but the scope of the book does not allow him to elaborate a deeper analysis. Sirovič intends to embrace the whole of Kierkegaard's philosophical message. The result is a brief analysis of the main lines in Kierkegaard's authorship including life events, publications, life stages, and concepts such as existence, faith, God, the single individual, incarnation, truth, crowd, and the moment. Sirovič does not provide any relevant bibliographical references to secondary literature. He uses only references to Kierkegaard's primary texts.

Sirovič interprets Kierkegaard's life stages as strictly separated. He considers this to be a problem, because, according to him, "we can consider these contradictory stages of existence as unified, but there is no possibility to occupy them at the same time."[5] This has resulted in another problem, of which Kierkegaard is accused. Sirovič claims: "there is an ascendant hierarchy of existential perfection. It flows from the aesthetic through the ethical up to the religious stage. What will remain from the lower stage after someone decides to live in a higher or the highest

---

3 Sirovič, *Søren A. Kierkegaard: Filozoficko-kritická analýza diela*, p. 9.

4 Ibid., pp. 10–11.

5 Ibid., p. 44.

one?"[6] Kierkegaard's difficulty is recognized mainly as in connection with the relation between the aesthetic and the religious (Christian) existence: "He is not willing to admit that every lower value recognized as genuine can be incorporated into the higher stage."[7] Sirovič concentrates his criticism of Kierkegaard on his view about the ethical stage of life. From Sirovič's point of view Kierkegaard is against self-sufficient morality and the ethical stage is always only a kind of a transitional stage, which should be overcome. Sirovič considers the ethical and the religious stages as intertwined: the two stages permeate each other. This problem probably occurred due to the fact that Sirovič reflected on Kierkegaard's ethical and religious stage primarily from the perspective of *Fear and Trembling*.

Kierkegaard is also blamed for a lack of faith. Sirovič is convinced that human abilities are given by God, and so they are both "natural" and "transcendent," that is, both we and God can develop them. But, according to Sirovič's interpretation, Kierkegaard does not believe that it is possible for God to interfere in the development of the personality of a human being. Sirovič notes that Kierkegaard always writes that we have to develop our natural abilities on our own by ourselves. Sirovič claims that ethical principles are always religiously oriented, at least immanently. Considering secular morality, Sirovič thinks that its foundation is religious even if we are not aware of it. Sirovič suggests that Kierkegaard did not postulate a systematic theory of natural law, which is grounded in a metaphysical theory of creation and rooted in the Bible. If an individual is understood as a being, who participates in eternal Being, the problem of the relation between the ethical and the religious way of life disappears. It seems that the author does not remain faithful to his methodological ambition and is unable to analyze and criticize Kierkegaard from a purely philosophical perspective.

Søren A. Kierkegaard: A Philosophical-Critical Analysis of his Authorship is a good starting point for studying Kierkegaard. The book contains basic information about Kierkegaard's personality and philosophy. The value of the book lies also in its being a pioneer monograph on Kierkegaard in Slovak. Sirovič produced his book at a time when the intellectual situation in Slovakia was still influenced by the communist era. Kierkegaard was more or less unknown. Also thanks to this book, Kierkegaard's philosophy became increasingly popular in Slovakia. Even though Sirovič presents Kierkegaard as a thinker who asked questions but did not provide the answers, he sees him as someone who raised interest in human philosophical problems. Sirovič's attempt to revive Kierkegaard at the beginning of the twenty-first century was successful. After 2004 many articles, studies, contributions, books, and reviews on Kierkegaard were published in Slovakia. It can be said finally that František Sirovič truly created a basis for reflection, analysis, and critique of Søren Kierkegaard's work and life.

Zuzana Blažeková

6 Ibid., p. 45.

7 Ibid.

Review and Critical Discussion

Karol Bošmanský, review in *Katolícke noviny*, no. 31, 2004, p. 20.

V. Secondary Literature in Spanish

Cèlia Amorós, *Søren Kierkegaard o la subjetividad del caballero. Un estudio a la luz de las paradojas del patriarcado* [Søren Kierkegaard or the Subjectivity of the Knight: A Study in the Light of the Paradoxes of Patriarchy],

Barcelona: Anthropos 1987, 264 pp.

Cèlia Amorós (Valencia, b. 1944) is the most influential feminist philosopher in the Spanish language, a pioneer of gender studies in Spain, and current Professor at the Universidad Complutense de Madrid and the Universidad Nacional a Distancia (UNED). Her line of analysis and research is inscribed into the so-called "equality feminism," an heir to the revolutionary ideals of modernity specifically in the context of the emancipation of women as a measure of all freedom. From the perspective of gender, Amorós detects in Western philosophical discourse the vices and distortions corresponding to the "patriarchal" domination system. What the author calls "patriarchal reason" or "patriarchal logos," that summarizes in her view the history of universal philosophy, constitutes the expression of a sexist ideology, subservient to a discriminatory socio-cultural organization.[1] From this hermeneutical context emerges the work that is the focus of our interest: *Soren Kierkegaard or the Subjectivity of the Knight: A Study in the Light of the Paradoxes of Patriarchy*, whose origin must be traced to Amorós' lectures on Kierkegaard at the Universidad Nacional a Distancia. Among Kierkegaardian studies, the originality of the present text is marked by its reading of Kierkegaard through the lens of a gender perspective, as is made manifest by the work's subtitle: *in the Light of the Paradoxes of Patriarchy.* Amorós addresses Kierkegaard in the light of her feminist philosophy, in which the legitimacy of patriarchal rationality is strongly questioned and in which

---

1 Cf. Cèlia Amorós, *Hacia una crítica de la razón patriarcal*, Barcelona: Anthropos: 1985.

Kierkegaard's philosophy itself is presented as one of the critical representatives of that ideology. Amorós' thesis might be summarized in the notion that *the subjectivity of the knight* constitutes one of the sacrificial victims caused by the patriarchal system itself.

The text consists of a historical introduction followed by four chapters which attempt to deconstruct the symbolic cores of patriarchal rationality supporting Kierkegaardian thought. Chapter 1 approaches the relation/dis-relation between Kierkegaard and Regine Olsen, assumed by Amorós as the foundational myth of Kierkegaardian thought, based on sacrifice and death, in this case the sacrifice and death of Regine. The latter's sacrifice determines the original event on which the whole Kierkegaardian symbolic is founded, woven on anxiety, melancholy, death, the impossible ideal, remembrance, the unhappy conscience, and so on. The denial of women as a foundational event reproduces Romantic misogyny and courtly love, ideologically defined by the identification of the feminine character with temptation, the flesh, sensitive immediacy, sin, and consequently, by a tormented and contradictory relation/dis-relation with women. Regine's seduction and desertion, as Abraham's *Fear and Trembling* on Mount Moriah, disclose the fact that sacrifice and death are in truth the institutional and legitimizing myth of the Kierkegaardian "knight"—the knight of Romantic love or the knight of faith. In this figure patriarchal lordliness is reincarnated. Nevertheless, the paradoxical element in this mortal ideology is that the knight's subjectivity itself succumbs to it, and thus Amorós concludes, "courtly love is inconceivable without obstacles. Since there are no real obstacles here, Kierkegaard constitutes himself as the obstacle: the extremely peculiar constitution of his subjectivity opposes itself to the fulfilment of love and will therefore end by recreating itself as an obstacle and loving itself in a narcissistic way as a magnified obstacle."[2] This fundamental paradox of patriarchal rationality, that is to say, the self-denial of its subject, is in the last resort the leading thread of Amorós' Kierkegaardian hermeneutics and, along the same line, the leading thread of her whole feminist criticism.

Chapter 2 goes back to the figures of Don Juan-seduction and Abraham-sacrifice—as the two great mythemes of the Kierkegaardian symbolic, whose common denominators are anxiety and death, because "seduction is conceived in a recurrent way as a sort of sacrifice."[3] The other common denominator stressed by the author in these pages is the "anti-genealogical or agenealogical"[4] nature of Kierkegaardian characters. In fact, they all emphatically reject all descent. Don Juan, on his part, does not want histories or succession; the same applies to Faust; and even in Abraham's case, Isaac does not operate as a carnal descendant but as the passage from the carnal sphere to the spiritual one, which reinforces the rejection of natural generation. Amorós attempts to disclose "the recurrent character of the association among themes such as seduction—the cult of the instant—sacrifice and what we

---

2 Cèlia Amorós, *Søren Kierkegaard o la subjetividad del caballero. Un estudio a la luz de las paradojas del patriarcado*, Barcelona: Anthropos 1987, p. 84.

3 Ibid., p. 141.

4 Ibid., p. 143.

might call the genealogical trauma, the horror to become a father as well as to insert himself in the genealogical succession—deeply related in its turn to the horror of a carnal relation with women, from which consequences might result."[5] In this anti-genealogy resides, according to the author, the symbolic core of the Kierkegaardian mythical complex, whose biographical hold must be sought in Kierkegaard's traumatic relationship with a blasphemous father and a servant mother, impure and unnamable, from which his phobia to marriage and paternity derives. To sum up, in his life as well as in his thought, Kierkegaardian existence has neither an origin, nor a history, nor consequences: it is cursed in his father, nameless in his mother and closed to "assuming for himself the fact of being the origin of anybody or perhaps of nothing."[6] The knight's subjectivity is thus "ex-posed" to the void of his own nothingness.

In Chapter 3, Amorós observes Kierkegaard's "anti-philosophy," that is, the resistance to an objective, merely abstract knowledge, and the overcoming of it in relation to a subjective, concretely existential knowledge. There are at least two reasons for this. The first consists in Kierkegaard's reaction against Hegelianism and modern philosophy in general, understood as an abstract and de-subjectified thought. The second one responds to his zeal regarding a Christianity whose truths would be incomprehensible to philosophical speculation, because they would correspond to the sphere of life itself, to its own existential transformation. Thus, Kierkegaard proposes "a knowledge having a direct relation to the life of real and concrete individuals...an existential knowledge stemming from concrete human existence."[7] Precisely in this desperate reaction of subjectivity in order to re-establish itself upon a vital knowledge, identical to its existence, Amorós decodes the crisis of patriarchal rationality, which is rather its own crumbling.

The last chapter of the text ends in the paradox of Kierkegaardian thought, that is just one of the many paradoxes of patriarchal reason itself, in other words its self-denial. In fact, the singular individual is mortally sick to himself through sin; the repetition of his freedom realizes life and death, the finite and the infinite, in an ambiguous way; and his faith expels him from the logic of things and the moral order. But if freedom and faith end by sinking into an irrational negativity, existence then annuls itself, and in this resides the ultimate paradox of Kierkegaardian thought. In the face of the historical deployment of modern rationality, individual subjectivity took refuge in its own anxiety, and from there it denounced the exhaustion of a paradigm which was already untenable, but its exit is no more tenable than the former. Along with Kierkegaard, the whole of later existentialism "bears witness to the crisis of genealogy as a devaluation of recognition deployed in the figures of the Spirit's patriarchal logos."[8] Existentialism has revealed the historical rupture of patriarchal ideology, suffered in individual subjectivity itself. Nevertheless, the ultimate paradox of this reason is that neither irrationality nor the absurd represents a real alternative.

---

5 Ibid., p. 152.

6 Ibid., p. 157.

7 Ibid., p. 189.

8 Ibid., p. 242.

The epilogue of the book concludes that "the Kierkegaardian paradox is perhaps the image of patriarchal paradox, characteristic of a crisis of genealogical legitimacy, in which the son becomes the father's denouncer, while at the same time he forbids himself to judge him."[9] But even more paradoxical than the death of the father is the fact that—in patriarchal ideology as well as in its Kierkegaardian epigone—the son had already been denied in the father. Seduction, sacrifice, and anti-genealogy determine the self-denial of the system by its own mortal logic. Ideology does not leave any options: the subjectivity of the knight will eternally despair of his exposited ex-istence.

One of the most thorough feminist readings of Kierkegaard, whose weight dwells both in its consistency and its originality, is expressed in these terms. The fluency and simplicity of Amorós' essay avoids great scholarly scaffoldings as well as ostentatious academic superstructures. Its impact lies rather in a criticism that, as the author prefers to say of feminism, appeals to "the common sense of humankind."[10]

María J. Binetti

9 Ibid., p. 259.

10 Amorós, *Hacia una crítica de la razón patriarcal*, p. 10.

Reviews and Critical Discussions

Miyares, Alicia, review in *Arbor. Ciencia, Pensamiento y Cultura*, vol. 133, 1989, pp. 149–52.

Sachetti, Alejandro, review in *Cuadernos Hispanoamerianos*, vol. 476, 1990, pp. 122–4.

Valcárcel, Amelia, *La política de las mujeres*, Madrid: Cátedra 1998, p. 9.

María José Binetti, *El itinerario hacia la libertad. Un estudio basado en el* Diario *de Søren Kierkegaard según la interpretación de Cornelio Fabro* [The Itinerary of Freedom: A Study Based on the Diary of Søren Kierkegaard According to Cornelio Fabro's Interpretation],

Buenos Aires: CIAFIC Ediciones 2003, 216 pp.

This work is a general overview of Kierkegaard's thought as interpreted by the Thomist philosopher and theologian Cornelio Fabro (1911–95). The study is based on Fabro's Italian translation of Kierkegaard's works,[1] especially Kierkegaard's journals. It uses Fabro's hermeneutical keys, notably Catholicism and Thomism, in order to offer a personal version of the Dane that focuses on the concept of freedom as well as the individual's self-constitution, which is developed through a creative-existential process generated by decision and faith in relation to God. This task gives way to the construction of an existential and subjective truth in a remarkably Christian style, distanced from the intellectualist abstractions and excesses of modernity and close to what is called "metaphysical realism."[2] The book is unique

---

I would like to thank Matthew Nowachek for helpful comments on an earlier draft of this article.

1 Søren Kierkegaard, *Opere*, trans. by Cornelio Fabro, Florence: Sansoni 1972, includes parts of *Either/Or* ("Diapsalmata," "The Tragic in Ancient Drama Reflected in the Tragic in Modern Drama"), *Fear and Trembling*, *The Concept of Anxiety*, *Philosophical Fragments*, *Concluding Unscientific Postscript to Philosophical Fragments*, *The Sickness unto Death*, *Practice in Christianity*, "The Gospel of Sufferings," *For Self-Examination: Recommended to the Present Age*, and *The Changelessness of God*)

2 María José Binetti, *El itinerario hacia la libertad. Un estudio basado en el* Diario *de Søren Kierkegaard según la interpretación de Cornelio Fabro*, Buenos Aires: CIAFIC Ediciones 2003, p. 22; p. 73; p. 158.

to Spanish research, and it is one of very few works in the international field that studies Fabro's interpretation of Kierkegaard.[3] Fabro's importance in Spain resides in that his Italian translation of Kierkegaard's works represents an essential starting point for the Spanish reading of Kierkegaard. In addition, an indirect Spanish translation of Kierkegaard's journals based on Fabro's Italian translation[4] has been the only Spanish edition of Kierkegaard's personal writings up until the publication of a complete edition of this material by the Universidad Iberoamericana, which remains yet to be completed.[5]

The book is the M.A. thesis presented at Universidad de Navarra by the Argentinian CONICET researcher María José Binetti, who is considered to be one of the most notable specialists on Kierkegaard in the hispanophone world. Although she distances herself from Fabro's Catholic and Thomist view in her later works, Binetti has preserved the centrality of the concept of freedom that is present in this book in order to offer a personal reading of Kierkegaard which vindicates his proximity to the *frühromantisch* and Hegelian conception of the individual.[6] However, *El itinerario de la libertad* did not receive any attention by critics in the press, and it was apparently never reviewed.

The study generally fulfills its purpose of offering an overview of Kierkegaard's thought through a conceptual reflection which links together several of his central themes through a reading of the journals. The exposition emphasizes the elements that generate the existential dynamic where subjectivity is constructed through a continuous process of self-becoming. It employs a terminology which aims at bringing Kierkegaard closer to the idealist approach by qualifying his thinking as a "metaphysics of freedom."[7] Nevertheless, the volume commits some of the errors

---

3 There is only one Spanish-language work, similar to Binetti's, which studies Fabro's Kierkegaard, namely, the Ph.D. dissertation of José García Martín, entitled *La doctrina sobre el individuo en el Diario de S.A. Kierkegaard* (Universidad de Navarra, 2007), which was directed by Tomás Melendo. But this work has never been published. See Dolores Perarnau Vidal and Óscar Parcero Oubiña, "Spain: The Old and New Kierkegaard. Reception in Spain," in *Kierkegaard's International Reception*, Tome II, *Southern, Central and Eastern Europe*, ed. by Jon Stewart, Aldershot: Ashgate 2009 (*Kierkegaard Research: Sources, Reception and Resources*, vol. 8), p. 51.

4 Søren Kierkegaard, *Diario íntimo*, trans. [from the Italian] by María Angélica Bosco, Buenos Aires: Santiago Rueda 1955 (reissued with an Introduction by José Luis López Aranguren, Barcelona: Planeta 1993). Cf. Vidal and Oubina, "Spain: The Old and New Kierkegaard. Reception in Spain," p. 33.

5 Søren Kierkegaard, *Colección de papeles de Kierkegaard. Los primeros diarios*, vol. I (1834–37) and vol. II (1837–38), trans. and ed. by María José Binetti, Mexico City: Universidad Iberoamericana 2011–13.

6 See, for example, Maria José Binetti, *El poder de la libertad*, Buenos Aires: CIAFIC 2006, or María José Binetti, "Kierkegaard como romántico," *Revista de Filosofía*, vol. 34, no. 1, 2009, pp. 119–37, as well as María José Binetti, "Hacia un nuevo Kierkegaard: la reconsideración histórico-especulativa de J. Stewart," *La mirada Kierkegaardiana: Revista de la Sociedad Hispánica de Amigos de Kierkegaard*, no. 0, 2008, pp. 1–15.

7 Binetti, *El itinerario hacia la libertad*, p. 9.

common to first publications, and this reduces the quality of the work. First, its methodology is a "literal exegesis,"[8] where Kierkegaard's and Fabro's texts are compared. Although it offers, on many occasions, a very detailed and efficient exposition, on other occasions it mixes up the voices of the two thinkers. Binetti's efforts to differentiate them are at times disappointing: her own voice falls silent, and it is limited in most cases to reproducing Fabro's commentary without any critical counterpoint. Although Binetti's disagreements with the most problematic aspects of Fabro's thesis are insinuated, the absence of direct and consistent criticism of Fabro's excessively Catholicizing interpretation significantly devalues the precision and rigor of the book. While at the beginning of the study Fabro is praised as "the soul and sense of distinction,"[9] at the end of the book, Binetti recognizes "the uncertainty of many of his affirmations."[10] While Fabro claims that Kierkegaard did not "develop deeply any decision or idea,"[11] Binetti suggests later that this indecision is inherent to Fabro's interpretation,[12] but not to the Kierkegaardian *corpus*. Yet, this and other similar critical suggestions are weak and never developed beyond a few mentions of Fabro's theoretical background.[13]

The inattention to historiography is the second remarkable methodological problem from which the book suffers. On the one hand, the study does not show accurately and clearly Fabro's hermeneutical keys, nor does it explain why someone who does not consider himself a Kierkegaard researcher[14] and who only appreciates the Dane as a minor author, was actually concerned to translate and to comment upon his work. There is no clarification of Fabro's influence on the intellectual context of his time, and Binetti only enumerates hurriedly the philosophical views to which Fabro is opposed. This shortcoming calls into question the pertinence and interest of the study. The work risks becoming an ambiguous exposition which disregards the particularities of Fabro's thought, both those aspects that are appropriate and those that are openly wrong. The value of the book, then, does not reside in the exposition of Fabro's interpretation of Kierkegaard, but rather in a presentation of Kierkegaard's anthropology. The problem, however, is that Fabro's thesis is not clearly differentiated from Kierkegaard's. However, there is no explanation about the particularities of the journals as means for understanding Kierkegaard's thought, nor is the relation between Kierkegaard's personal writings and Kierkegaard's published works outlined in any detail. In addition, the quotations from the journals are mixed up with fragments from the published works. Third, there are many allusions to Spanish and Italian partial editions of the Dane's *œuvre* without reference the original work to which they belong.

The work presents Kierkegaard as a Christian thinker worried about criticizing the vices of modernity that would lead philosophy to atheism or to intellectualism.

---

8 Ibid., p. 9.
9 Ibid., p. 8.
10 Ibid., p. 210.
11 Ibid., p. 18.
12 Ibid., p. 210.
13 Ibid., p. 18.
14 Ibid.

This idea has two problematic points. First, the author makes use of the imprecise description "the Danish existentialist" to refer to Kierkegaard,[15] but Kierkegaard's relation to existentialism is exposited ambiguously and with blind spots. It is explained that Fabro considers Kierkegaard the only genuine existentialist thinker because Kierkegaard conserves a theist and Christian basis in his thought.[16] "Later existentialism"[17] is described by Fabro as a degeneration of Kierkegaard's existentialism, and then he adds that the "rationalism" inherited by Socrates is "the crack through which existentialism had leaked."[18]

Finally, the description of the concept of freedom as the "vertebral column"[19] of Kierkegaard's thought is excessive and is based on an unjustified preference for particular works such as *The Sickness unto Death* or *The Concept of Anxiety*. In this way, the Dane is situated far too closely to Romantic or idealist approaches, distorting on occasion what is characteristic of his thought. This interpretative focus, which is one of the peculiarities of the work, was significantly enriched and corrected in Binetti's subsequent works.

In short, *El itinerario hacia la libertad* should be read cautiously in order to avoid its problematic points as well as the omissions that undermine a critical engagement with Fabro and thereby diminish the rigor of this text as an academic work. Only this careful reading will make possible the book's very profitable and productive reflections.

Juan Evaristo Valls Boix

---

15 Ibid., p. 8; p. 9; p. 13; p. 22; p. 24; p. 26; p. 34; p. 38; p. 50; p. 59; p. 67; p. 73; p. 84; p. 113; p. 191; p. 195; p. 197; p. 199; p. 209; p. 210; etc.

16 Ibid., p. 17.

17 Ibid., p. 27; p. 28.

18 Ibid., pp. 36–7.

19 Ibid., p. 23.

Reviews and Critical Discussions

Undetermined.

María José Binetti, *El Poder de la Libertad. Una introducción a Kierkegaard* [The Power of Freedom: An Introduction to Kierkegaard],

Buenos Aires: CIAFIC ediciones 2006, 270 pp.

The work *El Poder de la Libertad. Una introducción a Kierkegaard* by María José Binetti aims to be an introductory handbook to Kierkegaard's living thought. This work was composed in the context of Binetti's doctoral thesis, which was presented and approved in 2004 at the Faculty of Philosophy and Literature at The University of Navarra in Spain. The original doctoral thesis *El Poder de la Libertad. Un estudio del pensamiento de Søren Kierkegaard con especial referencia al Diario* was 557 pages with four large chapters, but in its final published version it was condensed to 270 pages and divided into sixteen chapters.

This printed text continues in the same direction as Binetti's dissertation: its leitmotif is the concept of *freedom*. This study is an analysis of Kierkegaard's main philosophical categories related to the very essence of personal subjectivity, the individual, and inwardness, that is, to forms or ways in which the *free spirit* becomes self-aware and develops. Binetti gives profound analyses of Kierkegaard's work, concentrating principally on Kierkegaard's journals and notebooks from the *Papirer* edition, which she uses to sustain the conviction that freedom represents a transcendental priority in Kierkegaardian thought.

In general terms, the work's main idea is that freedom is the cornerstone of personal subjectivity and the keynote for existential understanding of the individual. Binetti uses this standpoint as an initial platform to revise and illuminate some of the principal categories in Kierkegaard's philosophy. In doing so, she proves how these concepts constitute special manners or modes in which the *free spirit* unfolds in order to provide a steady bridge of exploration for crossing the threshold of self-discovery—an act realized through freedom.

Binetti's exposition provides a general and useful overview of the most important theoretical elements in the Danish thinker's perspective about human reality. Therefore, Binetti's book is an excellent introduction which currently forms part of the worldwide list of scholarly manuals to Kierkegaard's work; however, although this work is intended to be classified as a basic introductory handbook to Kierkegaard's philosophy, we cannot say this is an easy text. Nevertheless, this book does not oblige its reader to have previous knowledge about Kierkegaard's thinking, but indeed it is necessary to have some experience with philosophy. This introduction is less accessible for the uninitiated, but for those who have experience in philosophy it is more than helpful in allowing one to acquire accurate and specialized knowledge about the Danish author's philosophy.

Each of the text's sixteen chapters represents a determined perspective on different aspects of Kierkegaard's life and work. Together they provide the reader with the principal elements useful for the study of Kierkegaard's philosophy. In Chapter 1, Binetti begins with a brief description of Kierkegaard's life. In Chapter 2, she proceeds to elucidate the complex and ambiguous relationship between Kierkegaard and Hegel. In Hegel's strong objectivistic perception everything is determined by the external reality, while Kierkegaard, by contrast, pursues a personal subjective knowledge and inner self-realization as the principle through which real freedom and the inner self are affirmed. Once stepping firmly upon the territory of personal subjectivity, Binetti stops to explain Kierkegaard's concept of *irony* as one of the principal qualities in the development of interiority. According to Binetti, *irony* represents one of the rhetorical recourses used by Kierkegaard in the indirect manner of communicating the truth to his reader, always with the purpose of awakening the reader's sense of liberty. After she explains the concept of *irony*, Binetti reveals the important goal of indirect communication and how Kierkegaard uses it as a vehicle to transmit his message. Therefore, indirect communication provides a basis for developing and concluding the different modes of communication, explained in the fifth chapter.

For Binetti, existence is seen by Kierkegaard as *a becoming*, insofar as spiritual existence is particularly a transcendental becoming ruled by freedom. For this reason, the next four chapters are dedicated to treating the problems of the self—its struggle of being and becoming—and to discussing infinite possibility as freedom and its relation to subjectivity, as well as sin and its dialectical position.

In Binetti's view, subjective freedom begins with possibility and its corresponding knowledge of itself as possible reality, which results in *anxiety*. Anxiety appears through the fear of losing the self and suffering a separation from the absolute. This fear predisposes one to fall into despair and anticipates sin which gives the impulse for the spirit's dialectical becoming. Inevitably, the individual is forced to see the necessity of making a decision. This necessity puts him face to face with his own freedom.

Between the possibility and the decision, the individual is constantly suffering from anxiety and despair. The way to dissolve human despair can be found in the power of faith; here is where subjectivity takes back, repeats, and recovers the lost completeness of the one and authentic reality. This is because faith has leapt above itself; it has reached out far beyond, succeeding in binding human, ephemeral time to the all-surpassing reality which is eternity, linking the finite with the infinite and carrying human emptiness before the presence of the absolute. The personal self is measured by infinite dimensions, which transcend the individual; inevitably human reason fails in the face of the divine.

From Chapters 10–12 Binetti's central theme is that the decision taken through freedom drives man to create and behold his subjective identity; these chapters add clarity to the work and strengthen Binetti's principal thesis. Chapter 13 connects with temporality and its relation with Kierkegaardian categories which were already presented in the previous chapters. Time, the moment, eternity, and repetition are shown as the most emblematic elements of temporality, significantly implied in the depiction of *the particular existent individual*, a concept discussed by Binetti.

The Kierkegaardian subjective figure is described in Chapter 14, where the individual with his interiority works to build his own world-view in the form of subjective truth, which can only be genuine when realized in the parameters of freedom. Having explained the subjective figure of the singular existent, Binetti in the next chapter continues to analyze the dynamics between the individual and his particular position in relation to the other.

In the last chapter, Binetti explains the natural relationship between the individual and his fellow man established through an ethic of *love,* whose principal foundation relies on freedom. In this chapter Binetti also explains that above faith is love, which creates a force capable of framing and realizing what faith only outlines with uncertainty. The paradox of love overcomes all differences since it makes a powerful union of the individual with the other. As the bond of perfection and basis of every single unity, love restores the divine resemblance without losing the individual's subjectivity; this is because subjectivity is in itself a gift given from God to man.

El Poder de la Libertad: una introducción a Kierkegaard is important as an introductory approach to the Christian Danish thinker because of its special treatment of the material presented in the *Papirer*—which is used in its original language and in translation—and also because of the large number of bibliographical references it contains.

Due to its recent publication, there are not yet other texts in which Dr. Binetti's handbook is mentioned or discussed. However, the text has been useful for its original purpose of helping those students who are starting to become familiar with Kierkegaard, and thus it has been quoted in several academic works. Binetti's work represents an original effort of unveiling freedom—among other conceptual perspectives—as a principal category on which Kierkegaard's thought is based.

Alejandro González Contreras

Reviews and Critical Discussions

Undetermined.

José Luis Cañas Fernández, *Søren Kierkegaard. Entre la inmediatez y la relación* [Søren Kierkegaard: Between Immediacy and Relation],

Madrid: Trotta 2003, 125 pp.

José Luis Cañas' work, *Søren Kierkegaard: Between Immediacy and Relation*, published in 2003, aims to understand, from a methodological point of view, the structure of Kierkegaard's thought as a poetical-religious dialectic characterized by a tension between the categories of immediacy and relation. From this perspective, the author believes that the influence and importance of Kierkegaard can be better understood, not only for existential philosophy and existentialism, but also for phenomenology and personalism, and for the so-called philosophy of the absurd and dialogical thought. This gives some sense of the contribution of this work by José Luis Cañas to the literature about the influence of Kierkegaard. Cañas says, "it is possible that no one has yet addressed the depth of the method that structures Kierkegaard's thought."[1]

José Luis Cañas' book is explicitly influenced by the works about Kierkegaard by contemporary Spanish philosophers such as Rafael Larrañeta, Francesc Torralba, Manuel Suances, Juan Manuel Burgos, and Alfonso Lopez Quintás.[2] In particular, Cañas' use of the categories of immediacy and relation comes from the idea of levels of reality and the so-called playful-ambital (*lúdico-ambital*) thought of Alfonso López Quintás.[3] Even certain interpretations of Kierkegaard's categories such as

---

1 José Luis Cañas Fernández, *Søren Kierkegaard. Entre la inmediatez y la relación*, Madrid: Trotta 2003, p. 15.

2 Some of those mentioned by José Luis Cañas are the following: Rafael Larrañeta, *La interioridad apasionada. Verdad y amor en Søren Kierkegaard*, Salamanca: San Esteban/ Universidad Pontificia 1990; Francesc Torralba, *Kierkegaard en el laberinto de las máscaras*, Madrid: Fundación Emmanuel Mounier 2003; Manuel Suances, *Søren Kierkegaard I: Vida de un filósofo atormentado*, Madrid: Universidad Nacional de Educación a Distancia 1997; Juan Manuel Burgos, *El personalismo. Autores y temas de una filosofía nueva*, Madrid: Palabra 2000. Alfonso López Quintás, *Vértigo y éxtasis*, Madrid: PPC 1987.

3 See Alfonso López Quintás, *Inteligencia creativa*, Madrid: BAC 1999. For Quintás an ambit represents a kind of horizon or field of possibilities.

anxiety and despair are related and explicitly understood under Quinta's categories, such as "vertigo" and the relationship with God as "ecstasy."[4]

José Luis Cañas' way of interpreting Kierkegaard, following the thought of López Quintás, succeeds in presenting synthetically the coming into existence of the single individual without reducing Kierkegaard's thought to ideologies, either individualist, or existentialist, or pro-Catholic, or pro-Lutheran. Kierkegaard is portrayed much better as a Christian-dialogical-personalist thinker. Kierkegaard's thought about the existence of the human person is a movement of freedom between two dimensions that structure its condition: immediacy and the relational. Immediacy dispossesses human life from its personal quality: that is why a relational way of thinking is required, which is understood as a dialogical act with another human being. This means a relationship where each person invites the other, in reciprocity, to trust, to give something, creating a relationship that allows them to experience a dimension of reality higher than immediacy, as Quintás says, creating unity and intensifying singularity.[5]

José Luis Cañas' book is structured so that the reader can follow this existential movement, the "leap" required to pass from one field of reality to another. The two categories are presented as two extreme points of the situation of choice that Kierkegaard proposes in *Either/Or*: either a man is immediacy or is relational. Or to put it in terms of the two ways of understanding the existential sense of stages as explained by Alfonso López Quintás: immediacy and the relational are fundamental attitudes or levels of reality that imply a peculiar logic for the moments of human activity.[6] These extreme points are in tension in Kierkegaard's life as an author, in the structure of his work, and in his conception of indirect communication.

Cañas proposes to interpret Kierkegaard's life from the perspective that the development of his work and his rejection of Regine could only be understood in terms of the relationship he seeks with God.[7] Related to Kierkegaard's work, these two extreme ideals of existence are, first, the immediate man in the figure of Don Juan and with the analysis that Cañas made of the first part of *Either/Or*, and, second, the figure of Abraham in *Fear and Trembling*, as the relational man whose fullness as faith in God is a paradox in his existence. Between these two extreme points, anxiety and despair are explained as existential limit situations that allow one to make the leap of freedom from one ambit to another.

For José Luis Cañas, in the first part of *Either/Or*, Kierkegaard presents, as characteristic of the immediate man, an existential process in which immediacy, anxiety, and despair are connected like an experience of vertigo. The interpretation of this by López Quintás is considered by Cañas as one of the best interpretations of the aesthetic man of Kierkegaard.[8] This aesthetic man is defined by a lying game in the figure

---

4 See José Luis Cañas Fernández, *Søren Kierkegaard. Entre la inmediatez y la relación*, Madrid: Trotta 2003, p. 47; p. 72; p. 68; p. 110; p. 117.

5 See ibid., p. 27.

6 See ibid., pp. 24–5.

7 See ibid., pp. 35–7.

8 See ibid., p. 46.

of Don Juan and Johannes the seducer, who both fall into an existential crisis by a reductionist passion that prevents them from communicating and giving continuity to their own existence.

Cañas understands anxiety and despair as emotional stages that make present to the immediate man his relational character. But anxiety and despair are also directly related as expressions of guilt, sin, and repentance. Cañas claims that in the Spanish language a more accurate way of interpreting them is with the word "agony" (*agonía*).[9]

José Luis Cañas' interpretation is very suggestive, but there are some questionable statements that are not fully grounded; for example, the idea that anxiety is the immediacy of sin or that despair is the extreme limit of anxiety.[10] It seems that Cañas is looking for a continuity between the two stages as types of emotions; however, in Kierkegaard's works, *The Concept of Anxiety* and *The Sickness unto Death*, there are some important differences. Even if anxiety and despair both refer to the stages of the human synthesis as spirit, anxiety is not caused by our own free will as is the case with despair. This means that despair is more than an emotion and in no way could be a consequence of anxiety or another mode of it, as if they were different levels of the same stage.[11]

Finally, the relational stage can be explained as the ethical-religious and represented by the figure of Abraham, who makes an authentic and passionate movement of faith and commitment. This is an example of freedom that lifts us out of immediacy and a transfiguration that leads to a unique relationship with God, what López Quintás has called "ecstasy."

Rafael García Pavón

---

9 See ibid., p. 90. Cañas explains that agony has the meaning of being a mood of the presentiment of death or of spiritual reality. In this sense agony will have the two meanings of despair and anxiety, as inner impulses toward the presence of something not immediate, but indeterminate, because it could be death or spiritual life.

10 See ibid., pp. 87–8.

11 See *SKS* 11, 159 / *SUD*, 44.

Review and Critical Discussion

Suances Marcos, Anselmo M., review in *La Mirada Kierkegaardiana*, no. 0, 2008 (on-line journal).

Catalina Elena Dobre, *La experiencia del silencio* [The Experience of Silence],

Mexico City: Editorial Corinter 2009, 136 pp.

La experiencia del silencio belongs to a number of monographs that Catalina Dobre has written on Kierkegaard's thought. This work was issued by Corinter, a Mexican publishing house, in 2009, and includes a Preface by Professor Rafael García, one of the most influential scholars on Kierkegaard studies in Latin America. Dobre is a long-standing member of the Sociedad Iberoamericana de Estudios Kierkegaardianos in Mexico City and an associate editor of the *Søren Kierkegaard Newsletter* published by St. Olaf College.

Without a doubt, silence is a recurrent topic in Kierkegaard studies and generally in philosophy. Silence has been the focus of several works by Alastair Hannay,[1] Ettore Rocca,[2] and Joakim Garff,[3] to name a few. In Latin America, however, research on the notion of silence, specifically its role in Kierkegaard's works, is only in its incipient phase. In the Spanish-speaking world, we can find articles on silence by scholars Patricia Dip,[4] Luis Guerrero,[5] and Miriam Jerade,[6] but *La experiencia del silencio* is the very first monograph written in Spanish on the subject.

---

1 Alastair Hannay, "The Knight of Faith's Silence," in his *Kierkegaard*, London and New York: Routledge 1982, pp. 54–89.

2 Ettore Rocca, *Kierkegaard. Silenzio e comunicazione*, Bologna: University of Bologna 1997.

3 Joakim Garff, "Johannes de silentio: Rhetorician of Silence," in *Kierkegaard Studies Yearbook*, 1996, pp. 186–210.

4 Patricia Dip, "Abraham y la ética del silencio en el pensamiento de Søren A. Kierkegaard," in *The Proceedings of the Twenty-First World Congress of Philosophy*, vol. 10, ed. by Ioanna Kuçuradi, Stephen Voss, and Cemal Güzel, Ankara: Philosophical Society of Turkey 2008, pp. 515–26.

5 Luis Guerrero, "Kierkegaard–Derrida: El silencio como contrapunto de la filosofía," *Revista de Filosofía*, no. 113, 2005, pp. 101–19; republished in *Kierkegaard and Great Philosophers*, ed. by Roman Králik, Abrahim H. Khan, Peter Šajda, Jamie Turnbull, and Andrew J. Burgess, Mexico City, Barcelona and Šal'a: Sociedad Iberoamericana de Estudios Kierkegaardianos, University of Barcelona and Kierkegaard Society in Slovakia 2007, pp. 196–212 (*Acta Kierkegaardiana*, vol. 2).

6 Miriam Jerade Dana, "Violencia y responsabilidad: releer el silencio de Abraham," *Acta poética*, vol. 31, no. 1, 2010, pp. 101–34.

It is important to underscore that Dobre's approach to silence is not a systematic one. She attempts to discuss silence from silence instead. This means silence is not taken as a concept in need of definition, but as something that has to be lived and, indeed, experienced. The book, as its title suggests, aims to carry out an experiment on silence. Thus, the author's goal is to talk about silence while trying not to encapsulate it within conceptual formulations. In this regard, Dobre explains: "The path is not an easy one. What can be more difficult than to touch with words the halt of words, to touch with thinking the halt of thinking, to penetrate with inwardness that which is beyond inwardness?"[7] It is in this manner that Dobre sets forth the main perspective from which she deals with the topic of silence: language, thought, and intimacy or inwardness.

In her attempt to explore every path to silence, Dobre begins by suggesting some key questions: What is silence? How can we understand it? Where does it come from? Where does it go? Is it here or in the beyond? Can we feel it, see it, or listen to it?[8] To answer these questions, Dobre approaches the subject mainly from Kierkegaard's perspective, but also from Picard's and Guardini's, among others. Along the way, she demonstrates that the answers to these issues are not unique, but manifold.

According to Kierkegaard, silence is an essential part of communication. Referring to Kierkegaard's thought, Dobre claims that "his writing, his communication, his language emerge from silence."[9] If it is not possible to discover the category of silence in a direct fashion, it might be feasible to do it indirectly. In this way, silence is present in Kierkegaard's communication, manifestly and secretly; it is the origin and the end of communication, the space wherein language is put at rest and moves on. How is this possible when at first sight Kierkegaard is a noisy author, an author who speaks with a multitude of voices? The answer offered by Dobre is the following: Kierkegaard associated silence with human life. He considered it as a field where the individual could find his or her inwardness.[10] The claim that to read Kierkegaard is to listen to many voices is correct. But, at the same time, he remains silent. Undoubtedly Kierkegaard's mute words compel the reader to judge for himself or herself, but in order to do this it is necessary to reflect in inwardness, away from the noise, in silence. Therefore, communication in Kierkegaard moves from the author's silence to the reader's silence.

Immersed in this relation between silence and inwardness, Dobre points out that silence is not only an encounter with oneself, but also with God. The story of Abraham shows how the Father of Faith had to keep silence in front of Sara and Isaac, and, hidden within himself, listened to God's voice. In this way, Dobre tries to demonstrate that silence is not only a condition of communication, but that it allows a new existential stage as well: the religious stage.[11] Nevertheless, there is a demonic silence too. Whereas in divine silence the individual is able to find God and his or

---

7 Catalina Dobre, *La experiencia del silencio*, México City: Corinter 2009, p. 17.
8 Ibid., p. 19.
9 Ibid., p. 23.
10 Ibid., p. 24.
11 Ibid., p. 71.

her own self, in demonic silence he or she does not listen to God's voice: there is no encounter with one's own inwardness, no self.[12]

Dobre also underscores the importance of silence in the existential sphere as a notion that permeates the entirety of Kierkegaard's thought. She suggests that silence is a dialectical category that marks both the beginning and end of communication, a place where the individual can find himself or herself or lose touch with his or her inwardness, where it is possible to listen to the divine voice or get caught by demonic silence, where the infinite meets the finite in the instant.[13]

It is clear that the purpose of the book is not to talk about silence from a scholarly or conceptual point of view, but rather from an experiential and existential perspective. The author's references to Kierkegaard are not made in order to discuss concepts or to debate different views on this particular topic. Dobre invokes Kierkegaard as a teacher and guide for an actual life experience. Thus, the essential aim of this work is to invite the reader to get away from noise and experience the silence. With all this, Dobre's work marks a promising start in the research and further development of the notion—and experience—of silence in Kierkegaard's thought in the Spanish-speaking world.

Fernanda Rojas

12 Ibid., p. 89.
13 Ibid., p. 101.

Reviews and Critical Discussions

Undetermined.

Catalina Elena Dobre,
La repetición en Søren A. Kierkegaard. O cómo recuperar lo imposible [Repetition in Søren A. Kierkegaard: Or How to Recover the Impossible],

Saarbrücken: Editorial Académica
Española 2012, 92 pp.

The book *Repetition in Søren A. Kierkegaard: Or How to Recover the Impossible* by Catalina Elena Dobre explores with depth and detail the category of repetition in the well-known work by Kierkegaard, *Repetition.* Repetition expresses, for the author, the paradox of being singular in existence within the framework of time and temporality. This means that the individual can only become himself in the present, be completed as himself in the past, or create an image of himself in the future, simultaneously in one and the same unique time. Therefore, this present is the dialectic of the inner time of oneself as the dynamic tension of between past and future. On the one hand, the individual's past is considered something that does not admit change any more; and, on the other hand, the individual's future is considered something that could change at any time. The contradiction is between two tendencies of movement, one in the past, when one dwells in what one has already achieved, and the other in the future, when one wants to change everything already done; therefore, repetition would be the act of recovering something impossible: one's own singularity, which comes into existence in a present time that we could consider unique. Catalina Elena Dobre's text is divided into six chapters that develop the category of repetition from the beginning.

In Chapter 1, "Kierkegaard in Few Words," the author takes us to the center of the *dramatis personae* in the Kierkegaardian *oeuvre* in order to situate the category of repetition. It is a context in which Hegelian thought dominates as a quasi-religious mode of living comfortably under the security of the rational progress of necessity. The person facing existence with his singularity, with anxiety for the future and openness to the transcendent, is annihilated by the promise of the progress of the system. But, for Kierkegaard, Dobre says, this is precisely the way of reproducing all the evils since such a person fails to face existence as a movement in time, in which every person must choose himself in his own inwardness.

In Chapter 2, "Repetition, an Exercise of Understanding," the author invites us to understand the meaning of the word "repetition" as Kierkegaard uses it. While this term has multiple senses in Danish such as "resume," "rediscover," or "revive," for Kierkegaard it is understood only by living the passion, the *pathos*, which involves the act of trying to understand the repetition of oneself in time. And this *pathos* is due to the tension provoked by the claim of remembrance to be repetition or, in terms of what Kierkegaard takes from the history of thought, the tension between reminiscence and repetition. By reminiscence, what we were is re-discovered, and we go back to what was already in us, but by repetition, as a category of the future, we seek to begin again, not to be re-discovered, but to get to know ourselves for the real first time.

In Chapter 3, "*Repetition* a '*sui generis*' book," Catalina Elena Dobre takes us into the *pathos* of the book, into the mode in which *Repetition* is written, by which Kierkegaard indirectly communicates to us the scope of the repetition. What kind of book is *Repetition*? A literary work, a book of letters, a treatise on psychology, philosophy, or theology? Or is it, rather, a book without categories because they all come together in a mode of writing like a great theater play to represent existence itself? Is existence the synthesis of all of them? It is in opening up to this mode of writing that Kierkegaard makes us denote the crucial elements of repetition, which are presented in the next three chapters of Catalina Elena Dobre's book as follows: the stages of repetition, the dialectic of repetition, and the time of repetition.

In Chapter 4, "The Stages of Repetition," the author reminds us that Kierkegaard did not attempt to give a system of existence, and because of this, existence has to be thought of in the form of stages or conceptions of life. These are in some way dimensions inherent to the human condition, but they require the choice of each individual to acquire their correct order. There are, in general, are three stages: the aesthetic, the ethical, and the religious, and therefore three types of repetitions, of which only the third is the truly authentic one and to which every single individual is called. From this perspective, in the literary structure of the book, the pseudonymous author Constantin Constantius represents someone who has tried repetition in an aesthetic sense, or even in an ethical sense, and has failed miserably. He narrates in *Repetition* his experiment of repeating at different times the same circumstances of past experiences, to discover if the same past meaning could be present again, and his surprise is that it is not possible in any way. This repetition in an aesthetic sense and in mere ethical categories, like duty to society, is absurd and impotent in the movement of existence, because what is required is a leap of faith; one should not repeat the finite, the immanent, or the possibilities and conditions of the world or our wishes for the future, but the very possibility of receiving oneself beyond the worldliness of the immediacy of existence. Searching for this new beginning is the genuine repetition. As Dobre says: "The infinite repetition is the movement of faith, a movement that goes beyond reason, or, at best, repetition is a movement that makes us embrace the possibility of the impossible."[1]

In Chapter 5, "The Dialectic of Repetition," the author tells us that repetition should be understood as a movement in the field of existence, that is, not in the way

---

1 Catalina Elena Dobre, *La repetición en Søren A. Kierkegaard. O como recuperar lo imposible,* Saarbrücken: Editorial Académica Española 2012, p. 62.

in which things are derived from nature ontologically, but how it is that each one becomes a self. And this dialectic takes places because, for Kierkegaard, the human being is understood as a synthesis of opposites (soul-body and spirit) that cannot be resolved or unified by logical mediation or by means of thought, or a logical deduction, but through the leap of freedom that positions the individual with a personal responsibility for his existence.

This choosing of oneself is what makes that future, *qua* abstract, become a future that is concrete. Because it makes the past acquire new possibilities for the future, in the end past and future are both horizons of possibilities. In other words, repetition is a movement of freedom and not of the necessity between possibility and actuality, and what begins again continues to be possible, and this is what it means to be spirit.

In Chapter 6, "The Time of Repetition," the author argues that repetition is an event in time that implies a relationship between all the moments of time—past, present, and future—simultaneously. Therefore, the concrete effect of repetition is that time is qualified as the subjectivity or the inwardness of the single individual—not time as a succession or as an abstraction, but time such as temporality in tension. This time, the eternal instant, in which everything begins again, is when, in choosing oneself, one has chosen to believe that a past is possible and in this way becomes historical, repeating, not its past facts, but their past conditions of becoming, which are possibilities, changing in this way, our inner way of remembering and expecting. This brings into play again the temporal relationships in which they are experienced as a unit, that is to say, as eternity, as a deep experience of meaning and one that gives the possibility of redemption.

Catalina Elena Dobre's conclusion is that repetition is not itself redemption but its possibility. In the act itself we are again able to believe in the past, in which we might have lost youth, virtue, or innocence: that is, we are able to recover our own innocence by choosing ourselves and not being circumscribed by the situations of the world.

Rafael García Pavón

Review and Critical Discussion

García Pavón, Rafael, review in *Revista de filosofía. Universidad Iberoamericana*, no. 137, vol. 47, 2014, pp. 243–52.

Luis Farré,
Unamuno, William James y Kierkegaard y otros ensayos
[Unamuno, William James and Kierkegaard and Other Essays],

Buenos Aires: Editorial La Aurora 1967, 270 pp.

Unamuno, William James y Kierkegaard was published by Luis Farré in 1967. Farré had a distinguished career as a professor of philosophy in Argentina, teaching at the University of La Plata and the Evangelical Theological Faculty of Buenos Aires. He was above all an essayist, as the style of this work (and the scarce reference to secondary literature) makes clear. His viewpoints cannot be said to belong to any specific philosophical school. Concerned about the human and political crisis of the century, he looked at these issues with a strong emphasis on their spiritual dimension. It is this emphasis that attracted him to Kierkegaard, as becomes visible in the essays collected in this work.

Three of the pieces contained in the book directly deal with Kierkegaard. The other five pieces deal with diverse Protestant theologians and the contemporary spiritual situation of Roman Catholicism. We can begin with the third piece on Kierkegaard, the fourth chapter of the book, since not much of this piece stands in need of commentary. Its title is "A Man Called Sören Kierkegaard." It is a short biographical essay written after Farré had access to Kierkegaard's so-called *Diaries*. Originally published in the Argentinian newspaper *La Nación* in 1964, it reflects Farré's critical appreciation (and also his limited knowledge) of this side of Kierkegaard: Alexander Dru's translation is used, and there is no hint of Farré knowing how limited an approach to the Kierkegaardian papers this was. The essay basically commends the authenticity of Kierkegaard's life, but repeatedly claims that his demands are too high.

"Unamuno, William James y Kierkegaard," the essay which lends its title to the book as a whole, is also the longest piece of the collection. It was originally published as a journal article in 1954. It is important to keep that date in mind instead of 1967, since it explains the omission of the much more scholarly work on Unamuno and Kierkegaard published by Jesús-Antonio Collado in 1962. If we consider the original date of publication, Farré's is actually among the earliest published discussions about Kierkegaard's relation to Unamuno.[1] However, there was already

[1] Other important early contributions to this discussion are Carlos Alberto Erro, "Unamuno y Kierkegaard," *Sur*, vol. 8, no. 49, 1938, pp. 7–21; Joan Estelrich i Artgiues

frequent conversation about their relationship, and in the Preface of his book Farré states that his goal is to draw attention to their differences, given that enough was being said about their similarity.[2]

The essay stands slightly more in the service of our understanding of Unamuno than of James and Kierkegaard. But Farré discusses these three authors at length, stressing similarities and dissimilarities between them. Sometimes the points that Farré touches on lead him to bring Kierkegaard and Unamuno close together. Neither of them, for instance, claims to be a philosopher in the way James did. But for the most part he depicts them as kindred spirits who nevertheless are divided on important issues. Unamuno's moral thought, for example, is portrayed as closer to the positions of James than to Kierkegaard's.[3] The Spaniard's quest for immortality, on the other hand, is portrayed as his own distinctive theme.[4] When it comes to the religious life, one can see Farré's moderate preference for Kierkegaard emerge. Whereas Unamuno would consider doubt to be the quintessential religious disposition, for Kierkegaard that position is unquestionably occupied by faith. Doubt is not absent from Kierkegaard's thought, but Farré sees Kierkegaard as quickly leaving it behind.[5] The religiosity of both Unamuno and James are finally described by Farré as aesthetic: they look at religion as springing from human need (cultural or psychological), and thus, "no matter how much they stress the individual's grief and religious sentiment, they are reduced to this category."[6]

It is hard to avoid the conclusion that throughout the essay the three authors are being ranked, with Kierkegaard in the first and Unamuno in the second place. "James cannot with justice be placed at their side," Farré writes.[7] Together, however, the three are celebrated as a triumvirate far more profound than the various existentialisms of the twentieth century.

The second piece dealing with Kierkegaard (and the third essay of the work as a whole) is entitled "Hegel, Kierkegaard, and two Spaniards: Ortega y Gasset and Unamuno." Here Farré very usefully shows how Ortega's critique of Kierkegaard depends on his own dislike of Unamuno. While the point may seem trivial, it is significant for the fact that it does not tie rejection or adoption of Kierkegaard to sympathy or antipathy towards existentialism. Indeed, Farré suggests that Unamuno and Ortega "had a very limited knowledge about this movement."[8]

In Spain one could find enthusiastic efforts to bring Unamuno and Ortega as close to each other as possible (especially after their deaths). Farré starts by rejecting this

---

"Kierkegaard y Unamuno," *Gaceta Literaria*, vol. 4, no. 78, 1930; J. MacGregor, "Dos precursores del existencialismo: Kierkegaard y Unamuno," *Filosofía y Letras*, vol. 22, nos. 43–4, 1951, pp. 203–19.

2 Luis Farré, *Unamuno, William James y Kierkegaard y otros ensayos,* Buenos Aires: Editorial La Aurora 1967, p. 9.

3 Ibid., pp. 50–1.

4 Ibid., pp. 70–5.

5 Ibid., p. 82.

6 Ibid., p. 86.

7 Ibid., p. 94.

8 Ibid., p. 158.

and stressing their differences in temperament and intellectual disposition. Ortega is portrayed as a coldly abstract thinker in the tradition of Hegel, and Unamuno as a stormy and passionate thinker. Since Farré is writing a book that commends the work of Unamuno, James, and Kierkegaard, one would have expected this comparison to turn out negatively towards Ortega. But Farré finishes this essay with a reflection on the way in which contemporary philosophy was closing itself to argument. We who have chosen the path of philosophy, he writes, and have a desire for clear argument and firm explanation, but one that is rooted in lived reality. This, he suggests, calls for a "rapprochement of Hegel and Kierkegaard, and, as epigones, of Unamuno and Ortega y Gasset."[9] This may seem close to the position Farré was initially rejecting. But towards the end of the essay we can see that his initial criticism was aimed at the nationalistic celebration of both authors as Spanish thinkers. Their respective strengths, however, can plausibly be combined.

These two essays, thus, both reject a simplistic identification of different authors (of Unamuno and Kierkegaard as passionate thinkers, of Unamuno and Ortega y Gasset as Spanish thinkers), but they both in the end argue that attention can be fruitfully given to each of them. Contrary to what his title might suggest, Farré's work thus presented Kierkegaard in a way that would not necessarily support a unilateral agenda.

Manfred Svensson

[9] Ibid., p. 160.

Review and Critical Discussion

Evans, Jan E., *Miguel de Unamuno's Quest for Faith: A Kierkegaardian Understanding of Unamuno's Struggle to Believe*, Eugene, Oregon: Wipf & Stock 2013, pp. 56–61.

María García Amilburu (ed.), *El concepto de la angustia: 150 años después* [*The Concept of Anxiety:* 150 Years Later],

special issue of *Thémata, Revista de Filosofía*, vol. 15, 1995 (Seville: Universidad de Sevilla), 146 pp.

The Concept of Anxiety: 150 Years Later was not only a commemorative work of the 150th anniversary of the publication of the famous work by Kierkegaard under the pseudonymous author Vigilius Haufniensis, but it was also a point of departure for the Spanish-speaking world's response to the Kierkegaard renaissance.[1] As Amilburu notes, this publication appeared at a time when, in the Hispanic world, there were no complete translations of the works of Kierkegaard. The main motivation for the editor of the book, Maria Garcia Amilburu, to put together seven authors from Spain and Latin America to write about *The Concept of Anxiety* was to indicate the importance that Kierkegaard studies should have in the Spanish language. Although two of the authors are not Spanish speakers, Arne Grøn and Julia Watkin, their presence here is entirely justified since they were at that time promoters of international Kierkegaard research: Grøn from the University of Copenhagen and Watkin the editor of the *International Kierkegaard Newsletter*.

The text consists of different topics about the implications that anxiety has for the human condition: temporality, suffering, destiny, providence, freedom, worldliness, the demonic, and self-realization with God. In the following we refer to the featured articles in the order in which they appear in the text.

The article by Arne Grøn, "*The Concept of Anxiety* in the Work of Kierkegaard," presents the thesis that even though it is a centerpiece of Kierkegaard's thought, *The Concept of Anxiety* is not a completed work in the sense that it takes up topics from the previous works giving them a new development that are not at all wholly worked out in the book. It thus remains open to be completed by other works such as *The Sickness unto Death*. These topics converge to define what man is, and at the same time they are treated in a new way such that *The Concept of Anxiety* opens up new horizons of reflection about what this definition might imply. In particular, Grøn tries to present an interpretation of a second ethics that is in harmony with *Works of Love*.

[1] The Kierkegaard renaissance refers to the growing international interest that took place in the 1990s, where publications, translations, forums, and congresses grew exponentially.

The text by Rafael Alvira, "About the Radical Beginning: Considerations about *The Concept of Anxiety* in S.A. Kierkegaard," presents the thesis that anxiety, as outlined by Kierkegaard, could be better understood in Spanish culture as anguish (*ansiedad*), because it refers to an inner impulse toward something and not only to an inward experience. This view is used in the thesis Alvira argues for, namely, that *The Concept of Anxiety* could be interpreted as the state of the beginning of understanding or knowledge of the truth. Alvira shows that in Kierkegaard this resembles the Socratic method, but with the difference that in Kierkegaard the idea of love of wisdom is missing. It is clear that Alvira's thesis takes the pseudonymous author a bit out of context, since such conclusion—the absence of the love of wisdom—does not hold to the extent that it regards the book as an existential movement.

The article by Begonya Sáez Tajafuerce, "Fulfillment and Temporality in *The Concept of Anxiety*," makes a thorough analysis of how the idea of self-realization is identified ethically with the meaning of the moment. Here the moment is not what we commonly understand as something ephemeral, but as the presence of the interrelationship of eternity within the flow of the temporal becoming; the moment acquires an original dialectic that explains more specifically the idea that the human being is spirit and inwardness. Temporality is neither the chronology, nor the conception of time in Plato's metaphysics, nor is it a condition of perception, but "the legitimate horizon for legitimate subjective action."[2]

The article by Teresa Aizpún, "Freedom in *The Concept of Anxiety*," argues that the topic of freedom in Kierkegaard has to be understood as a form of conditioned freedom because of the reality of sin. For Aizpún, to be free means to become conscious of oneself as affected by sin and to become aware that the source of the self does not depend of our will. This gives rise to an openness of consciousness to a radical otherness. Aizpún concludes that freedom, which is identified with this process of awareness, has to be self-creation. However, without giving too many arguments Aizpún ends by saying that the idea of spirit in Kierkegaard does not become freedom at all but rather a silent inactivity.

The text by Rafael Larrañeta, "Kierkegaard: Tragedy or Theophany: From the Innocent Suffering to the Pain of God," presents the idea of suffering in the work of Kierkegaard in the three stages: aesthetic, metaphysical-ethical, and religious. Aesthetic suffering has to do with the nature of the lack of reflection, principally denoted by the sense of the classic tragedy, for which the origin of suffering is not the fault of the individual. Ethical and metaphysical sufferings are characterized by reflection on the possible meaning of actions. Therefore, suffering is the experience of needing to become a way of life that depends on our choice in the time we have available, and at the same time, the risk of not choosing on time; this always keeps the one who chooses in a situation of contradiction; one reaches the point where the radical question of suffering is not resolved and requires a religious stage. At the religious

---

2 Begonya Sáez Tajafuerce, "Autorrealización y temporalidad en *El concepto de la angustia*," *El concepto de la angustia: 150 años después,* ed. by María García Amilburu, *Thémata, Revista de Filosofía*, vol. 15, 1995 (Seville: Universidad de Sevilla), p. 51.

level, suffering is characterized as the highest form of life and inwardness, by which suffering is a choice between tragedy and theophany.

The article by Virginia Careaga, "Destiny and/or Providence," presents the dialectical relations between freedom and necessity, where anxiety is the opening of necessity to the sphere of faith and therefore of providence as the ultimate act of being.

As the title implies, the text by Julia Watkin, "The Problem and Reality of Destiny in *The Concept of Anxiety*," presents a reflection on the category of destiny. According to Watkin, destiny is equivalent to the category of nothingness in *The Concept of Anxiety*, because it is an abstract and imaginative way of justifying the meaning of existence. However, Watkin argues that by asking about destiny the individual becomes aware of the categories of freedom and existential responsibility, when they are related to the ideas of sin and guilt.

The text by Leticia Valádez, "The Criticism of Worldliness in *The Concept of Anxiety*," argues that worldliness is a way of life that is present in all the stages of life, without identifying it with any of them. What characterizes the worldly life is a lack of understanding of each of the stages; that is why there can be different types of worldliness: from a worldly aesthetics to a worldly religion. In *The Concept of Anxiety*, worldliness means lack of spirit, of possibilities, and not wanting to be educated by anxiety. Therefore, worldliness means the neglect of the difficulties of the religious life, since one is confronted with the radical choice of being oneself in the infinite possibilities by the means of anxiety.

The text by Montserrat Negre, "The Demonic in *The Concept of Anxiety*," is a description of the state of development of the individual as a demonic personality. This means denying what grounds us. The originality of Kierkegaard, according to Negre, is to relate the demonic to anxiety as a vital situation.

The closing text by Carlos Diaz, "The Anxiety of Kierkegaard and Ours," which is written with a very peculiar and even existential style, presents Kierkegaard as a kind of older brother who makes us pay attention to what is important in life: love in its fullness.

This volume was a central point of reference for later studies on *The Concept of Anxiety*, and some of the articles continue to be used, for example, the one about temporality. Because it was one of the first works in the Hispanic world to explore anxiety from the existentialist perspective, it opened up a new understanding of Kierkegaard's book and the importance and complexity of its categories for the human condition, even though some of the articles made some objections from an existential position. It was also one of the first collected volumes to be put together by Hispanic and Latin American Kierkegaard scholars.

Rafael Garcia Pavón

Reviews and Critical Discussions

Undetermined.

Rafael García Pavón, *El problema de la comunicación en Søren A. Kierkegaard. El debate con Hegel en El concepto de la angustia* [The Problem of Communication in Søren A. Kierkegaard: The Debate with Hegel in *The Concept of Anxiety*],

Rome: IIF-Press 2012, 228 pp.

El problema de la comunicación en Søren A. Kierkegaard aims at reconstructing the indirect discussion between G.W.F. Hegel and Søren Kierkegaard through a study of *The Concept of Anxiety* in order to analyze Haufniensis' psychological insights and its structure as a reflection on the problem of communication. The Hegelian conception of psychology as the objective spirit of the human being is criticized from a Kierkegaardian consideration of existential communication, which structures the work and affords a central role to its pseudonymity. The book is one of several studies in Spanish on the topic of indirect communication and Kierkegaard's authorship,[1] and it distances contemporary Spanish research from many persistent clichés in the Spanish reception of Kierkegaard which continue to stress the existentialist, tragic, or passionate character of the author. By doing this, Rafael García Pavón's work

I would like to thank Matthew Nowachek for helpful comments on an earlier draft of this article.

[1] There is a significant number of relatively recent Spanish studies about Kierkegaard's use of pseudonyms and indirect communication. Some of the most important are Begonya Saez Tajafuerce, *Søren Kierkegaard: la seducció ètica*, Barcelona: Universitat Autònoma de Barcelona 1997; Francesc Torralba, *Punt d'inflexió. Lectura de Kierkegaard*, Lleida: Pagès Editors 1992; Luis I. Guerrero, *La verdad subjetiva. Søren Kierkegaard como escritor*, Mexico City, Universidad Iberoamericana 2004. García Pavón's work stands out by focusing uniquely on *The Concept of Anxiety*, while Saez Tajafuerce's study is probably the only one that takes seriously the role of Kierkegaard as an author and develops an aesthetic research rather than offering a bare general interpretation of Kierkegaard's *œuvre* preceded by a presentation of Kierkegaard's style.

defends a critical reading that relates *The Concept of Anxiety* to the purposes and intentions of its author, his other works, and the composition process of Kierkegaard's *corpus* as a whole. García Pavón is professor and researcher in the Faculty of Humanities from the Universidad Anáhuac Norte, México and this work is a revised version of his Master's thesis in philosophy for the Universidad Panamericana (1999). He obtained his Ph.D. at the Universidad Iberoamericana with his dissertation *The Category of Contemporaneity and the Existential Status of Faith in the Thought of Søren A. Kierkegaard*.[2] Unfortunately, critics in the press have not paid any attention to the present study, which could play a significant role in the renewed Spanish-speaking reception of Kierkegaard's work.

The book achieves its goals well and offers a detailed reflection on the discussion between Kierkegaard and Hegel from the perspective of Vigilius Haufniensis. Its structure is solid and well-organized, and it is based strictly on the reconstruction of the arguments of both Hegel and Kierkegaard: first, it presents the conception of psychology in the intellectual context of the nineteenth century, which was strongly influenced by Hegel's idealism; second, it studies Kierkegaard's counterargument, paying special attention to the pseudonymous character of *The Concept of Anxiety*, and extends this exposition with a general view of Kierkegaard's problem of communication.[3] This reconstruction is intended to show that the pseudonymous character of *The Concept of Anxiety* is designed by Kierkegaard as a critique of the Hegelian conception of the human being as described in the *Encyclopedia of the Philosophical Sciences*, against which it develops a conception of human psychology understood as the possibility of freedom.[4] García Pavón's exposition deals rigorously with the exchange of arguments and clearly connects Kierkegaard's conception of the individual with his communicative purposes as an author. The study gets rid of outdated opinions and myths, and it bases its research on a direct analysis of the work of both Hegel and Kierkegaard.

Nevertheless, several problems with the study undermine the value of its expositive virtues. First, it draws on the first edition of the complete works of Kierkegaard from 1901–6,[5] and the papers from 1968–70,[6] and it makes use of neither the current Danish critical edition nor the latest Spanish and Italian translations.

Second, it ignores the latest research about Kierkegaard's Danish intellectual context and his contemporary interlocutors.[7] This is probably the greatest problem

---

2 Rafael García Pavón, *La categoría de contemporaneidad y el estatuto existencial de la fe en el pensamiento de Søren A. Kierkegaard*, Ph.D. Thesis, Universidad Iberoamericana, México D.F. 2009.

3 Rafael García Pavón, *El problema de la comunicación en Søren A. Kierkegaard. El debate con Hegel en El concepto de la angustia*, Rome: IIF-Press 2012, p. 34.

4 Ibid., p. 102.

5 *Søren Kierkegaards Samlede Værker*, vols. 1–14, ed. by A.B. Drachmann, J.L. Heiberg, and H.O. Lange, Copenhagen: Glydendalske Boghandel Nordisk Forlag 1901–6.

6 *Søren Kierkegaards Papirer*, vols. 1–16, ed. by P.A. Heiberg, V. Kuhr, and E. Torsting, Copenhagen: Gyldendal 1909–48; supplemented by Niels Thulstrup, Copenhagen: Gyldendal 1968–78.

7 See Jon Stewart, "Quellensforschung y la relación de Kierkegaard con Hegel," *Ironía y destino. La filosofía secreta de Søren Kierkegaard*, ed. by Fernando Pérez-Borbujo, Barcelona: Herder 2013, pp. 43–77.

with the study. On the one hand, many analyses show a considerable knowledge about Danish Hegelianism and the different intellectuals that Kierkegaard criticized, such as Hans Lassen Martensen or Johan Ludvig Heiberg.[8] García Pavón's study draws on Bruce Kirmmse's work[9] and other contemporary studies in order to take account of historical details. However, García Pavón defends the thesis of early studies that consider Kierkegaard as a direct opponent of Hegel rather than a critic of the philosophers and theologians from Copenhagen: "there is a discussion about the relationship between Hegel and Kierkegaard where extreme stances have been adopted which deny Kierkegaard's critique of Hegel and consider that his polemic was actually against the Danish Hegelians."[10] It is true that García Pavón moderates his position when he indicates that Kierkegaard's critique is directed against "the ideas"[11] of Hegel and that, since Kierkegaard's age was "conditioned by the Hegelian argument," *The Concept of Anxiety* can question "indirectly those who, in the nineteenth century, [are thinking] under Hegel's influence."[12] Yet, there is not a single reference in the García Pavón's work to the actual object of *The Concept of Anxiety*'s criticism: Adolf Peter Adler,[13] nor to his work from 1842 entitled *Popular Lectures on Hegel's Objective Logic*,[14] which was later mentioned in *The Book on Adler*. García Pavón just exposits the old idea defended by Cornelio Fabro and Reidar Thomte, among others, that Haufniensis is criticizing Hegel's *Science of Logic* and its conception of "actuality" (*Virkelighed* in Danish, *Wirklichkeit* in German),[15] as well as Hegel's *Encyclopedia*.[16] Moreover, García Pavón quotes the very passage of *The Concept of Anxiety* in which Kierkegaard refers indirectly to Adler's work.[17] The study avoids a direct discussion of Adler's thought, and in addition an accurate exposition of the Danish interlocutors of Kierkegaard is considered secondarily and overshadowed by a discussion of the general intellectual context in Germany.

Finally, García Pavón's conception of indirect communication, even if rigorous and clear, still requires some clarifications. First, the pseudonymous character of *The Concept of Anxiety* has probably been excessively emphasized, since it is described

---

8 García Pavón, *El problema de la comunicación en Søren A. Kierkegaard*, p. 27, p; 99, p. 201, note 143.

9 Bruce H. Kirmmse, *Kierkegaard in Golden Age Denmark*, Bloomington: Indiana University Press.

10 García Pavón, *El problema de la comunicación en Søren A. Kierkegaard*, p. 126, note 155.

11 Ibid., p. 144.

12 Ibid., p. 126.

13 Stewart, "Quellensforschung y la relación de Kierkegaard con Hegel," pp. 53–6. See also Jon Stewart, *Kierkegaard's Relations to Hegel Reconsidered*, New York: Cambridge University Press 2003, Chapter 9, pp. 378–418.

14 Adolph Peter Adler, *Populaire Foredrag over Hegels objective Logik*, Copenhagen: C.A. Reitzel 1842 (*ASKB* 383).

15 García Pavón, *El problema de la comunicación en Søren A. Kierkegaard*, pp. 74–5 (note 9).

16 Ibid., p. 68.

17 *SKS* 4, 324 note / *CA*, 16 note.

as "essential for understanding the content"[18] of *The Concept of Anxiety*. The author knows the circumstances in which *The Concept of Anxiety* was published and the sudden change of Kierkegaard's name for the pseudonym immediately prior to the book's printing,[19] but he undermines this information and insists that the pseudonym plays a central role in the work shaping the contents and its whole structure, even if the pseudonym was included only after the book was written. Second, although García Pavón mentions Climacus' works, there is no allusion to some of Kierkegaard's main writings which deal with the problem of indirect communication such as "The Concepts of *Esse* and *Inter-esse*,"[20] the "Lessons about the Dialectics of Ethics and Ethical-Religious Communication,"[21] or simply *The Concept of Irony*.

In short, *El problema de la comunicación en Søren Kierkegaard* has some conceptual and historiographical problems, but it achieves its purposes and offers a rich study of Kierkegaard's indirect communication as based generally on the latest international research, an indispensable task to guarantee an accurate and critical contribution to Spanish research on indirect communication and to offer a fair account of Kierkegaard's thought.

Juan Evaristo Valls Boix

---

18 García Pavón, *El problema de la comunicación en Søren A. Kierkegaard*, p. 181; p. 183.

19 Ibid., p. 181.

20 *SKS* 27, 269–71, Papir 277:1–282.

21 *SKS* 27, 389–430, Papir 364–371:2.

Reviews and Critical Discussions

Undetermined.

Rafael García Pavón and Catalina Elena Dobre, *Søren Kierkegaard y los ámbitos de la existencia* [Søren Kierkegaard and the Areas of Existence],

Mexico City: Centro de Filosofía Aplicada 2006, 125 pp.

Søren Kierkegaard y los ámbitos de la existencia is a collection of essays written by Catalina Elena Dobre and Rafael García Pavón. Catalina Elena has a Ph.D. in Philosophy from Iasi University, Romania. She is Collaborator on the *Quaderno di Filosofia Morale* in Italy and Editor of the journal *Anales de Filosofia* from Galati University, Romania. She was also associate editor of the *Kierkegaard Newsletter* in December 2005. Rafael García Pavón has a Ph.D. in Philosophy from the Universidad Iberoamericana, Mexico. He is a full professor at the Universidad Anáhuac Norte, Mexico. He is a specialist in applied ethics and Coordinator of the Center for Applied Ethics at the Universidad Anáhuac Norte, Mexico.

The Introduction explains that this work is not only the result of intellectual and existential growth, but also engages the authors in the task of divulging Kierkegaard in Mexico, especially among researchers. The topics presented in this work express Pavón and Dobre's varied interests devoted to Kierkegaard. The text is composed of eight essays: "1. Una tentativa hermenéutica de *La Repetición* en Søren Kierkegaard," "2. La seducción como obra de arte en *La Alternativa* de Søren Kierkegaard," "3. La actualidad de la comunicación en Søren Kierkegaard," "4. Søren Kierkegaard, una propuesta de hermenéutica existencial," "5. La dignidad de la persona como poética de la libertad en el planteamiento ético de Søren Kierkegaard," "6. Haciendo Justicia a la categoría de transición," "7. Angustia y tragedia: un humanismo para apáticos," "8. Ética aplicada como hermenéutica existencial." These essays can be read separately or as a whole; they are connected by Kierkegaard's notions of existence and pathos. They contain interesting reflections on topics such as repetition, choice, good, evil, communication, God and the single individual. The authors explain:

> So, the following pages are a collection of articles created in the repetition of the encounter, with the same passion, passion for existence that the Dane Søren A. Kierkegaard has injected to ours. In the continuity of the natural and sometimes passionate dialogue, [he]

> has given us the possibility of becoming more aware that our existence can only be by means of repetition, from and in love.[1]

"Una tentativa hermenéutica de *La Repetición* en Søren Kierkegaard" is the title of the essay that opens this book. As it states, the main goal of this reflection is to develop an analysis of Kierkegaard's category of repetition. In order to achieve this, hermeneutical approaches are employed at different levels. The first level is constituted by an interpretation of Kierkegaard's work *Repetition.* In this sense, *Repetition* is classified according to Kierkegaard's criteria and it is also classified by taking into consideration the content and objective stated in this book, that is, an aesthetic book inquiring whether repetition exists or not and what its meaning is.[2]

The second hermeneutical level is the interpretation of the category of repetition, where both the work and the concept are bound together by the description of the latter as another exegetical guideline for the former: "This experience has its origin in recollection (*anamnesis*). And what Constantinus is trying to do is to integrate the present into an idealized past which, throughout a dialectical movement, can return to the present and can be accomplished in the future."[3]

And, as long as Kierkegaard's work becomes clearer, the category of repetition becomes more accessible: "What is important is that the book helps us understand that repetition is related to freedom in an essential way but, at the same time, to the single individual. Then, it is not an abstract category but an existential one."[4] Finally, as this category becomes clearer, a third hermeneutical level arises with the interpretation of an existential experience lived by the individual, who is on a quest for himself ethically and religiously:

> Without faith, repetition cannot be possible. The kind of faith that is treated by Kierkegaard is Abraham's and Job's faith; it is the result of an infinite double signification, and it also is the result of a paradoxical and absurd movement. What is interesting is that Job and Abraham received everything in a double manner, but not in a future way but here in this world, in immanence. Repetition is received when you feel that your interiority is more than exteriority, but this is repetition's mystery and provocation. And here we have the question whether repetition is possible. Yes, but only when we are prepared to receive God, in the moment we are ready to make changes in our soul. Yes, it exists but only when we believe that repetition is a gift of faith.[5]

In the article, "La seducción como obra de arte en *La Alternativa* de Søren Kierkegaard," seduction is analyzed from many different viewpoints: concerning the seducer, the seduced, and its literary expression. This is done in the interest of depicting how seduction is related to the single individual's existential determinations and

---

1 Rafael García Pavón, and Catalina Elena Dobre, *Søren Kierkegaard y los ámbitos de la existencia*, Mexico City: Centro de Filosofía Aplicada 2006, p. 11. (All of the translations that appear in the text are by the author.)

2 Ibid., p. 21.

3 Ibid., p. 21.

4 Ibid., p. 17.

5 Ibid., p. 25.

also how these different views can contribute to consider Kierkegaard's writing task as the one of a seducer.

Of course, the definition of seduction is developed following the Kierkegaardian model:

> Seduction is a work of art that makes possible the revelation of spirit's internal possibility of becoming; this in the intimate presence of the single individual as possibility. In other words, seduction is the creation of possibilities, or situations of possibility, of becoming oneself in this metaphysical sense; this creation is what we can call the *ambitus* of love.[6]

If seduction is considered in a metaphysical way, in other words, as the medium by which a human being is going to develop the possibilities of possibilities, then, what is the role of a seducer? The seducer is the one who brings out the possibilities of someone else's inner being. These possibilities can only be developed in a poetical way: "The seducer is someone who takes something—let it be said the interesting—of effective reality and reconstructs it *ad infinitum* by means of his poetic power in such a way that this reconstruction is a mode of non-being. This creation is 'reality's nothingness.'"[7]

This poetical nothingness is an image which belongs to the realm of possibilities, and the one poetically recreated, that is, the seduced, can observe, ignore, choose or overcome them, always in the mood for anxiety, by which possibilities of possibilities can only be experienced because "anxiety is a genuine tragic category. The tragic is defined as the revelation of the single individual belonging to a fundamental substantiality."[8]

Bearing all this in mind, it is not impossible to conclude that, for the authors, seduction is also the main characteristic upon which Kierkegaard develops his task as an author. "The most interesting thing to say, at the end of this work, is that, for Kierkegaard, seduction neither belongs to a specific realm, nor is it a way of falling in love, but rather seduction is also his attitude towards his authorship."[9] This conclusion is broadened in the following essay, called "3. La actualidad de la comunicación en Søren Kierkegaard," where Kierkegaard's art of communication is depicted.

Following the tendency of the former essays, the methodology employed in order to analyze communication in Kierkegaard takes elements from hermeneutics, on one side, and, on the other, Kierkegaardian existential categories, resulting in a symbiotic relationship, where comprehension, understood as the realization and projection of oneself into an idea,[10] and language, result in silence, the realm in which interiority, love, and authenticity can take place in an existing individual: "And then, if the condition of communication is silence, communication transforms itself in

---

6 Ibid., p. 28.
7 Ibid., p. 32.
8 Ibid., p. 41.
9 Ibid., p. 42.
10 Ibid., p. 46.

a way in which our mystery is revealed absolutely but also in a way that awakens love in the other, because silence is the infinite movement which gives us the possibility of interiorizing our life."[11]

"Søren Kierkegaard, una propuesta de hermenéutica existencial" is one of the core parts of this book not only because it presents an original standpoint by the authors, but also because it explains the criteria by which all these reflections have been enriched with two different philosophical traditions producing as result a notion called existential hermeneutics. This kind of exegesis is based upon the thesis that hermeneutics is interpretation, but this can only take its point of departure in oneself and it will end up in oneself by means of contemporaneity, which is an analogue to comprehension: "the individual confronts himself with his free choice about Christ; he stands in front of the true decision of existing in its most profound and authentic sense: choose to believe or not."[12]

"La dignidad de la persona como poética de la libertad en el planteamiento ético de Søren Kierkegaard" is an essay that explores one of the conclusions that can be drawn from the existential hermeneutics stated above. As long as this choice is made freely, whatever it is, it constitutes the individual essentially. In other words, the construction of personality is based upon freedom, and the different ways of expressing it are poetics that embellish this process in which personality is transfigured by the passion of authenticity: "Ethical life is then the life, the personality of which has been validated by the choice of energy and passion."[13] As this poetic validation is neither something still and dead, nor a concept, nor a result, it is necessary to explain it as much as it allows us to apprehend it. This is one of the aims in the essay called "Haciendo Justicia a la categoría de transición." Here, transition is explained as progress, a way of living passionately and as the living part of personal life.

The last two essays in this book are applications of the majority of the reflections that appear in the preceding pages. In "Angustia y tragedia: un humanismo para apáticos" we find an effort to show how the principles of existential hermeneutics are portrayed by Nikos Kazantzakis' *Zorba the Greek*.

In the last essay of this book, "Ética aplicada como hermenéutica existencial" we find that many of the conclusions drawn from the different essays constitute a response to the question: What ethical view can arise from taking existential hermeneutics as a foundation? This is a very solid attempt to understand how authenticity, contemporaneity, language, dialogue, and hermeneutics can work to help individuals whose aim is to live individually and passionately in societies without losing themselves.

This work is proof of how Kierkegaard's existential proposal can be enriched and brought to contemporary discussions in the fields of aesthetics, psychology, and ethics by many different readings and interpretations, which can lead to very important contributions such as the so-called existential hermeneutics.

Azucena Palavicini Sánchez

11 Ibid., p. 47.

12 Ibid., p. 53.

13 Ibid., p. 56.

Reviews and Critical Discussions

García Pavón, Rafael, review in *Revista Internacional de bioética, deontología y ética médica*, vol. 17, no. 2, 2006, pp. 149–52.
Palavicini Sánchez, Azucena, review in *Open Insight. Revista de Filosofía*, vol. 2, no. 2, pp. 199–201.

Rafael García Pavón, Catalina E. Dobre, Luis Guerrero Martínez, and Leticia Valadez (eds.), *Conversaciones sobre Kierkegaard* [Conversations about Kierkegaard],

Mexico City: Rosa María Porrúa Ediciones 2013, 150 pp.

Conversaciones sobre Kierkegaard is an homage to Søren Kierkegaard on the bicentennial of his birth. Its purpose is to show the continued relevance of Kierkegaard's thought through the testimony of thirty international researchers who specialize in Kierkegaard. The contributions stem from asking the question "What are the most important concepts and the unique nature of Kierkegaard that make him relevant and valuable after 200 years?"[1] In addition, the work includes a short biography focused on Kierkegaard's relation to his father and Regine Olsen, a collection of images of the author's manuscripts, and a report with photographs on the commemorative exhibition entitled "El individuo frente a sí mismo. Søren Kierkegaard a 200 años de su nacimiento," which took place in April 2013 at the same time that an international congress with the same name was celebrated at the Universidad Iberoamericana de México.[2] The book's aim is the popular dissemination of Kierkegaard's works and the social vindication of his thought beyond the narrow parameters of specialized research. The editors maintain that their work was inspired by the famous international congress organized by UNESCO in 1964 entitled "Kierkegaard vivant."[3] Even if there have been other more significant international congresses about Kierkegaard in Spain or South America, such as, for example, the conference entitled "Las publicaciones de

---

I would like to thank Matthew Nowachek and Jon Stewart for helpful comments on an earlier draft of this article.

1 Catalina Elena Dobre, "Y Kierkegaard está vivo todavía...," in Rafael García Pavón, Catalina E. Dobre, Luis Guerrero Martínez, and Leticia Valadez (eds.), *Conversaciones sobre Kierkegaard*, Mexico City: Rosa María Porrúa Ediciones 2013, p. 11.

2 The papers of the congress were published as *El individuo frente a sí mismo: El pensamiento de Søren Kierkegaard*, ed. by Catalina Elena Dobre, Leticia Valadez, Rafael García Pavón, and Luis Guerrero Martínez, Mexico City: Rosa María Porrúa Ediciones 2013.

3 Published as Jean-Paul Sartre et al., *Kierkegaard vivant: colloque organisé par l'Unesco à Paris du 21 au 23 avril 1964*, Paris: Gallimard 1966.

Søren Kierkegaard de 1843"[4] or the congress *Encuentros de Filosofía en Denia*, held in 1987 and dedicated to *Fear and Trembling* and "The Seducer's Diary," none of them has produced this kind of publication that is specifically aimed at the general public.

Nevertheless, despite its good intentions, the work only keeps its promises to a very minimal degree. It could be useful for new students who want to become informed about some of the main Kierkegaardian topics as a starting point for their studies and research. In addition, it could help the non-specialist public to obtain a very broad image of Kierkegaard in order to begin to read his works. However, the book has some limitations, which makes it confusing and inadequate as a fruitful presentation of Kierkegaard's thought. First, the articles are excessively short—always less than three pages—and they present superficial and not very clever opinions that offer neither new perspectives of interpretation nor attractive developments of traditional topics. Second, the chapters are not well coordinated or thematically structured, and many of them repeat one another. Furthermore, others are contradictory and in the majority of cases are imprecise and get lost in unnecessary commentary and allusions without showing clearly the issue they would like to treat.

Third, the quality of the contributions is considerably varied: although the work has chapters by experts such as George Pattison, C. Stephen Evans, John D. Caputo, Ettore Rocca, and Alastair Hannay, there is no contribution from contemporary French, Danish, or German research, and the work includes chapters by completely unknown intellectuals and by others far from familiar with Kierkegaard's work. This shortcoming significantly reduces the intellectual quality of the volume. In addition, it does not distinguish between research areas, and it mixes contributions from theologians, philosophers, biographers, and historians, resulting in an irregular and conceptually imprecise exposition, that frequently carries with it a Christian and spiritualizing tone. Furthermore, the book has many errors of translation and orthography in some chapters, as well as many confused or excessive claims such as "we read Kierkegaard today in the same way Unamuno read the Danish philosopher, in order to understand the meaning of life";[5] "the Christian way does not intend to go beyond the philosophical way, but rather, it intends something different: not to follow reason but to lose it";[6] and "Kierkegaard's life could be summed up by saying that his existence was a sacrifice, a holocaust in order to follow the exigencies that the truth demanded of him."[7]

There are, however, two positive aspects of the book. On the one hand, Kierkegaard's biography, even if a very basic introduction, is generally correct, and it is profusely illustrated with quotations from Kierkegaard's personal writings which are not otherwise translated into Spanish. The problem is that, insofar as it

---

4 Published as a monograph number of the Mexican periodical *Tópicos*: *Las publicaciones de Søren Kierkegaard de 1843*, ed. by Leticia Valadez, *Tópicos. Revista de filosofía*, vol. 3, no. 5, 1993 (Mexico City).

5 García Pavón et al. (eds.), *Conversaciones sobre Kierkegaard*, p. 46.

6 Ibid., p. 50.

7 Ibid., p. 94.

is restricted to the exposition of Kierkegaard's relationship with his father and his fiancée, it is a far too common, partial, and outdated interpretation, which ignores very important aspects of Kierkegaard's intellectual groundings, his position in the nineteenth-century Danish intellectual and social context, and his work as a writer—both of pseudonymous and signed works. In spite of this, the biography puts the philosophical stress on other questions related to the Dane's youth and his literary beginnings, presenting the dramatic image of a wounded and tormented philosopher. However, the volume has some really lucid and clever chapters which show well some of Kierkegaard's philosophical discoveries and his best intellectual intuitions. Chapters such as those of Caputo, Rocca, Green, and Hannay really make this publication valuable and interesting, but their brevity, unfortunately, does not allow for deeper commentary.

In short, this work has only a documentary and testimonial value: it is a document from the bicentennial of Kierkegaard's birth and a testimony of the numerous intellectuals who, from many different perspectives, study his thinking and vindicate his work nowadays. Nevertheless, its critical value is significantly reduced due to its unclear structure, its vague contributions as well as its errors and confusions, which prevent it from being more than a mere superficial presentation. Despite this, the book could still offer a set of basic guidelines for the amateur researcher.

This work has the look of a volume of proceedings where the goal was, at all costs, to include the contributions of absolutely everyone involved, regardless of any criteria for relevance or quality. This is not necessary a bad thing in itself, but if this is the goal, then the editors are enjoined to organize it in a careful manner such that the individual contributions make sense in the context of the publication. More time and effort should have been spent in organizing the contributions under general headings and perhaps, in the Introduction, in explaining to the reader how they can be used by someone who wishes to have a general introduction to Kierkegaard. In this sense it seems that the goals of the volume were not carefully thought through, and its execution was a bit hasty.

Juan Evaristo Valls Boix

Review and Critical Discussion

Anonymous, "Analizan vigencia de la obra del filósofo danés Søren Kierkegaard," *Crónica.com.mx*, March 4, 2014.

Carlos Goñi,
El filósofo impertinente. Kierkegaard contra el orden establecido [The Impertinent Philosopher: Kierkegaard against the Established Order],

Madrid: Trotta 2013, 176 pp.

El filósofo impertinente is a general overview of Søren Kierkegaard's life and work in accessible and common language. It was published by the printing house Trotta in commemoration of the bicentennial of Kierkegaard's birth, and its intention was to update the old readings of Kierkegaard that were still current and have been accepted in Spain for several decades. It could also be understood as a complementary commentary to the critical edition of Kierkegaard's complete works that Trotta began publishing in 2006, which represented the first translation of many of Kierkegaard's works directly from Danish into Spanish.[1] Carlos Goñi's book could be seen as a sort of basic guide for reading an author whose works were, for the first time, edited with rigor and accuracy. Critics in the press generously praised the book, which was described as an "intelligent contribution,"[2] a "magnificent introduction to the life and work of the Danish thinker,"[3] and as "one of the most lucid and clear introductions to Kierkegaard's work that we have found."[4] Carlos Goñi was also praised as someone who "does something that, to be honest, is only achievable for the best connoisseurs of the Dane's work,"[5] because "he knows how to transmit without betrayal the keys of the Kierkegaardian philosophy."[6] Carlos Goñi is a doctor in philosophy at the Universitat de Barcelona, where he defended

---

I would like to thank Matthew Nowachek for helpful comments on an earlier draft of this article.

1 *Escritos de Søren Kierkegaard*, trans. and ed. by Rafael Larrañeta, Begonya Saez Tajafuerce, and Darío González, Madrid: Trotta 2006ff.

2 Jacobo Muñoz, review in *El cultural*, May 24, 2013, p. 78.

3 José María Carabante, review in *Nueva Revista de política, cultura y arte*, no. 143, June 2013, p. 90.

4 Anonymous, review in *Revista Leer*, no. 243, p. 49.

5 Carabante, review in *Nueva Revista de política, cultura y arte*, no. 143, June 2013, p. 90.

6 Ibid.

his dissertation *Tiempo y eternidad en Søren Kierkegaard* in 1994.[7] He has also published *El valor eterno del tiempo. Introducción a Søren Kierkegaard.*[8]

It was certainly important in Spain to renew knowledge about Kierkegaard with a basic and updated introduction in that Kierkegaard was still being read exclusively from the existentialist standpoint or from the traditional Catholic perspective and thereby remained subject to myths and clichés. It was very commendable to offer to Spanish philosophical research a simple reading which accurately described a life which used to be deformed by sentimentalist interpretations and an *œuvre* whose Spanish editions have been for the most part characterized by their lack of rigor, indirect translations, and partial exegesis. In these sense, Goñi's direct and clear style, as well as his chronologically ordered exposition, are necessary for establishing a starting point for a new Spanish reception of Kierkegaard.

Goñi's work nevertheless is far from achieving its purposes. First, the work is philosophically vague and inexact, shows a notable ignorance of Kierkegaard's philosophical context, and repeats a series of clichés about the author that transforms him into a sort of frenzied irrationalist. It points out that "the existential dialectics of the aesthetic, the ethical and the religious [is] the way to understand the complete works of Kierkegaard."[9] While explaining *The Moment*'s critique of Danish society, Goñi claims:

> in conclusion, for the love of God you should renounce desire and life. The Nietzschean proposal points to the opposite: for the love of life and desire, you should renounce God. Both programs have the same ontological strength...nevertheless, the German philosopher's approach would prove more successful, as Kierkegaard himself predicts: the weakness of established Christendom leads to atheism.[10]

The book offers an account of *Fear and Trembling* with claims such as "Johannes de silentio refers directly to Abraham's faith as an example of one's duty to God.... He realizes that human beings do not respect the moral law by themselves, but rather they respect the law because it participates in divine wisdom and goodness, [which serve as] the authentic foundation [for the law]";[11] or, that Abraham's episode "obliges ethics to run through its own limits."[12] The book describes Hegel as a "rationalist"[13] and an "abstract essentialist," and Kierkegaard as a critic of rationalism: "Kierkegaard goes against rationalism: against Hegel...."[14]

---

7 Carlos Goñi, *Tiempo y eternidad en Søren Kierkegaard*, Barcelona: Publicaciones Universitat de Barcelona 1995.

8 Carlos Goñi, *El valor eterno del tiempo. Introducción a Søren Kierkegaard*, Barcelona: Promociones y Publicaciones Universitarias (PPU) 1996.

9 Carlos Goñi, *El filósofo impertinente*, Madrid: Trotta 2013, p. 90.

10 Ibid., p. 157.

11 Ibid., p. 68.

12 Ibid., p. 66.

13 Ibid., p. 64; p. 70.

14 Ibid., p. 64.

Moreover, the author retains the myth that Kierkegaard was worried about the possibility of conceiving a son with a prostitute.[15] In addition, there is insufficient contextualization without any kind of accurate allusion to Kierkegaard's intellectual contemporaries.

Second, the study portrays Kierkegaard as a kind of hero and savior of his time. It affirms that through his breakup with Regine Olsen, he "was detached from the mundane in order to live in pure ideality,"[16] and that "Kierkegaard must drink the chalice of the separation of Regine in order to fight against the established order and to become the authentic impertinent philosopher."[17] It maintains that, "thanks to *The Corsair*, the impertinent philosopher reloads the barrel chamber and returns forcefully to the battlefield. As a timorous soldier, to whom wounds give more strength, Kierkegaard pounces impetuously on his enemy, and that is how he resurrects himself from the crucifixion which he bore during the first months of 1846."[18] His vocation consists in a fight in which "he is against everybody...he only counts on the intimate conviction that God is directing his steps. He knows his mission can cost him his life, and he is prepared for this."[19]

Finally, the study makes intolerable errors such as attributing *Works of Love* to Anti-Climacus,[20] and, even though the author continuously quotes the original Danish titles, he uses the old Spanish translation of the text without correcting their numerous errors.[21]

In short, *El filósofo impertinente* starts the good task of rescuing the figure of Kierkegaard from oblivion and error, but nevertheless the work betrays Kierkegaard's thought and repeats the prejudices and confused imagery that dominated Kierkegaardian exegesis in previous decades. This is also made evident by the work's outdated bibliography. The study presents a heroic Kierkegaard full of irrationalism and Romantic sentimentalism, and it defends exclusively a personal and biographical approximation of Kierkegaard's *œuvre* with a style that, far from being simple, is colloquial, immoderate, and confused. This imbues the book with a sentimentalism that, in addition to the inadmissible philosophical and historical errors, confirms the prejudices from the past about Kierkegaard rather than fighting against them. This is not the clear and ordered exegesis which could offer an updated, fair, and exact version of Kierkegaard for the specialist or non-specialist Spanish reader. In comparison with erudite studies of international research, such

15 Ibid., p. 41.

16 Ibid., p. 40.

17 Ibid., p. 43.

18 Ibid., p 106.

19 Ibid., p. 136.

20 Ibid., p. 111; p. 112; p. 114; p. 170.

21 Ibid., p. 67. This could be shown when, while quoting *Fear and Trembling*, the author leaves untranslated the term *Anfægtelse* as the translator Vicente Simón Merchán does in *Temor y temblor*, Madrid: Alianza Editorial 1987.

as Hannay's biography[22] or Kirmmse's work on the Danish Golden Age,[23] this monograph—which actually could have consulted both of these other works—results in a completely unsatisfactory exposition and critique, and thus makes clear the deplorable situation in which Spanish research on Kierkegaard found itself. In this regard, some other introductions to Kierkegaard have recently been published which achieve the goals of updating and revising the image of Kierkegaard in a way that Goñi's introduction does not. Two of the most significant are Rafael Larrañeta's *La lupa de Kierkegaard*[24] and Darío González's preliminary study to a compilation of Kierkegaard's works published by the publishing house Gredos.[25] These other works, composed with an eye to the background in international contemporary research, show the right way to carry out future Kierkegaardian research.

Juan Evaristo Valls Boix

22 Alastair Hannay, *Kierkegaard*, London and New York: Routledge 1991. There is a Spanish translation: Alastair Hannay, *Kierkegaard, una biografía*, trans. by Nassim Bravo Jordán, Mexico City: Universidad Iberoamericana 2010.

23 Bruce H. Kirmmse, *Kierkegaard in Golden Age Denmark*, Bloomington: Indiana University Press 1990.

24 Rafael Larrañeta, *La lupa de Kierkegaard*, Salamanca: San Esteban, 2002. The work of revision undertaken by Larrañeta is also present in his article "El verdadero rostro de Kierkegaard," *Revista de Filosofía*, vol. 10, no. 18, 1997, pp. 83–112.

25 Søren Kierkegaard, *Diapsálmata; Los estadios eróticos inmediatos o El erotismo musical; Repercusión de la tragedia antigua en la moderna; Siluetas; El más desgraciado; El primer amor; La validez estética del matrimonio; Referencia acerca del matrimonio en respuesta a algunas objeciones; Temor y temblor*, introduction by Darío González, Madrid: Gredos 2010. While González's study is considerably better than Goñi's one, the publishing house Gredos has just reprinted old Spanish translations of Kierkegaard's works from the 1960s made by Demetrio G. Rivero and Vicente Simón Merchán.

Reviews and Critical Discussions

Anonymous, review in *Revista Leer*, no. 243, July 2013, p. 49.
Carabante, José María, review in *Nueva Revista de política, cultura y arte*, no. 143, June 2013.
Fernández Muñoz, Jesús, review in *Thémata. Revista de filosofía*, no. 49, 2014, pp. 347–50.
Moreno Claros, Luis Fernando, review in *El País. Babelia*, June 2013.
Muñoz, Jacobo, review in *El cultural*, May 24, 2013.
Stegmeier, Igor, "'Todo filósofo debe ser impertinente,'" *Diario de Navarra*, April 30, 2013.

Luis Guerrero Martínez, *Kierkegaard. Los límites de la razón en la existencia humana* [Kierkegaard: The Limits of Reason in Human Existence],

Mexico City: Publicaciones Cruz O. 1993, 307 pp.

Kierkegaard. Los límites de la razón en la existencia humana is the second book by Mexican scholar Luis Guerrero. This monograph was published in 1993 by Publicaciones Cruz O., and coedited by the Universidad Panamericana and the Sociedad Iberoamericana de Estudios Kierkegaardianos. As president of this society, Luis Guerrero was one of the pioneers in Kierkegaard studies in Mexico and has supervised many research projects in several Latin American countries. Referring to this particular work, José García argues that "it was the first interpretative map of the works by Søren Kierkegaard in Mexico."[1] Therefore, this monograph should be read as a general introduction to the thought of Søren Kierkegaard. The reader will be able to find both a brief summary of each of the Danish philosopher's works and an analysis of the dialectical categories and existential stages typical of Kierkegaard's anthropology.

Although the book has a central theme, namely, the relationship between faith and reason in Kierkegaard's thought, the author begins by offering the reader a general contextualization of the historical and philosophical background in which the work of Kierkegaard developed. Guerrero refers to specific circumstances that marked the life of the Dane and had a deep impact on his authorship. Next he makes a brief tour around each one of Kierkegaard's works (including his journals), summarizing and explaining the central topics and main ideas covered in them. All of this has the purpose not of substituting the reading of these works, but of encouraging it.[2] Finally, in order to address the central issue of his book in detail, he proceeds as follows: (1) he explains the dialectical definition of "self" in Kierkegaard by exploring the dual categories of body-soul, finite-infinite, possibility-necessity, and temporality-eternity;

1 José García, *Recepción de Kierkegaard en Iberoamérica*, Madrid: Editor Bubok 2012, p. 62.

2 Cf. Luis Guerrero Martínez, *Kierkegaard. Los límites de la razón en la existencia humana*, Mexico City: Publicaciones Cruz O. 1993, p. 15.

(2) he puts forth a phenomenological explanation of the existential stages: the aesthetic, the ethical, and the religious; and (3) he shows how the fulfillment of the synthesis of the aforementioned dialectical categories that constitute the individual can only take place through a third party, namely, when the individual lays his own foundation on God through faith, which involves going beyond reason. Thus, Guerrero claims that, by analyzing human existence, Kierkegaard reveals the limits of reason.[3]

The statement with which Guerrero concludes is in fact the same main thesis suggested throughout the entire book, that is, faith—through which the individual relates to God—implies an overcoming of reason. According to Kierkegaard, Guerrero argues, there is only a self when the individual has his or her foundation in God. However, since the individual is at first a set of dialectical categories that is yet to be synthesized, he or she is free to choose a fulfilled existence before God, remain living without God, or simply refuse his or her own self.[4] Alluding to this dialectical structure, Guerrero underscores a key concept in Kierkegaard's thought: the freedom of the individual.

Once the concept of freedom has been set forth, the notions of anxiety and despair emerge; these, in turn, require a proper understanding of the concept of sin. Guerrero analyzes at length the anthropological dimension of sin. Ethics, he claims, is incapable of understanding sin, and reason alone is unable to overcome it. On the contrary, it is reason itself that states that a human's existence before God is scandal, but not wanting to live before God is sin itself. He who chooses to exist without God, despairs, since he lives in sin, and he who lives in the possibility of sin, feels anxiety. The only way to overcome anxiety and despair is to want to live before God, which is only possible through faith.

Guerrero moves on to explain the forms of existence: the aesthetic, the ethical, and the religious. The author discusses in detail the qualitative leap between the first two. This is the awakening of consciousness to an eternal self. As is well known, the immediate, finite, and sensuous is what matter to those who live in the aesthetic stage. To live in accordance with the general is the ultimate aim of the ethical. Even though the religious does not imply an absolute withdrawal from the previous two stages, it involves a leap, an awareness of an eternal self that is reconciled with the temporal and finite in God. At this point it is underscored once again that existential fulfillment can be attained only through faith, when the synthesis between the temporal and eternal becomes actual and the individual believes in a revelation given in the past, has hope in the future, and is charitable in the present with those around him or her.[5]

Thus, each topic in this monograph calls attention to Kierkegaard's interest in establishing limits for reason. However, as José García stresses, Guerrero makes clear that "the explicit purpose that Kierkegaard assumes as his philosophical, literary and theological task is—as shown in *The Point of View*—to explain how to become a Christian through faith and what this implies, pointing out the way reason must be

3 Cf. ibid., p. 13.
4 Cf. ibid., p. 83.
5 Ibid., p. 261.

overcome and is to become subject to the demands of faith."[6] This is a line of thought maintained throughout the works by Kierkegaard, including those signed by pseudonyms. The methodology employed by Kierkegaard to do this is faithfully captured in this study by Guerrero. His explanation of the constituent dialectical categories of the human being and the different existential stages reveals Kierkegaard's aim rationally to demonstrate the limits of reason.[7]

This book is undoubtedly a pillar of scholarly Kierkegaard studies in Latin America. It has been quoted countless times by both scholars and students in this region of the world interested in the thought of the Dane. Given the variety of topics, the book might be said to sacrifice depth and become vague in some respects, but its introductory character is ideal for those who are seeking an accessible and reliable source of information to start reading Kierkegaard. Furthermore, its comprehensive mapping of Kierkegaard's thought makes Guerrero's book a handy resource for the research and study of every significant topic that Kierkegaard's work offers the reader.

Fernanda Rojas

6 Ibid., p. 12.
7 Cf. ibid., p. 14.

Reviews and Critical Discussions

García, José, *Recepción de Kierkegaard en Iberoamérica*, Madrid: Editor Bubok 2012, pp. 61–9.
Valadez, Leticia, review in *Tópicos. Revista de Filosofía*, no. 6, 1994, pp. 181–3.

Luis Guerrero Martínez, *La verdad subjetiva. Søren Kierkegaard como escritor* [The Subjective Truth: Søren Kierkegaard as Writer],

Mexico City: Universidad Iberoamericana 2004, 266 pp.

La verdad subjetiva. Søren Kierkegaard como escritor (The Subjective Truth: Søren Kierkegaard as Writer) is the second major work by Luis Guerrero Martínez, one of the most prominent Kierkegaard researchers in Mexico. This work was published in 2004, ten years after his first major book about Kierkegaard, *Kierkegaard. Los límites de la razón en la existencia humana* from 1993.[1] Both works show Guerrero's varied interests on Kierkegaardian topics.

As its full title states, *La verdad subjetiva. Søren Kierkegaard como escritor* is a work which develops a view about the issue of author and pseudonyms, taking into consideration subjective truth as the principal, but not the only, category. The development of this position stresses the importance of communication in Kierkegaard's philosophy: "this book is composed of different essays that were written with the objective of pointing out Kierkegaard's task as communicator of philosophy, or better, showing how philosophy in Kierkegaard becomes first and foremost, communication."[2]

The text is divided into the following parts: "1. El desdoblamiento de la comunicación existencial," "2. El lenguaje estético," "3. Entre la paradoja y la argumentación," "4. A Glance at Danish Literature," "5. Appendix," and each of these is further subdivided into individual sections. The first chapter, "El desdoblamiento de la comunicación existencial," explains the methodology used in this book. First, Guerrero presents many biographical and historical events that were influential in Kierkegaard's life as well as intellectual growth, events that made it possible for him to become an author. Second, he analyzes, within this context, different concepts in Kierkegaard's thought in order to develop these notions.

---

1 Luis Guerrero Martínez, *Kierkegaard. Los límites de la razón en la existencia,* Mexico City: Publicaciones Cruz O 1993. (All of the translations that appear in the text are by the author.)

2 Luis Guerrero Martínez, *La verdad subjetiva. Søren Kierkegaard como escritor*, Mexico City: Universidad Iberoamericana 2004, p. 8.

Guerrero considers that socio-cultural disorientation, thoughtless individuals living in a closed society, and excessive academicism are factors that inspired Kierkegaard to develop ideas such as the single individual, indirect communication, or human existence as something unique and personal:

> One of the greatest paradoxes of Kierkegaard's disorientated epoch is...that the ones who had official authority, had lost the real authority...and the ones who, aware of that situation, had no authority to make a call for attention....How then can one talk with authority if, precisely, what needs to be communicated is the defense of individuality, freedom and the personal relationship with God?[3]

Not only is this question paradoxical, but Kierkegaard's answer is as well. Taking into account individuality and freedom as it has, Kierkegaard's philosophy cannot be formulated in certain or demonstrable concepts but rather in notions that essentially can preserve his main concerns. These notions are indirect communication and its basis, subjective truth. In demonstrating how Kierkegaard's philosophy can be viewed as communication, Guerrero develops indirect communication and subjective truth, showing the dependence of the former on the latter in this first part. And, in the second part, *La verdad subjetiva. Søren Kierkegaard como escritor* presents the manifold links between these two categories and Kierkegaard's work.

An example of this is the section "El estilo literario de Søren Kierkegaard," where Guerrero's goal is to explain the idea of subjective truth in Kierkegaard's work. This task is enriched with biographical information and entries from the *Papirer*. Another example is the section "seudónimos, ironía y comunicación indirecta," where the relationship between irony and indirect communication is explored by means of presenting an individual's diagnosis of his epoch, specifically by pointing out its abuses and deficiencies: "Kierkegaard's proposal is based on his analysis and criticism of society. Each of his works is thought to be not the speculative development of any concept, but the pursuit of the best way to make his readers aware of his social criticism."[4]

Since irony is a key concept in Kierkegaard's thought, it is also studied in Plato's *Meno*, where it is employed by Socrates and viewed in contrast with *Fear and Trembling*. This analysis includes two aspects: reason's failure to overcome religion and the criticism of institutionalized religion.

From Guerrero's perspective, there is not only the need to consider Kierkegaard's authorship from one point of view, that is, the author's, but there is also the reader's point of view, and it is equally important to bear it on mind when someone is trying to establish a position regarding Kierkegaard's work as an author. The exposition in "Las edades de la vida: infancia, juventud y madurez" expresses widely this concern, and even if at first sight, this analysis seems to depart from the argumentative track of *La verdad subjetiva*, this anthropological analysis establishes the conditions, in a

3 Ibid., p. 43.
4 Ibid., p. 80.

variety of existential terms, that could lead a reader to relate, or not, to the subjective truth. Certainly, this leads to different understandings of Kierkegaard's work:

> Despite the fact that there are many texts that recognize youth in the category of immediacy and in this sense the young man has not gone further than the child, qualitatively speaking, youth has the privilege of being psychologically constituted as possibility, a key characteristic of Vigilius Haufniensis; as passion is to Johannes de Silentio and as inwardness is to Johannes Climacus, so also subjectivity is opened towards the divine for Anti-Climacus and for Kierkegaard in *Works of Love*.[5]

In the second part, "El lenguaje estético," Guerrero presents three different analyses of Kierkegaard's aesthetics focusing on seduction: "La seducción como arte musical," "La seducción reflexive," and "Seducción y abandono." Each of these analyses deals with central issues in Kierkegaardian aesthetics. These studies are basic for Guerrero's understanding of the relationship between aesthetics and authorship, since he considers that aesthetic publications, especially *Either/Or*, Part One, are very important in Kierkegaard's career as an author and, hence, as the expression of his philosophy viewed as communication. All these studies are informed by *The Point of View for My Work as an Author* as a hermeneutical point of departure. In "La seducción como arte musical: El Don Giovanni de Mozart" the already mentioned musical figure is studied in terms of imagination as the faculty responsible for reflection and personality. Imagination, in Guerrero's view, is the source of seduction, and of works of art, but it also gives birth to the relationship between two kinds of existence: ethical and aesthetic. Then, seduction is studied differently in "La propuesta estética de El Diario de un seductor." Here Guerrero's exposition is about the literary criteria that generate seduction in this realm. This is expressed in Cordelia and the seducer's relationship by means of the terms of seduction and abandonment.[6] This analysis tries to exhibit the contrasts between direct and indirect communication. Yet, there is another way by which Guerrero approaches seduction, and it is shown in "Seducción y abandono. La pena como categoría estética." Here he explores sorrow produced by abandonment: "sorrow—which is different from angst—refers to the past, especially to recollection....Always in the context of sorrow as a poetic object, life and death construct their own time, which leads melancholically towards absence, independently of projecting itself to the future or the past."[7]

The third part of the work, "Entre la paradoja y la argumentación," contains two chapters. The first consists of a logical analysis of "The Socratic Definition of Sin" from *The Sickness unto Death*. The second one broadens this analysis by studying the logical structure of Anti-Climacus' discourse, and Guerrero explores how it is presented in order to criticize society and also to state his own point of view on certain matters.

"A Glance at Danish Literature" is presented by Guerrero as the conclusion of *La verdad subjetiva. Søren Kierkegaard como escritor* and also as the last of the

5 Ibid., p. 101.
6 Ibid., p. 123.
7 Ibid., p. 133.

many paths and perspectives explored in order to approach the issue of Kierkegaard's authorship. This last section is introduced by an analysis that shows an integral vision of Kierkegaard's task as an author, its relation to indirect communication and to subjective truth. Another thing that is important to mention is that the translation of the fragment "A Glance at Danish Literature," made by Leticia Valadez Hernández, was the first part of the *Postscript* ever published in Spanish, in Mexico. This translation appears in the book itself and gives a good overview of the problem of Kierkegaardian authorship.

The Appendix of this book was already presented in Guerrero's first book, *Kierkegaard. Los límites de la razón en la existencia humana*. It consists of a list of the different works by Kierkegaard published in Spanish.

La verdad subjetiva attempts to present the best understanding of the issue of Kierkegaard's authorship, in breadth and in depth. This work is worthwhile for anyone interested in Kierkegaard's authorship but also in the aesthetic Kierkegaardian productions. Due to its methodology and composition, the different sections of the book can be read as individual pieces devoted to specific topics.

Despite the fact that this text is addressed to scholars, its clarity makes it accessible to a non-specialized public that would easily be aware of the substantial issues in Kierkegaard's thought after reading this text.

Azucena Palavicini Sánchez

Review and Critical Discussion

Vilchis Peñalosa, Javier, review in *Revista de Filosofía*, vol. 37, no. 112, 2005, pp. 171–7.

Luis Guerrero Martínez (ed.), *Kierkegaard. Individualidad versus globalización* [Kierkegaard: Individuality versus Globalization],

special issue of *El garabato*, no. 12, 2000, 20 pp.

The monographic issue of *El garabato* dedicated to Kierkegaard is focused on the topic "Individuality versus Globalization." It is one of the few special issues in hispanophone journals about the Danish thinker, preceded only by *Las publicaciones de Søren Kierkegaard de 1843*, published in *Tópicos*,[1] a monograph about *The Concept of Anxiety* edited by the Sevillian periodical *Thémata*,[2] and another one in the Catalan periodical *Enrahonar*.[3] In this case, the monograph is a very short publication (20 pages) addressed to a non-specialized public and devoid of any kind of criticism or research goal, although it contains papers by international researchers such as Arne Grøn and Gordon Marino, and others written by Spanish and Latin Kierkegaard scholars such as Francesc Torralba, Leticia Valadez, Luis Guerrero, Rafael García Pavón, and Manuel Suances.

The edition and form of the issue are notably questionable. First, the papers contain very few basic bibliographical references, and all critical apparatus is lacking. In addition, the length of the articles is always less than three pages, which renders the issue a popular magazine rather than a philosophical review. Moreover, the graphic design of the review devalues the (presumable) quality of its content: one can find advertisements for matchboxes and homemade pictures of folkloric dances on the covers, as well as images of paintings by Expressionist artists such as Munch throughout the review. These images obviously transmit to the reader the existentialist and sentimentalist cliché that made Kierkegaard known more than thirty years ago. Finally, only two of the essays deal directly with the topic of the monograph issue, that is, "Individuality versus Globalization," while the rest are about different aspects of Kierkegaard's thought put together apparently without any

1 Leticia Valadez (ed.), *Las publicaciones de Søren Kierkegaard de 1843*, special issue of *Tópicos. Revista de Filosofía*, vol. 3, no. 5, 1993.

2 María García Amilburu (ed.), *El concepto de la angustia: 150 años después*, special issue of *Thémata, Revista de Filosofía*, vol. 15, 1995.

3 Begonya Sáez Tajafuerce (ed.), *Enrahonar*, no. 29, Barcelona: Universidad Autònoma de Barcelona 1998.

link or connection: Kierkegaard's vocation as a writer, the motto "The Thorn in the Flesh," the difference between depression and despair, and Kierkegaard's ethics of subjectivity. It seems that there is no editorial concept in this quite random selection of papers.

Concerning the content, even if the general tone of the articles is informative, there are important differences in quality among them. First, Grøn's contribution is clear and clever, and aims at showing how Kierkegaard has been "rediscovered" in the twentieth century beyond existentialist philosophy. It considers Kierkegaard's ethics as an "ethics of subjectivity,"[4] in which the ethical is not a simple stage, but rather a "radical determination of human existence."[5] Second, Torralba's paper offers a very existentialist image of Kierkegaard focused on the concept of the individual, which is opposed to the category of the crowd. The article could be worth reading for non-specialized public, but some of its passages are very confusing, and its philosophical allusions as well as its description of some features of Kierkegaardian anthropology are simplistic. Third, the article coauthored by Valadez and Guerrero tries to show the important role that Kierkegaard's vocation as a writer plays in his philosophy, one of the most personal characteristics of Kierkegaard's authorship. However, the text is generally superficial, vague, and poor in arguments, which are frequently replaced by Kierkegaard's personal declarations supposedly extracted from the journals.

Fourth, the purpose of García Pavón's paper is to show Kierkegaard's critique of the concepts of crowd and reflection by means of the concepts of irony and singular individuality. In addition, it considers Kierkegaard as a direct adversary of Hegel and Hegelianism, as well as a thinker whose aim is understood as the task of recovering individual responsibility that is lost in modern societies due to the birth of a sort of collective and mass subject. The article could be motivating reading for beginners in philosophy, but it must also be said that it is facile when it tries to offer philosophical portraits of other thinkers such as Hegel, and, moreover, its rhetorical figures are ambiguous and indeterminate. Fifth, Marino's piece is observant, interesting, and intelligent. It aims at presenting, from a Christian point of view, the difference between despair and depression, and offers a lucid and updated reading of *The Sickness unto Death*, contributing to a clarification of the boundaries between philosophy and modern psychology. Finally, Suances' work is an article of Catholic spirituality rather than a philosophical text. It deals with Kierkegaard's upbuilding discourse "The Thorn in the Flesh" and considers with overemphasis its central motif as a "crucial point which explains the whole structure of Kierkegaard's thought."[6] The article, which quotes the French translation of Kierkegaard's writings,[7] is full of sentimentalism and written with a poeticizing tone that makes it puzzling and vague;

---

4 Arne Grøn, "Kierkegaard: Ética de la subjetividad," *El garabato*, no. 12, 2000, p. 5.

5 Ibid.

6 Manuel Suances Marcos, "El problema kierkegaardiano de 'La espina clavada en la carne,'" *El garabato*, no. 12, 2000, p. 18.

7 Søren Kierkegaard, "L'écharde dans la chair," in *Œuvres Complètes*, vols. 1–20, ed. by Paul-Henri Tisseau, Paris: Éditions l'Orante 1966–86, vol. 16, pp. 297–327.

it converts Kierkegaard into a writer close to a sort of expressionism or dramatic existentialism.

In short, despite some very good contributions, the strong problems of methodology, structural coherence, and philosophical rigor make this monographic issue of *El garabato* a rather poor contribution to the dissemination of Kierkegaard's thought. Even if the aim of providing popular information about Kierkegaard is important and respectable, it is difficult to understand why articles by major researchers are edited in such a form, and why a basic thematic coherence is ignored in a publication of only twenty pages. At least, the issue offers the possibility of motivating and encouraging the reading of Kierkegaard's writings for those who do not know him yet.

Juan Evaristo Valls Boix

Reviews and Critical Discussions

Undetermined.

Luis Guerrero Martínez (ed.), *Søren Kierkegaard. Una reflexión sobre la existencia humana* [Søren Kierkegaard: A Reflection on Human Existence],

Mexico City: Universidad Iberoamericana 2009, 350 pp.

One of the most influential thinkers of the twentieth century claims that liberal education consists in studying with proper care the "great books" that were left to us by the "greatest minds."[1] During this study, the most experienced students should help the least experienced ones, even the beginners. These great minds, the philosopher continues, are rather hard to find. We would even be very lucky if we could count even one in our own time. As far as our discussion is concerned, Søren Kierkegaard was, beyond any doubt, one of them.

The book *Søren Kierkegaard. Una reflexión sobre la existencia humana* is a collective research work about the Danish philosopher's thoughts on various aspects of human existence. As the coordinator and editor of the project, Luis Guerrero Martínez, points out in his "Introducción" that each article presents and depicts Kierkegaard's main themes, works, reception from or influence upon his most important interlocutors from the philosophical, literary and theological traditions he knew so well. Thus, throughout the book one can read names like Socrates, Augustine, Luther, Kant, Goethe, Fichte, Hegel, Feuerbach, Marx, Nietzsche, Rosenzweig, Heidegger, Sartre, among others, and thus the reader can contrast their philosophical conceptions to those of Kierkegaard. There are many conceptions connected with Romanticism and German idealism, which bring one to the thinker's aesthetic and ethical views, as well as the multiple connections to Jesus Christ and God, which lead one to elaborate on Kierkegaard's attitude towards Christianity and religion.

As the Introduction states, the text, as a whole, aims at bringing together some of the most important Kierkegaardian researchers working in Spanish. Inasmuch as the interest in his thinking has increased worldwide, specialists from the Spanish-speaking countries have increasingly turned their attention to the philosopher. Accordingly, the

---

1 Cf. Leo Strauss, *Liberalism Ancient and Modern*, Chicago: University of Chicago Press 1995, p. 3.

book compiles fourteen unpublished articles that were written in Spanish by today's most outstanding Kierkegaard researchers and disseminators, specifically from Spain, Mexico, and Argentina. This poses a novel attempt in Kierkegaard studies since it is the first collection that has been written completely by hispanophone authors. It appears in the context of a larger project led by Luis Guerrero Martínez. Guerrero Martinez's project includes both the creation of the SIEK—*Sociedad Iberoamericana de Estudios Kierkegaardianos*—and the development of an annual seminar on various topics at the Universidad Iberoamericana in Mexico City, as well as translations and other works on Kierkegaard that are being issued by the university's publishing house.

The book includes a thorough list of Kierkegaard's complete works in Danish and their use in the volume, preceded by a biographical overview of the collaborators in the project. The articles, each with its own approach showing its author's particular writing style and philosophical interpretation, are as follows.

(1) "Søren Aabye Kierkegaard: Obra, seudónimos y comunicación indirecta" (Kierkegaard: Work, Pseudonyms and Indirect Communication) by Catalina Elena Dobre concludes that Kierkegaard's indirect communication allows both the reader and the author himself to judge the work by themselves. (2) "Dialéctica de la existencia (antropología: el ser humano como síntesis)" (The Dialectic of Existence (Anthropology: The Human Being as a Synthesis)) by Dolors Perarnau Vidal proposes that men and women are a synthesis as far as their beings, works, and relationships are concerned. (3) "El problema terminológico y semántico del concepto de individuo en los *Diarios* de Søren A. Kierkegaard" (The Terminological and Semantic Problem of the Concept of the Individual in Kierkegaard's *Journals*) by José García Martín analyzes the importance of spirit as a human quality in the classification of the individual, the exemplary individual, and the singular individual. (4) "Inmediatez y conciencia del yo en Kierkegaard" (Immediacy and Awareness of the Self in Kierkegaard) by Patricia C. Dip also examines the central role of spirit and its relation to the ego in the triads that Kierkegaard inherits from German Idealism. (5) "Verdad subjetiva, interioridad y pasión" (Subjective Truth, Interiority and Passion) by Óscar Parcero Oubiña examines the concept of subjective truth as it occurs in the passionate inwardness of human beings, which is manifested in the personal interest in this truth. (6) "Kierkegaard: poeta del devenir existencial" (Kierkegaard: Poet of Becoming Existential) by Elsa Torres Garza argues that Kierkegaard's various pseudonyms exhibit the possibility of choice for human existence across an aesthetic *pathos*, a demonic *pathos*, or else an existential one. (7) "La suspensión de lo ético. Lectura de *Temor y temblor* (Frygt og Baeven) (1843)" (The Suspension of the Ethical: A Reading of *Fear and Trembling*) by Francesc Torralba Roselló offers a reading of the teleological suspension of the ethical stage and the absolute duty to God in Kierkegaard's writing. (8) "El amargo sabor de la eternidad. Dimensiones y praxis de la angustia en el pensamiento de Søren Kierkegaard" (The Bitter Taste of Eternity: Dimensions and Praxis of Anguish in Kierkegaard's Thought) by Ángel E. Garrido-Maturano argues that along with the central role of spirit in Kierkegaard's anthropology comes the anxiety, which is analyzed from its ontological and existential dimensions. (9) "Subjetividad, existencia, Dios y pecado en el pensamiento de Kierkegaard" (Subjectivity, Existence, God and Sin in Kierkegaard's Thought)

by Gonzalo Balderas Vega ponders the close relationship between the existence of subjectivity and its reference to the eternal in its own constitutive dialectic. (10) "Sobre la verdadera formación de un poeta: Una pequeña querella en contra de Hans Christian Andersen" (On the True Formation of a Poet: A Small Claim against Hans Christian Andersen) by Nassim Bravo Jordán traces Kierkegaard's Romantic and Hegelian influences by examining his early work *From the Papers of One Still Living*. (11) "El instante y la temporalidad, como síntesis de eternidad y tiempo en el devenir del individuo en singular, en *Migajas filosóficas* y *El concepto de la angustia*" (The Moment and Temporality, as a Synthesis of Eternity and Time in the Becoming of the Singular Individual, in *Philosophical Fragments* and *The Concept of Anxiety*) by Rafael García Pavón shows the topic of the moment and temporality on becoming a self. (12) "Mociones de los espíritus en Kierkegaard y San Ignacio" (Motions of the Spirits in Kierkegaard and San Ignacio) by Jorge Manzano, SJ suggests that both Kierkegaard and San Ignacio refer to those movements that, stemming from the interior of the human being, urge one to carry out certain actions with free will. (13) "Un punto de encuentro: el pensador reflexivo y la crítica al academicismo" (A Point of Encounter: The Reflective Thinker and the Critique to Academics) by Luis Guerrero Martínez combines Kierkegaard's critique of the objectification of knowledge developed by the Hegelian system with the always present critique of academics. (14) "La influencia de Kierkegaard en la filosofía contemporánea (siglos XX y XXI)" (Kierkegaard's Influence on Contemporary Philosophy (20th and 21st Centuries)) by María José Binetti covers Kierkegaard's vast influence on considerations about human existence in contemporary phenomenology, hermeneutics, postmodern deconstruction, Hegelianism, Marxism, and analytic philosophy.

Finally, the book presents a list of Spanish translations of the Danish philosopher's works and a list of its major translations into other languages. However, not every article provides a bibliography of secondary literature at the end. From all the concepts and issues dealt with, we can conclude that *Søren Kierkegaard. Una reflexión sobre la existencia humana* gives rise to a general understanding of different aspects of Kierkegaard's analysis of human existence. With regards to this, the different authors present Kierkegaard's philosophy in a detailed and critical way by arguing for their own readings and those of other researchers. Given the vast amount of secondary literature on this topic—mostly in languages other than Spanish—its terminological and methodological thoroughness makes the present book a good alternative to begin with, being much more than a mere introduction to Kierkegaard's thought, since prior knowledge about the history of philosophy in general, and the Danish thinker in particular, is needed to approach the subject. With this background, our authors become those "most experienced students," referred to by Strauss, the ones who will help the least experienced ones to study Søren Kierkegaard. To sum up, the current book is a compilation of theme-oriented articles that proves to be a valuable introduction to the Danish philosopher's anthropological and metaphysical thoughts. The work paves the way for further questions and studies upon Kierkegaard's different periods and views, encouraging the dedicated reader to fathom, deepen, and expand the philosopher's inexhaustible legacy.

Guadalupe Pardi

Reviews and Critical Discussions

Undetermined.

Asunción Herrera Guevara, *La historia perdida de Kierkegaard y Adorno. Cómo leer a Kierkegaard y Adorno* [The Lost History of Kierkegaard and Adorno: How to Read Kierkegaard and Adorno],

Madrid: Biblioteca Nueva 2005, 203 pp.

La historia perdida de Kierkegaard y Adorno aims to recover from oblivion the ethical dimension of Søren Kierkegaard's and Theodor L.W. Adorno's philosophy in order to contribute a new research perspective based on the discourse ethics of Jürgen Habermas and to continue the moral discussion about the good life in light of the concept of suffering. The work, written by Asunción Herrera Guevara, professor at the Universidad de Oviedo and specialist in the third generation of critical theory, is one of the first Spanish studies on the relation between Kierkegaard and Adorno and, more generally, critical theory.[1]

The work is divided into three parts: first, it criticizes the obscure image of Kierkegaard and rereads the Danish thinker by reconsidering many of the aspects of his thought that have been forgotten in traditional interpretations.[2] This part is a preliminary introduction that tries to set up the comparison between Kierkegaard and Adorno, and to consider them as philosophers of the "damaged life," as well as to present Adorno as the "materialist Kierkegaard of the twentieth century."[3] The volume concludes by explaining the constellation Kierkegaard–Adorno–Habermas in an effort to shed light on contemporary ethical problems.[4] Critics in the press praised the book and positively assessed its effort to put Kierkegaard's thought into dialogue with contemporary philosophy.[5] In addition they hailed it as an "original

---

I would like to thank Matthew Nowachek for helpful comments on an earlier draft of this article.

1 Iván Teimil García, "Un nuevo 'viejo' pensamiento," *Isegoría*, no. 34, 2006, p. 309.

2 Asunción Herrera Guevara, *La historia perdida de Kierkegaard y Adorno. Cómo leer a Kierkegaard y Adorno*, Madrid: Biblioteca nueva 2005, p. 13.

3 Ibid., p. 14.

4 Ibid.

5 Mariano C. Melero de la Torre, review in *Teorema: Revista internacional de filosofía*, vol. 26, no. 1, 2007, p. 142.

interpretation of this author" and a "complete and rigorous view,"[6] in short, as an important contribution to the Spanish reception of Kierkegaard.

In spite of the author's good intentions, the work does not achieve its goals. Its first problem is its structure and methodology: the division of the book into three hermetic chapters, each one dedicated to one author, impedes a fruitful exposition of the relation between Kierkegaard and Adorno (as well as Habermas). While the first chapter remains focused exclusively on Kierkegaard, the Dane disappears almost entirely in the following chapters except for a few indirect references and vague comments. In addition, the volume concludes with a complex reflection on the question of the good life in contemporary societies of advanced capitalism, but the discussion gets lost in the details of the contemporary ethical debate completely disregarding either a Kierkegaardian or an Adornian approach. In this way, the book becomes asymmetrical and inconsistent: in the beginning, one finds a reconstruction of Kierkegaard's thought, but in the end this amounts to merely a discussion of practical philosophy in a Habermasian style about the good life and contemporary society. Finally, the bibliography is significantly outdated: the Danish edition of Kierkegaard's complete works is from the 1960s,[7] and the secondary sources are generally from the 1970s or even earlier.[8] In addition, the numerous references to Kierkegaard's journals are from a rudimentary and incomplete edition from 1955,[9] based on an indirect translation from the Italian.[10]

---

6 Teimil García, "Un nuevo 'viejo' pensamiento," p. 309.

7 *Søren Kierkegaard Samlede Værker*, vols. 1–14, ed. by A.B. Drachmann, J.L. Heiberg, and H.O. Lange, Copenhagen, Gyldendal 1962–64.

8 Herrera Guevara does not take into account the most recent results of international research on the relationship between Kierkegaard and critical theory, such as Martin Beck Matuštík, *Postnational Identity: Critical Theory and Existential Philosophy in Habermas, Kierkegaard, and Havel*, New York: Guilford Press 1993; Marcia Morgan, *The Aesthetic-Religious Nexus in Theodor W. Adorno's Interpretation of the Works of Søren Kierkegaard and Its Influence on Adorno's Aesthetic Theory,* Ph.D. Thesis, New School University, New York 2003; Hermann Deuser, *Dialektische Theologie. Studien zu Adornos Metaphysik und zum Spätwerk Kierkegaards,* Munich and Mainz: Kaiser-Grünewald 1980; Eller Beck, *Identität der Person. Sozialphilosophische Studien zu Kierkegaard, Adorno und Habermas*, Würzburg: Köningshausen & Neumann 1991. There are also important research papers such as Dominic Desroches, "Existence esthétique, musique et language. Retour sur la réception critique de Kierkegaard par Adorno," *Horizons Philosophiques*, vol. 16, no. 2, 1996, pp. 21–38; Geoffrey Arthur Hale, "Learning to Read: Adorno, Kierkegaard and *Konstruktion*," in his *Kierkegaard and the Ends of Language*, Minneapolis: University of Minnesota Press 2002, pp. 37–72; Klaus-M. Kodalle, "Adornos Kierkegaard–ein kritischer Kommentar," in *Die Rezeption Søren Kierkegaard in der deutschen und dänischen Philosophie und Theologie. Vorträge des Kolloquiums am 22. und 23. März 1982*, ed. by Heinrich Anz, Poul Lübcke, and Friedrich Schmöe, Copenhagen and Munich: Fink 1983, pp. 70–100; Alvaro L.M. Valls, "Testemunhos da presenca de Kierkegaard em Adorno," *Educaçāo e Filosofia* (Uberlândia), vol. 12, no. 23, 1998, pp. 197–219.

9 Søren Kierkegaard, *Diario íntimo*, trans. by María Angélica Bosco (from the Italian translation of Cornelio Fabro), Buenos Aires: Santiago Rueda 1955.

10 Jaime Franco Barrio, "Kierkegaard en Español," *Azafea*, no. 2, 1989, p. 219.

Moving on to other issues, the content of the book with respect to Kierkegaard is far from achieving the rigor of exposition touted in the press reviews. Its surprising ignorance about Kierkegaard's work is made manifest when the author seems to discover that "The Seducer's Diary" is a part of *Either/Or*.[11] Moreover, it displays a highly partial and superficial reading of the Kierkegaardian *corpus*. First, it reduces *Fear and Trembling* to an exposition about faith as fanaticism ("the ethical-religious existence would be confused with the madness of whoever...believes that his religious duty obliges him to dynamite, for example, the most important cities of the world"),[12] which is then "refuted"[13] with the ethic of love developed in *Works of Love*. However, while the author rejects faith for being absurd, she praises this love ethic for being a "scandal."[14] Second, the author puts excessive stress on *Works of Love* simply because it is a signed work, but she does not study in detail any of Kierkegaard's other signed works; she disregards a serious reading of the pseudonymous works and only studies Anti-Climacus: "the only pseudonym who reduplicates Christianity is Anti-Climacus; in him we find the true Christian faith."[15] Despite this claim, she dedicates just a single page to *The Sickness unto Death*. In short, "in this pseudonym and in the writings signed by Kierkegaard we find what is the authentic truth,"[16] while pseudonyms like Climacus are "one more pawn in the plan designed by Kierkegaard."[17]

Herrera Guevara's version of Kierkegaard is full of clichés as well as old and superficial interpretations. Kierkegaard is defined as "the philosopher who has gone down in history as a second Luther,"[18] a "thinker of the tragic,"[19] an ardent critic of the Hegelian system,[20] a "mystical thinker,"[21] a "melancholic and misunderstood being, an outcast who only can dialogue truly with God,"[22] and a "grieved"[23] philosopher. The author ignores the Danish intellectual context of the nineteenth century and the philosophical intellectual contemporaries of Kierkegaard, who are reduced to the German thinkers Hegel, Schelling, Hamann, and Trendelenburg.[24] All these problems result in an inadequate portrait that makes it difficult to read Kierkegaard's ethical

---

11 Herrera Guevara, *La historia perdida de Kierkegaard y Adorno. Cómo leer a Kierkegaard y Adorno*, p. 24.

12 Ibid., p. 42.

13 Ibid., p. 41. To understand the relation between *Fear and Trembling* and *Works of Love*, see, for example, Sharon Krishek, *Kierkegaard on Faith and Love*, Cambridge: Cambridge University Press 2009, specially pp. 75–109.

14 Herrera Guevara, *La historia perdida de Kierkegaard y Adorno. Cómo leer a Kierkegaard y Adorno*, p. 73.

15 Ibid., p. 66. See also p. 30.

16 Ibid., p. 65. See also p. 71.

17 Ibid., p. 41.

18 Ibid., p. 18.

19 Ibid., p. 19.

20 Ibid., p. 19; p. 20; p. 46.

21 Ibid., p. 45.

22 Ibid., p. 34.

23 Ibid., p. 173.

24 Ibid., p. 49; p. 50; p. 57.

observations in a contemporary context. The chapter devoted to Kierkegaard is notoriously ambiguous and is in need of a deeper explanation, for example, when Herrera Guevara claims "Kierkegaard, with his theological and Christian discourse, breaks with the classical ontological difference....The Danish thinker cries out for a *real reality*—the invisible one; the visible is not the false [reality]—the despicable, the bad, that one must deny, but rather it is the transposition of this unique [real] reality."[25]

In another vein, the presentation of the relation between Kierkegaard and Adorno is unsatisfactory. Not only is the reflection about Kierkegaard from the former chapter reduced to bare allusions to the chapter on Adorno and the following ones, but there is no place in the entire book dedicated to a study of Adorno's doctoral thesis, *Kierkegaard. Konstruktion des Ästhetischen.*[26] This is Adorno's main statement about Kierkegaard, and one would think that it would be the centerpiece of the analysis, but instead it is neglected entirely. Similarly, the book makes not a single mention of Adorno's famous critique of Kierkegaard's doctrine of love. All of this is paired with the failure of the author to point out the continuity between the two thinkers on topics such as language, aesthetics, and indirect communication, which are only exposited in a superficial, irregular, and unconnected way. The comparison between Kierkegaard and Adorno is reduced to the common denominator of both authors under labels such as thinkers of the "damaged"[27] and "anguished"[28] life, as well as "sad philosophers."[29] Likewise, Adorno is described with Kierkegaardian clichés such as melancholic or ironic: "both are thinkers of the damaged life....The vague and persistent sadness that is reflected in their thoughts is not sensationalism or egoism, but misfortune. The way in which they express their melancholy separates them from the method of communication characteristic of those who believe in the truth of the System, bringing Kierkegaard and Adorno closer to an ironist tradition."[30]

Neither the good intentions of the work nor the relevance of the topics it considers prevents it from being a superficial and uncritical study full of clichés and poor arguments. After reading the book, one receives the impression that Kierkegaard is still a suffering and obscure philosopher who cannot contribute to contemporary reflection, and that Adorno and Habermas still remain at a great distance from him. The book gets lost in its multiple aims, and it is more exact in its observations about contemporary ethics than in any of its opinions about Kierkegaard and Adorno. In short, it acts merely as a thin cover over the gaping hole that remains in the Spanish intellectual context about the forgotten history of Kierkegaard's influence on Adorno and critical theory.

Juan Evaristo Valls Boix

[25] Ibid., p. 53.

[26] Theodor L.W. Adorno, *Kierkegaard. Konstruktion des Ästhetischen*, Frankfurt am Main: Suhrkamp 1986.

[27] Herrera Guevara, *La historia perdida de Kierkegaard y Adorno. Cómo leer a Kierkegaard y Adorno*, p. 88.

[28] Ibid., p. 89.

[29] Ibid., p. 167.

[30] Ibid., p. 89.

Reviews and Critical Discussions

Melero de la Torre, Mariano C., review in *Teorema: Revista internacional de filosofía*, vol. 26, no. 1, 2007, pp. 141–4.
Teimil García, Iván, "Un nuevo 'viejo' pensamiento," *Isegoría*, no. 34, 2006, pp. 289–323.

Manuel Gutiérrez Marín, *Dios ha hablado. El pensamiento dialéctico de Kierkegaard, Brunner y Barth* [God has Spoken: The Dialectical Thought of Kierkegaard, Brunner and Barth],

Buenos Aires: Editorial La Aurora and Mexico City:
Casa Unida de Publicaciones 1950, 147 pp.

Dios ha hablado was published by Manuel Gutiérrez in 1950. It was issued by La Aurora and Casa Unida de Publicaciones, which for decades were the leading Protestant publishers of Latin America (some years later La Aurora published the first Spanish translation of *Philosophiske Smuler*). Together both publishing houses made contemporary Protestant theology available to the continent in a measure rarely surpassed today. *Dios ha hablado* is, indeed, likely the first introduction to dialectical theology published in the region. The work arose out of several lectures given by Gutiérrez at the Evangelical Theological Faculty of Buenos Aires. Gutiérrez, a Spaniard, had studied in Greifswald, Berlin, and Halle, and thus was fully up to date with the latest theological developments in Europe.

This is a reasonably learned work for the public he was addressing, visibly shaped by Gutiérrez's first-hand reading of Kierkegaard, with no references to secondary literature. The work opens with an (at the time fairly usual) attempt at describing dialectical theology as fundamentally a retrieval of distinctive themes of Reformation theology. After this first chapter on the Reformation, a chapter on Kierkegaard follows. As announced in the subtitle, it is the dialectical thought of Kierkegaard, Barth, and Brunner that is the object of detailed scrutiny in the work.

The main idea of the book—that Kierkegaard should be read as a proto-dialectical theologian—can be considered typical of the times. However, there are accents that come from the author's minority position as a Protestant writer in South America. Almost at the opening of the chapter on Kierkegaard, for instance, we find an emphatic rejection of current comparisons between Pascal and Kierkegaard. The reason for this rejection is quite clearly a confessional one: Pascal remained a quintessentially Roman Catholic thinker, Gutiérrez writes, so that "whenever comparisons between Pascal and Kierkegaard are attempted a catastrophe is waiting."[1] For Gutiérrez, himself a historian of the Reformation in Spain and a significant translator of Reformation writings into Spanish, comparisons of Roman Catholic authors with Kierkegaard are out of the question.

While this resistance to Roman Catholic parallels may be questionable (Gutiérrez even denies that Kierkegaard had any interest in Roman Catholicism),[2] the author's Reformation heritage also plays a positive role in the book. For someone writing in South America in the late 1940s, and portraying Kierkegaard as a forerunner of dialectical theology, there was a significant risk of making Kierkegaard too much of a twentieth-century figure. This tendency is compensated for by the effort to simultaneously place Kierkegaard in the lineage of the Reformation. Trying to establish this continuity, Gutiérrez emphatically rejects both those who would attribute a subjectivist position to Kierkegaard, and those who would otherwise relate him to twentieth-century existentialism.[3]

The later chapters, dedicated to Barth and Brunner, only rarely mention Kierkegaard. The often-quoted assertion of Barth that the closest he came to having a system was his adoption of Kierkegaard's "infinite qualitative distinction," is mentioned.[4] More interestingly, Gutiérrez does not depict Barth and Kierkegaard as rejecting metaphysics altogether. They are portrayed as "turning away from Hegel," but in order to approach "the humble metaphysics of Plato and the Bible."[5] While Gutiérrez does not expand much on such issues, he offers a balanced introduction to some of Kierkegaard's emphases. Together with Luis Farré's work on Unamuno, James, and Kierkegaard his book is a good example of non-existentialist reception of Kierkegaard in Latin America.

Manfred Svensson

1 Manuel Gutiérrez Marín, *Dios ha hablado. El pensamiento dialéctico de Kierkegaard, Brunner y Barth*, Buenos Aires: Editorial La Aurora; México: Casa Unida de Publicaciones 1950, p. 21.

2 Ibid., p. 22.

3 Ibid., p. 33.

4 Ibid., p. 43.

5 Ibid., p. 105.

Reviews and Critical Discussions

Undetermined.

Rafael Larrañeta, *La interioridad apasionada. Verdad y amor en Søren Kierkegaard* [Passionate Inwardness: Love and Truth in S. Kierkegaard],

Salamanca: Universidad Pontificia Editorial San Esteban 1990, ix + 266 pp.

Rafael Larrañeta Olleta (1945–2002) was a Spanish teacher with doctorates in Philosophy and Theology who dedicated a large part of his life to the study and translation of Kierkegaard's *oeuvre*. Amongst his works, the following stand out: *Una moral de la felicidad* (1979), *La preocupación ética* (1986), *Lecciones para la clase de Utopía* (2000), and *La lupa de Kierkegaard* (2002).[1]

Larrañeta's study, *La interioridad apasionada. Verdad y amor en Søren Kierkegaard* (Passionate Interiority: Truth and Love in Søren Kierkegaard), was published by Editorial San Esteban in 1990. To put Larrañeta's book in its proper perspective, one should recall that when it was published, the standard work on Kierkegaard in Spanish did not offer a full understanding of the theme he developed, and a proper translation of Kierkegaard's complete works had still not been published, something which is still in process. The author himself acknowledges that he was motivated to undertake this research because of both the absence of works by Spanish speakers which give an analysis of the relation between truth and love in Kierkegaard's *oeuvre* and the conviction that with his treatment he could demonstrate the total harmony of the Dane's philosophy.[2]

Thus he dedicates the first part of his book to discussing the problem of truth and the second to examining the problem of love in order to show the origin of both

[1] Rafael Larrañeta, *Una moral de felicidad*, Salamanca: Editorial San Esteban 1979; Rafael Larrañeta, *La preocupación ética*, Salamanca: Editorial San Esteban 1986; Rafael Larrañeta, *Kierkegaard*, Madrid: Ediciones del Orto, 1995; Rafael Larrañeta, *Tras la justicia: introducción a una filosofía política*, Salamanca: San Esteban and Madrid: Edibesa 1999; Rafael Larrañeta, *Lecciones para la clase de* utopía, Salamanca: Editorial San Esteban 2000; Rafael Larrañeta, *La lupa de Kierkegaard*, Salamanca: Editorial San Esteban 2002.

[2] Rafael Larrañeta, *La interioridad apasionada. Verdad y amor en Søren Kierkegaard*, Salamanca: Universidad Pontificia Editorial San Esteban 1990, p. 27.

notions on the basis of a shared philosophical argument. This argument assumes that the relation between reality and ideality, which has obsessed the history of philosophy, can only be understood when the "real and existential subjectivity" arises dialectically from it. In this sense both truth and love demonstrate the supremacy of "decision" over reason.[3]

In order to develop the first part of the work, Larrañeta begins by analyzing *Johannes Climacus or De omnibus dubitandum est*, with the aim of emphasizing that "the consciousness which is incapable of doubt cannot reach the truth."[4] Then he examines the *Concluding Unscientific Postscript* in order to show the subjective character of the question of truth which supersedes the classical view of truth understood as *adaequatio rei et intellectus* by introducing a third term, the "existing man." It is in man's consciousness, understood as the place in which the contradiction between thought and being is generated, that the search arises for the truth as rupture or leap into space, which Kierkegaard calls *Beslutning* (decision). Within this framework, Larrañeta follows Jaurata Marion in considering that Kierkegaard is not interested in expounding either an ontology or a theory of knowledge, but rather in showing how what exists is related *in concreto* to the truth.[5]

While the works examined in the first part are *Johannes Climacus or De omnibus dubitandum est*, the *Concluding Unscientific Postscript*, *Philosophical Fragments*, and *The Sickness unto Death*, in order to organize the second part, he takes up the scheme of Hans Friemond in respect to the works selected: *Either/Or*, *Stages on Life's Way*, and *Works of Love*, so as to highlight the progressive character of the supersession of the immediacy of Romantic love brought about by Christian love.[6]

From the outset Larrañeta accepts that his starting point is a kind of apologetic defense of the importance of the religious in the constitution of Kierkegaardian thought. This might explain that the author's intention is neither polemical nor critical but rather descriptive. The expository method that he uses is based on searching for the philosophical sources of the concepts which he works on and their subsequent articulation in Kierkegaard's work conceived as an organic whole.

For Larrañeta, interiority "is the underlying theme of the entire Kierkegaardian philosophy."[7] Because he takes this affirmation as the starting point and conclusion of his research, he does not manage to present the more complex dialectical aspects of Kierkegaard's thought. In order to do so, he should have avoided following a

---

3 Ibid., p. 227.

4 Ibid., p. 37.

5 Ibid., p. 129.

6 As "love" appears as the main topic of these works, it was said that *Either/Or* and *Stages on Life's Way* considered the esthetic and ethical aspects of love while *Works of Love* was dedicated to the religious stage. Hans Friemond, *Existenz in Liebe nach Søren Kierkegaard*, Salzburg and Munich: Verlag Anton Postet 1965, pp. 43–140.

7 Larrañeta, *La interioridad apasionada*, p. 230.

"unilateral" analytical path, that is to say, taking interiority for granted, but would have had rather to examine the relation between interiority and exteriority. In spite of understanding the underlying logic of Kierkegaard's argument, which he summarizes very well as the maintenance of the "triad" (reality, ideality, and consciousness), Larrañeta cannot apply this to his own focus which turns out to be explanatory rather than descriptive, and critical rather than apologetic.

In his defense of Kierkegaard, Larrañeta makes a shrewd summary of the former's most important philosophical works and demonstrates a broad grasp of the secondary sources, especially in German. The very choice of theme is relevant. However, having made the choice on the basis of too narrow a reading of Kierkegaard's work, he prevented himself from offering a broader perspective on the basis of which to discuss a number of themes. These include, amongst others, the following: the problem of decisionism elaborated by Karl Löwith in an article from 1935, in which he conceives of Kierkegaard and Marx as antecedents of the political decisionism of Carl Schmitt; the distinct modes of conceiving of the relation between love and truth as an expression of two types of universal history, the Indo-Hellenistic and the Christian, described by Max Scheler at the start of the twentieth century in *Love and Knowledge*; and the study of the Christian idea of love in contrast to the Hellenistic idea developed by Anders Nygren in *Agape and Eros*, published in 1953.

In summary, despite having undertaken a detailed analysis of the question proposed, Larrañeta's work merits revision in three aspects. On the one hand, reducing Kierkegaard's intention to the description of "passionate interiority" impedes the understanding of the difficulties which the Dane's thought runs into when it comes to articulating interiority and exteriority, paganism and Christianity, sensual love, the authentic, and the word of God. Instead of showing that the articulations between these opposites suppose a leap of faith which many consider without basis, not only does Larrañeta content himself with accepting the religious basis of Kierkegaard's philosophy without questioning it, but he does not concern himself with why the Dane has chosen the Christian religion without explaining why this would be superior to that of the Jew or the Muslim: "That Kierkegaard 'seizes the opportunity' and identifies this 'faith' which concludes his philosophy of subjectivity, this faith of passionate interiority, with the Christian faith, would not necessarily undermine his philosophical project."[8]

On the other hand, when Larrañeta analyzes the reading that Adorno makes of Kierkegaard's work, he does not show why Adorno's criticisms are not consistent. Instead, Larrañeta contents himself with rejecting them and maintaining that while Kierkegaard occupies himself with describing the "form" (*hvorledes*) of love, Adorno searches in action for the liberating transformation with which Kierkegaard is not concerned, and thus shows that he has not really understood it.[9] In the end,

8 Ibid., pp. 228–9.

9 Ibid., p. 218.

Larrañeta concludes that the transition from *Works of Love* to the philosophy and the theory of liberation would be natural but does not explain how. In summary, Larrañeta carries out an excellent work of investigation even when his personal adhesion to the thought of Kierkegaard impedes him from discerning its paradoxical character and replying to the just objections by scholars of the order of Adorno, who has the best understanding of the *oeuvre* of the Dane in the Marxist tradition and whose critical reading today is still indispensable.[10]

Patricia Dip

[10] K.E. Løgstrup (*Opgør med Kierkegaard*, Copenhagen: Gyldendal 1968) again takes up Adorno's criticism, which Larrañeta opposes, defending Thulstrup's position in "Les Œuvres del l'amour de Kierkegaard en regard du Nouveau Testament" (in *Orbis litterarum*, vol. 10, 1955, pp. 275–6). In this confrontation, Larrañeta defends Thulstrup without developing arguments but rather assuming his apologetic reading of Kierkegaard.

Review and Critical Discussion

Salamone, Maria Antonieta, "La interioridad apasionada. Verdad y amor en Soren Kierkegaard," in *La ética, aliento de lo eterno. Homenaje al profesor Rafael A. Larrañeta*, ed. by Luis Méndez Francisco, Salamanca: San Esteban 2003, pp. 493–506.

Rafael Larrañeta,
La lupa de Kierkegaard
[Kierkegaard's Magnifying Glass],

Salamanca: Editorial San Esteban 2002, 159 pp.

Rafael Larrañeta was a major figure in the Spanish reception of Kierkegaard. He is widely acknowledged as the person who was mainly responsible for the decisive turning point in Spanish Kierkegaard studies that took place in the last two decades of the last century. His contribution to the development of a rigorous academic tradition of Kierkegaard studies was particularly multifaceted, and one could argue that so was his work: among his many publications on Kierkegaard, we can find both in-depth studies, exclusively addressed to scholars, and more accessible presentations, intended to introduce Kierkegaard to students or the general reader. The conjunction of these esoteric and exoteric studies gives Larrañeta's work a very interesting balance that no doubt contributes to the significance of his labor for the Spanish reception.[1]

La lupa de Kierkegaard is the paradigm of this "acrobatic" production since it combines a scholarly advanced understanding of Kierkegaard's work with a light and accessible presentation. In fact, in its form Larrañeta's text is anything but a scholarly treatise. There are none of the usual references to other studies or even to Kierkegaard's works; not a single footnote can be found in the whole book—and yet it still retains its academic validity. The reason for this lies in the peculiar nature of the book and the role it plays within the whole work of Larrañeta, namely, a sort of *summa* of his long-term intellectual devotion to Kierkegaard.

It could be argued that only fate assigned the book that particular position (Larrañeta died tragically shortly after the book was published), but at the same time it is hard to deny that the work fits extremely well with that interpretation. In this respect, a glance at the table of contents makes clear two decisive aspects that shape the book: one, the whole work and life of Kierkegaard are approached (in only 159 pages, small format), and two, the main topics that had constituted Larrañeta's academic research are incorporated—the chapter "¿Tragedia o teofanía?"

---

[1] A more detailed presentation of Larrañeta's contribution to Kierkegaard studies can be found in Dolors Perarnau Vidal and Óscar Parcero Oubiña, "Spain: The Old and New Kierkegaard Reception in Spain," in *Kierkegaard's International Reception*, Tome II, *Southern, Central and Eastern Europe*, ed. by Jon Stewart, Aldershot: Ashgate 2009 (*Kierkegaard Research: Sources, Reception and Resources*, vol. 8), pp. 17–80.

being a clear example of this.[2] The approach is thus quite obvious, and could be summarized as follows: an attempt to consider the whole figure of Kierkegaard within the narrow limits of a brief non-academic presentation without relinquishing the gravity of a mature scholarly interpretation. Not an easy task, we could add.

The first chapter of the book, "Jutlandia," opens with the well-known story of Michael Pedersen Kierkegaard's dreadful sin. In order to introduce this sort of novelistic episode in Kierkegaard's biography, Larrañeta uses a novelistic style that immediately creates the proper mood: "*Aquel día, Michael Pedersen se sintió abatido. Su vista descansaba en las arenosas playas del bravo mar del Norte*" (That day, Michael Pedersen felt downhearted. His sight rested on the sandy beaches of the rough North Sea).[3] Soon the tone moves to a more descriptive one, in which the whole biography of Kierkegaard is little by little displayed, together with some historical facts that are explained here and there in order to help the reader understand the intellectual issues involved in Kierkegaard's life story. The rich background from which Larrañeta deals with the various topics makes the text more fecund for the reader, and this is manifest from the very beginning of the book.

Chapters 2, "Copenhague," 3, "Universidad," and 4, "Seducción," continue the biographical account, which includes some of the most controversial episodes of Kierkegaard's profile, such as, for instance, the love affair with Regine Olsen. As far as this and other polemical topics are concerned, it must be mentioned—and should be praised, as well—that Larrañeta avoids making definite statements based on what he personally might believe to be the correct interpretation. Instead, he provides the reader with critical assessments that cover different perspectives and possible readings of each subject in dispute among Kierkegaard scholars.

Chapter 5, "Migajas de verdad" (Fragments of Truth), is another good example of what was mentioned before about the possibility of tracing Larrañeta's previous work in this book. The chapter deals with the question of truth, and it does so by resorting mostly to *Philosophical Fragments*, the one work that Larrañeta had translated into Spanish some years before. In a way, Chapter 5 interrupts the biographical thread that dominates most of the text and comes back to the foreground with the treatment, in Chapter 6, of the conflict between the aesthetic and the religious. The same thing applies to the following chapters, which deal with anxiety, faith, and the single individual, to mention the major subjects approached in the subsequent pages. In all cases, Larrañeta creates a balance between following the narration of Kierkegaard's life story, on the one hand, and presenting the most important elements of his philosophy and theology, on the other.

Chapter 11, "Creyente" (Believer), discusses the question of Kierkegaard's personal and intellectual religiosity. This makes these pages a particularly interesting text for the average Spanish reader, who was—and, to a large extent, still is—used to a cliché image of Kierkegaard, namely, that of the melancholic, pessimistic believer

---

[2] Rafael Larrañeta, "Kierkegaard: Tragedia o Teofanía. Del sufrimiento inocente al dolor de Dios," *Thémata*, no. 15, 1995, pp. 67–77 (monographic issue *El Concepto de la Angustia: 150 años después*).

[3] Rafael Larrañeta, *La lupa de Kierkegaard*, Salamanca: Editorial San Esteban 2002, p. 11.

of an irrational Christianity. Larrañeta makes here yet another effort to show the reader "the real face of Kierkegaard," as he had already done in the past,[4] clarifying the relation between faith and reason, explaining Kierkegaard's self-conception as a Christian and, particularly, denying the well-known portrait of the pessimist: "*En lugar de un individuo desesperado, ácido, pesimista, resignado ante el mal, [el lector] descubrirá una personalidad jovial, alegre, entusiasta*" (Instead of a desperate, caustic, pessimistic individual resigned to evil, [the reader] will find a cheerful, happy, enthusiastic personality).[5] But for this, states Larrañeta, we need to include in our readings the various edifying discourses, whose rejection in the Spanish reception was a great mistake.

Emil Boesen, Kierkegaard's friend and companion in his last days, concentrates the attention of "El postrer amigo" (The Last Friend), which is the last chapter devoted to the biographical account (before it, we still find the previously mentioned "¿Tragedia o Teofanía?"). Larrañeta refers to Boesen as the only source of information for Kierkegaard's final days, and it is with this that he comes to the end of the portrayal of Kierkegaard's intellectual biography. Finally, a chronology and some complementary information end the book. It is worth mentioning that among these final notes, we find the only bibliographical reference in the volume: Joakim Garff's *SAK*, then recently published, is recommended by Larrañeta as a deeper introduction to Kierkegaard's life and work. Otherwise, as previously mentioned, we will not encounter any other references, not even to Kierkegaard's works, which are now and then quoted, but never with a footnote properly to identify the passage.

Bringing this review to a close, we should insist on the multifaceted nature of Larrañeta's contribution to the study of Kierkegaard's work, since that is precisely what we best find here. *La lupa de Kierkegaard* is not only a brief introduction to Kierkegaard's intellectual biography, one which any student could make good use of; it is also a good compendium of some 30 years of devoted academic research, and as such, it still has something to offer to Kierkegaard scholars, who will be able to confront their interpretations with that of an essential figure in the particular field of Spanish Kierkegaard studies.

Oscar Parcero Oubiña

---

4 Rafael Larrañeta, "El verdadero rostro de Kierkegaard," *Revista de Filosofía*, vol. 10, no. 18, 1997, pp. 83–112.

5 Larrañeta, *La lupa de Kierkegaard*, p. 117.

Reviews and Critical Discussions

Fernández Manzano, Juan A., review in *La ética, aliento de lo eterno. Homenaje al profesor Rafael A. Larrañeta*, ed. by Luis Méndez Francisco, Salamanca: Editorial San Esteban 2003, pp. 517–24.

Parcero Oubiña, Oscar, review in *Estudios filosóficos*, vol. 52, no. 149, 2003, pp. 160–2.

— review in *Anales del Seminario de Historia de la Filosofía*, vol. 21, 2004, pp. 208–10.

Santiago Guervós, Luis Enrique, review in *Contrastes*, vol. 8, 2003, pp. 219–20.

Fernando Pérez-Borbujo (ed.), *Ironía y destino. La filosofía secreta de Søren Kierkegaard* [Irony and Destiny: The Secret Philosophy of Søren Kierkegaard],

Barcelona: Herder 2013, 271 pp.

Ironía y destino. La filosofía secreta de Søren Kierkegaard is a compilation of five essays edited and prefaced by Fernando Pérez-Borbujo and published in Barcelona as a part of the bicentennial celebration of Søren Kierkegaard's birth. Additionally, the book is an indirect product of the studies developed in the national research project on Kierkegaard, "Schelling-Kierkegaard: la génesis de la angustia contemporánea," ("Schelling-Kierkegaard: the Genesis of Contemporary Anxiety"), which was completed in 2011 after three years of research led by Pérez-Borbujo at the Universitat Pompeu Fabra in Barcelona. Another relevant publication related to this project is the edition of Kierkegaard's notes to Schelling's lectures,[1] which is the first Spanish translation of these texts. As well as Pérez-Borbujo, other researchers related to that project collaborate in the present book, including Jacobo Zabalo Puig and Francesc Torralba.

Another important aspect of this publication is the participation of Luis I. Guerrero, María José Binetti, and Jon Stewart, each of whom contributes a chapter. With their contributions, the book brings to Spain the work of two of the most important Latin specialists in Kierkegaard and an example of the thorough historiographical research of Jon Stewart, which is generally unknown in Spain. Its publication by a printing house as well known and as popular as Herder, unlike many preceding studies about Kierkegaard printed in minor and secondary publishing houses, contributes to its diffusion of Kierkegaard's thought. The volume in fact aims to update and refresh the image of Kierkegaard in academic circles as well as to renew the interest in a thinker who has been normally disregarded in Spain, uncritically translated, or interpreted from partial perspectives such as the Catholic

I would like to thank Matthew Nowachek and Jon Stewart for helpful comments on an earlier draft of this article.

1 Søren Kierkegaard, *Apuntes sobre la Filosofía de la Revelación de F. W. J. Schelling (1841–1842)*, trans. by Óscar Parcero Oubiña, Madrid: Trotta 2014.

or the existentialist one. In addition, Kierkegaard has often merely been compared to other better known philosophers such as Heidegger or Sartre, making the Dane little more than a mere precursor to their philosophy. Press reviews praise the collection as a renewed and updated reflection on Kierkegaard[2] and "profitable reading,"[3] which displays "the competence of its authors and the notable knowledge they have about Kierkegaard's philosophy."[4]

The purpose of the book is situated between popular dissemination and an academic approach to Kierkegaard's thought. The Preface of the study underlines the ambiguous and enigmatic character of Kierkegaard's *œuvre* in order to explain how it has been studied from different exegetical traditions, which have not offered a convincing overall interpretation of the Dane. Similarly, Stewart's chapter is a historiographical exercise that shows—with a deep knowledge of the historical context of the works, the Danish nineteenth century, and the intellectual field of Copenhagen—the most egregious errors and misunderstandings which have been constantly repeated in Kierkegaard research. This chapter further shows many different biographical myths or confusions concerning Kierkegaard's allusions to Hegelian Danish philosophers or theologians and direct attacks on Hegel himself. The rest of the book deals with Kierkegaard's philosophy from a traditional perspectives: three respective chapters consider the existential stages described in 1845, namely, the aesthetic, ethical, and religious along with providing a general overview of Kierkegaard's works. The volume concludes with a chapter on Kierkegaard's social critique of his time and the institutionalized Christendom, which he carried out in part by means of irony. The contributions here try to clarify and update a complex *corpus* which is qualified in the Introduction as a "philosophy of the secret": "the interest perhaps resides in that, even today, 200 years after his birth, the meaning of Kierkegaard's works is still a mystery, as if it were impossible to figure out its secret. Even more, we could claim that Kierkegaardian philosophy is a 'philosophy of secret.'"[5]

The work's intention of dissemination and its critical purposes are unsuccessful due to its unclear structure and methodology. First, in spite of the book's commemoration of the 200 years of Kierkegaard's birth and his great influence on the twentieth century, the authors do not always employ the most recent critical edition of Kierkegaard works, *Søren Kierkegaards Skrifter*, but rather they often quote older editions. Moreover, the bibliography of secondary sources is also outdated: central aspects of Kierkegaard's work are illustrated with references to studies from as early as 1930, although the volume purports to want to correct past errors and old

---

2 Anonymous, review in *Diálogo filosófico*, no. 87, 2013, p. 185; Josep Boada, review in *Actualidad bibliográfica de Filosofía y Teología*, vol. 51, no. 101, 2014, p. 286; Gloria Luque Moya, review in *Estudios filosóficos*, vol. 63, 2014, p. 163.

3 Gloria Luque Moya, review in *Estudios filosóficos*, vol. 63, 2014, p. 164.

4 Josep Boada, review in *Actualidad bibliográfica de Filosofía y Teología*, vol. 51, no. 101, 2014, p. 287.

5 Fernando Pérez-Borbujo, "Introducción," *Ironía y destino. La filosofía secreta de Søren Kierkegaard*, Barcelona: Herder 2013, p. 9.

mistaken interpretations. On other occasions, chapters are just based on insufficient sources. Only Stewart's chapter adequately avoids these problems.

Second, the structure of the book—at least Chapters 2, and 4—reflects the cliché in Kierkegaard exegesis of the three existential stages without giving consideration to the time (1845) when Kierkegaard wrote *Stages on Life's Way* and its relation to preceding and subsequent works, imposing this structure on the whole authorship. In this way, the work explains the search for God in *Three Discourses on Imagined Occasions* without considering the authorial difference between this text and the other work from 1845 and without any comparison of them. In addition, there is no clear distinction between the topics of pseudonymity and immediacy in the chapter about aesthetics. Binetti's chapter, however, avoids the cliché because it defends, from the beginning, a personal interpretation of the continuity of the ethical through the complete writings of Kierkegaard and explains the evolution of this aspect through different works.

Concerning its exposition, the volume has just as many virtues as notable errors. Pérez-Borbujo's introduction is clear and useful for gaining an overview of the reception of Kierkegaard and for understanding the fecundity of his thinking and its impact on the twentieth century. With the same clarifying purpose, Stewart's contribution is by far the most careful, critical, and profitable piece of the volume: it should actually be required reading for anyone beginning an updated and rigorous study of Kierkegaard and for helping readers disabuse themselves of the confusions which have long dominated interpretation of the Dane. The final chapter by Luis I. Guerrero, modest and clear, is an acceptable exposition of Kierkegaard's critique of his society, which considers Kierkegaard as a sort of gadfly *à la* Socrates. In contrast to these virtues, other parts of the book are imprecise and reveal a poor understanding of Kierkegaard's peculiarities. They also ignore the most recent international research including the works of Hannay,[6] Kirmmse,[7] and Stewart.[8] The study, then, is affected by the very provincialism and lack of accuracy that the volume wants to combat: one can find excessive comparisons between Kierkegaard and Nietzsche, which designate the latter as "the closest thinker to Kierkegaard,"[9] unjustified and immoderate references to Kant and other writers like Sade or even Heraclitus, whose qualification as "the Obscure" is naïvely applied to Kierkegaard: "The great Heraclitus went down in the history of philosophy with the nickname 'the Obscure,'...and this obscurity has given room to an infinite hermeneutics. In the same manner, the Kierkegaardian *corpus* has gathered around itself a huge

6 For example, Alastair Hannay, *Kierkegaard*, London and New York, Routledge 1991. There is a Spanish translation of this work: Alastair Hannay, *Kierkegaard, una biografía*, trans. by Nassim Bravo Jordán, Mexico City, Universidad Iberoamericana 2010.

7 Bruce H. Kirmmse, *Kierkegaard in Golden Age Denmark*, Bloomington: Indiana University Press 1990.

8 For example, Jon Stewart, *Kierkegaard's Relations to Hegel Reconsidered*, New York: Cambridge University Press 2003.

9 Pérez-Borbujo, "Introducción," *Ironía y destino. La filosofía secreta de Søren Kierkegaard*, p. 29.

hermeneutic and interpretative production."[10] Far from resolving the supposed ambiguity of Kierkegaard's thought through an appropriate treatment of topics such as the authorship, or clarifying remarks of the development of his thought, the volume, except for Stewart's, Binetti's, and Guerrero's chapters, celebrates a mystery and a secret that consists simply in an incorrect and outdated study of Kierkegaard.

In short, this collection could be effective in spreading the profundity of the works of a versatile thinker to the non-specialized public[11] as well as introducing the reader to the direct reading of Kierkegaard's *corpus*. However, the study fails significantly in its pretension of offering critical or accurate approaches to Kierkegaard's works, and its aim of updating is successfully realized only in some chapters, while others continue to propagate traditional interpretations and old myths. Perhaps the book defends the relevance of a critical analysis of Kierkegaard's thought and the necessity of current and critical translation in the Spanish research, but it is not the best way to do it.

Juan Evaristo Valls Boix

---

10 Ibid., p. 9.

11 This is the case even if many of the aspects described in the different chapters are too specific to be understood by a common reader. By the way, other recent Spanish introductions to Kierkegaard's thought have been more profitable and without the many errors of this one; for example: Rafael Larrañeta, *La lupa de Kierkegaard*, Salamanca: San Esteban 2002, or Darío González's preliminary study to a compilation of works by Gredos publishing house: Søren Kierkegaard, *Diapsálmata; Los estadios eróticos inmediatos o El erotismo musical; Repercusión de la tragedia antigua en la moderna; Siluetas; El más desgraciado; El primer amor; La validez estética del matrimonio; Referencia acerca del matrimonio en respuesta a algunas objeciones; Temor y temblor*, Introduction by Darío González, Madrid: Gredos 2010.

Reviews and Critical Discussions

Anonymous, review in *Diálogo filosófico*, no. 87, 2013, p. 185.
Boada, Josep, review in *Actualidad bibliográfica de Filosofía y Teología*, vol. 51, no. 101, 2014, pp. 286–9.
García, María José, review in *Nova et Vetera*, no. 24, 2014, pp. 382–89.
Luque Moya, Gloria, review in *Estudios filosóficos*, vol. 63, 2014, pp. 163–4.

Francesc Torralba, *Kierkegaard en el laberinto de las mascaras* [Kierkegaard in the Labyrinth of Masks],

Madrid: Fundación Emmanuel Mounier 2003, 116 pp.

Kierkegaard en el laberinto de las máscaras (Kierkegaard in the Labyrinth of Masks) is an example of one of the many publications and interests belonging to the prolific author Francesc Torralba Roselló. For almost a decade Torralba's interest in Kierkegaard has been expressed in different specialized reflections on topics such as love, difference, anthropology, music, Christology, reflection and dialectics. *Kierkegaard en el laberinto de las máscaras* continues with this scholarly research because this text explores one of Kierkegaard's most interesting topics: communication. Moreover, this text can also be considered a good introduction to Kierkegaard's thought. The author writes:

> In this essay, the objective that we propose to ourselves is to present the internal structure of Kierkegaard's work and also to offer helpful leads for the best understanding of his communicative strategy. This book can be considered, then, as an introduction to the study of Kierkegaard, the objective of which is not, at all, to substitute the Dane's reading, but to bring it about, to suggest it or, in the best sense, to generate a will of studying in the reader.[1]

The text is divided into eleven parts, each one of which presents an element that helps to provide a general overview of Kierkegaard, his thought and his particular way of expressing it that leads to the problem of his authorship.

In the first section, "Kierkegaard el confidente," Kierkegaard is to be pictured as a religious author whose overwhelming and complex personality unfolds into different masks. This part has three subdivisions ("1.1. Poeta religioso," "1.2. Teórico de la comunicación," and "1.3. Intérprete del Cristianismo") that depict the most important aspects, on Torralba's view, of this thinker. All these subsections are related to Kierkegaard's pseudonyms by which he communicates his quest for what it means to be a Christian in the world through different voices, world-views, and perspectives.

---

[1] Francesc Torralba, *Kierkegaard en el laberinto de las máscaras*, Madrid: Fundación Emmanuel Mounier 2003, p. 14. (All of the translations that appear in the text are by the author.)

Because of all these different views, Kierkegaard knows how to express these characters and that is why Torralba describes his labor as a kind of artistry, specifically musicality:

> Definitely, musicality constitutes the most characteristic feature of Kierkegaard's lyrical dialectic. What is proper of music is to keep the plurality of voices in a harmonic unity, and this is precisely what happens in the Kierkegaardian *opus*. The unity and the harmony of his *corpus* are based on the simultaneity (*Samtidige*) and the concurrent voices (*samstemmen*), of sounds (*Lyder*) released altogether. The aesthetic works have a proper rhythm, lively and light. The ethical works display a different sonority, deeper, slower. In order to apprehend the whole, one needs to join both sonorities and find concordance. Kierkegaard's originality consists in the harmonic syntheses of both musicalities. This, then, opens a third way, a final reconciliation that is the religious (*det Religieuse*) perspective.[2]

Following this idea, Torralba develops the second section of this book, "El hilo de Ariadna." In this section the reader is introduced to the problem of authorship in Kierkegaard. Here we encounter the review of many efforts to give a solution to this problem. Not only Kierkegaard himself is mentioned and analyzed with the proposal made in *The Point of View for My Work as an Author*, but also scholars such as Cornelio Fabro, André Clair, and Alastair Hannay. Torralba states the three different coordinates by which the Kierkegaardian *corpus* should ideally be arranged, harmonized, or classified:

> On our point of view, an internal and systematic classification of the Kierkegaardian *corpus* should respect these three factors: first, the biographical, and this means that the order stated for the literary production should consider the author's existential itinerary. Second, the polynomic variable, and this implies that the production should be ordered according to the pseudonyms, and at last, the thematic constant, which means that the classification should be done by taking into consideration its thematic nuclei.[3]

Once these factors are settled, Torralba explores Kierkegaard's multiplicity. The point of departure for this study is presented in section three, "La novedad y la singularidad de Kierkegaard." Here, Torralba depicts the features that, on his point of view, make Kierkegaard unique as an author. These are introspection and self-analysis, which lead to a continual self-knowledge that is expressed along with Kierkegaard's work: "Kierkegaard spies himself throughout his authorship."[4] Due to this continual analysis of himself, "Kierkegaard identifies himself as the receiver of a voice."[5] This voice is spread and decomposed in many different tones that are the pseudonyms that Kierkegaard created. How are these pseudonyms managed and arranged?

In order to answer this question, Torralba analyzes a passage from the *Concluding Unscientific Postscript*, which gives the title for the next part of the book, "Una primera y última explicación." This explanation helps to show how Kierkegaard

---

2 Ibid., p. 29.
3 Ibid., p. 37.
4 Ibid., p. 48.
5 Ibid.

understands his work as an author and his relationship with the pseudonymous works. Kierkegaard is seen by Torralba as an author who writes because he has experienced somehow the many different ways in which his pseudonyms develop and consider their existential choices, but personally he does not subscribe to them. On Torralba's view, this work completes the general overview stated in *The Point of View for My Work as an Author*.

Even when it has been stated how the Kierkegaardian production has been arranged, an explanation of how the authorship's dynamic functions is still missing. In other words, how can it be possible for these works to be taken individually and conjointly with specific results? Chapter 5, "La dialéctica de la comunicación," is dedicated to clarifying these questions. According to Torralba, Kierkegaard's whole communication dynamic stands on a conception of truth. In other words, "He himself affirms that, by means of his work, he wishes to become a witness of the truth....He wishes to awaken in his readers this craving for truth, the clarifying exercise of that existential form that can satisfy human beings."[6] In this quest for the truth Kierkegaard does not search for an abstract truth. He is looking for a truth that touches human existence: "On Kierkegaard's judgment, the quest for existential truth requires a subjective kind of communication, that is, by means of subjectivities."[7] So, it is by virtue of these, *dramatis personae* or pseudonyms, considered not only as autonomous, as themselves, as persons apart from Kierkegaard that they can stand on their own, as literary works, but also as part of a personal project.

As an obligatory subject that has to be dealt with, *The Point of View for My Work as an Author* is presented as another part of Torralba's analysis of Kierkegaard's authorship in Chapter 6, "Su punto de vista como escritor." This chapter is divided into three parts ("1. Kierkegaard escritor religioso," "2. La práctica de la ambigüedad," "3. La obra como recepción de la palabra") that explain the content of *The Point of View for My Work as an Author*, according to Torralba. The author claims that this work is important since it is another interpretation of Kierkegaard's whole authorship based on his own criteria and also that this text is the proof that Kierkegaard's work was one connected and intimately related to his life and the complexities he experienced rather than one that expresses some kind of progression as in the aesthetic, ethical, and religious stages.[8]

On Torralba's view, there is a doubleness in Kierkegaard's thought, which, after a certain point, reveals itself not as an aesthetic but as a religious one. So, the relationship between his works and his concerns is either direct or indirect. This is how Kierkegaard conceives the categories of direct and indirect communication in *The Point of View for My Work as an Author*.

Another work, which is worthy of study, is "Armed Neutrality," and this analysis is presented in the chapter of the same name, "Neutralidad Armada." Here, Torralba's

---

6 Ibid., p. 56.
7 Ibid., p. 57.
8 Ibid., p. 66.

main goal is to depict how Kierkegaard develops his authorship as an opposition to the established church, as well as the culture, literature, and mass existence of his time.[9]

After the abovementioned, there are other efforts left that are presented in Torralba's work in order to present the complexity of the pseudonymous problem in Kierkegaard's authorship. This is the case in Chapter 8, "Un pseudonimo, lector de pseudonimos" and Chapter 9, "Cartografía de los Pseudónimos," where the labor of Johannes Climacus in "A Glance at a Contemporary Effort in Danish Literature" is carefully described as one interpretation that enriches the many different views of Kierkegaard's work. This pseudonym, of course, has to be explained, and this, specifically has to be in contrast to Anti-Climacus in order to see what is the scope that was used to interpret the Kierkegaardian *opus.* This is, mainly, the function of Chapter 10, "Climacus y Anticlimacus."

Finally, Chapter 11, "Kierkegaard, ¿dónde estás?" and Chapter 12, "Epílogo" function as conclusions, where a summary of the many different explorations is presented and left to the reader with the aim that he can draw his own conclusions and form his own view upon one of the most important subjects in Kierkegaard: communication. It is important to say that after these chapters, Torralba adds a time chart in order to locate chronologically the different Kierkegaardian works, and this is very useful for non-specialists. The text is rich in reflections and profundity. The analysis of the different approaches to Kierkegaard's work is quite sharp and, in this sense, Torralba's work can be considered one of the most important critical works in Spanish about the subject.

Azucena Palavicini Sánchez

9 Ibid., p. 84.

Review and Critical Discussion

Perarnau Vidal, Dolors, review in *Anales del Seminario de Historia de la Filosofía*, vol. 23, 2006, pp. 279–310.

Leticia Valadez (ed.), *Las publicaciones de Søren Kierkegaard de 1843* [Søren Kierkegaard's Publications from 1843],

special issue of *Tópicos. Revista de Filosofía*, vol. 3, no. 5, 1993 (Mexico City: Universidad Panamericana), 325 pp.

The monographic issue of the Mexican periodical *Tópicos* contains all the papers presented at the International Symposium "Las publicaciones de Søren Kierkegaard de 1843" organized by the Sociedad Iberoamericana de Estudios Kierkegaardianos and the Universidad Panamericana in Mexico City. This symposium was held on September 23–24, 1993, to commemorate the 150-year anniversary of the publication of Kierkegaard's pseudonymous works *Either/Or*, *Repetition*, and *Fear and Trembling*, as well as the edifying discourses of the same year. This congress was one of the first research activities on Kierkegaard in the Spanish-speaking context, and it can be regarded as a significant step forward for Spanish-language research.[1] It was preceded only by the congress "Encuentros de Filosofía en Denia," which was dedicated to Kierkegaard and held in May 1987. Yet, unlike this first congress, all of the lecturers at the conference in Mexico were Kierkegaard scholars. In addition, some of the main international Kierkegaard researchers participated in the conference, contributing the latest discoveries and perspectives in international research. In this sense, the special issue of *Tópicos* could be understood as a predecessor of the monograph on Kierkegaard edited by Begonya Sáez Tajafuerce five years later in the periodical *Enrahonar*,[2] which consisted in a compilation of essays by exclusively foreign contributors with the aim of improving and supplementing Spanish Kierkegaard studies with the best results of international research.

The monographic issue of *Tópicos* aims to offer some critical studies about Kierkegaard's authorship and his first thoughts about individual existence through

---

I would like to thank Matthew Nowachek for helpful comments on an earlier draft of this article.

1 Dolores Perarnau Vidal and Óscar Parcero Oubiña, "Spain: The Old and New Kierkegaard. Reception in Spain," *Kierkegaard's International Reception*, Tome II, *Southern, Central and Eastern Europe*, ed. by Jon Stewart, Aldershot: Ashgate 2009 (*Kierkegaard Research: Sources, Reception and Resources*, vol. 8), p. 49.

2 Begonya Sáez Tajafuerce (ed.), *Enrahonar*, no. 29, 1998 (Barcelona: Universidad Autònoma de Barcelona).

the well-known three stages (aesthetic, ethical, and religious) as they are exposited in the works of 1843. It also deals with the topic of pseudonymity. First, the book contains six papers about *Either/Or* written by Julia Watkin, Luis I. Guerrero (who contributes two articles), Alastair McKinnon, Ralph McInerny, and María García Amilburu, respectively. These articles explain primarily Kierkegaard's rhetorical strategies and pseudonymity, the indirect communication, and some of the features of the aesthetic existence, with an interesting comparison between the two different conceptions of woman in the two parts of the book. Although the contributions stand out for their intelligent, well-documented, and richly discussed reflections, Guerrero's and Amilburu's articles are notably less rigorous and less focused than the others, being a sort of basic reading of Kierkegaard's work.

Second, there is Arne Grøn's study of *Repetition* that deals with the ambiguity of the concept of "repetition" through a detailed and critical reading of the work. Third, the monograph presents the proceedings of a panel discussion about *Fear and Trembling*, which includes Leonardo Polo's talk followed by the contributions of the panel that included Ramón Xirau, Alastair McKinnon, and Basilio Rojo. Polo, who is not really a specialist on Kierkegaard, offers an uncritical and imprecise introductory overview of De silentio's work, disregarding some of the specific points of *Fear and Trembling*. The rest of the contributions to the discussion, made by speakers who are also rather distant from Kierkegaard research, are in the same way vague and unfruitful.

Fourth, *Tópicos* contains three papers on the three publications of edifying discourses of 1843. Authored by Leticia Valadez, Teresa Aizpún, and Abrahim H. Khan, respectively, these articles consider the different Christian aspects of religious existence, but unfortunately they do not compare this conception of religious existence with that of *Fear and Trembling*, and neither do they deal with the notoriously different character of this sort of sermon literature compared to the rest of the publications of the same year.

The issue ends with an introduction by Leif Korsback to *The Concept of Irony* and its relationship to the pseudonymous works. This study stands out for its historical detail, although it only contains a superficial appreciation of the philosophical content of the work. It must also be added that the issue reproduces the opening and closing speeches to the symposium delivered by several public authorities in a ceremonial style. These speeches, however, have only documentary and historical value.

The structure of the monograph is generally organized and balanced, and it offers several excellent secondary sources for critical research on Kierkegaard's early authorship, as well as other more basic articles. In addition, the contents of the papers are notable for thorough and deep reflections based on a profound knowledge of Kierkegaard's thought and international secondary sources, avoiding many of the current clichés about Kierkegaard that are repeated uncritically in the Spanish reception. The monograph therefore successfully achieves its purposes and undoubtedly marks a turning point in hispanophone studies on Kierkegaard.

Some small shortcomings of the issue must nevertheless be mentioned. First, *Fear and Trembling* receives little attention compared to the other works since it is presented only through a poor panel discussion composed mostly of authorities from the Universidad Panamericana who do not specialize in Kierkegaard research.

Second, concerning *Either/Or*, the monograph is far too focused on the aesthetic part and lacks a detailed analysis of the ethical dimension developed in the second part. Although many of the different pieces of *Either/Or*, Part One are explained and exposited, Part Two is merely mentioned in some of the papers, without any serious explanation of the ethical way of life as Judge William develops it in his letters. Third, the monograph shows only partially the different perspectives on contemporary research about Kierkegaard, and favors the method of computational analysis with two long articles (McKinnon's and Khan's). Nevertheless, there is no contribution from other exegetical traditions, such as analytical philosophy, postmodernism, reception studies, or biographical studies. Finally, it must be remarked that Korsback's study is slightly out of place in a publication about the works of 1843, especially since it is situated after the other papers and not before, a fact that does not respect the chronological order of Kierkegaard's publications. Even if interesting and helpful, it seems that its relevance in such a monographic issue remains unclear.

Yet, despite its limitations, the monograph "Las publicaciones de Søren Kierkegaard de 1843" was and still is a very important work in the Spanish reception of Kierkegaard. Its papers demonstrate a quality akin to international research, and the contributions of foreign Kierkegaard scholars are decisive for adequately updating what has been called the "Kierkegaard Renaissance."

Juan Evaristo Valls Boix

Review and Critical Discussion

Perarnau Vidal, Dolores and Parcero Oubiña, Óscar, "Spain: The Old and New Kierkegaard. Reception in Spain," *Kierkegaard's International Reception*, Tome II, *Southern, Central and Eastern Europe*, ed. by Jon Stewart, Aldershot: Ashgate 2009 (*Kierkegaard Research: Sources, Reception and Resources*, vol. 8), pp. 17–80; see p. 49.

VI. Secondary Literature in Swedish

John Björkhem, *Sören Kierkegaard i psykologisk belysning* [Søren Kierkegaard Seen from a Psychological Perspective],

Uppsala: Nybloms Förlag 1942, 123 pp.

John Björkhem's short monograph *Sören Kierkegaard i psykologisk belysning* was published in 1942 by Nybloms Förlag. It was released in the same year that Björkhem, who at various points in his academic career wore the hats of priest, psychologist, and medical doctor, completed his doctoral dissertation in psychology at Lund University. As a Kierkegaard scholar, Björkhem paled in comparison to many of his Swedish academic contemporaries, but as a researcher in psychology he was able to contribute an interesting perspective on Kierkegaard that served as a welcome challenge to what was becoming the accepted psychological view of the intriguing Dane. Although Björkhem's book received a fair amount of attention in the years immediately following its publication, its reliance upon what are now seen to be antiquated psychological categories is one reason that it has not carried over well into contemporary Kierkegaard studies.

Before outlining the argument of the text, a brief word is in order concerning Björkhem's intellectual context. Nine years prior to the release of *Sören Kierkegaard i psykologisk belysning*, the renowned Danish psychologist Hjalmar Helweg had published the important monograph *Søren Kierkegaard. En psykiatrisk-psykologisk studie.*[1] In this study, Helweg offered a patho-graphical diagnosis of Kierkegaard based in part on what was then the fashionable physiological-psychological typology developed by the German psychologist Ernst Kretschmer,[2] arguing that Kierkegaard

---

Research for this project was made possible by generous support from the Smith Family Fellowship.

1 Hjalmar Helweg, *Søren Kierkegaard. En psykiatrisk-psykologisk studie*, Copenhagen: H. Hagerups Forlag 1933. In Swedish: *Sören Kierkegaard. En psykiatrisk-psykologisk studie*, trans. by Julia von Sneidern, Stockholm: Sveriges Kristna Studentrörelses Förlag 1933 (*Modern religionspsykologi*, vol. 7).

2 See Ernst Kretschmer, *Körperbau und Charakter. Untersuchungen zum Konstitutionsproblem und zur Lehre von den Temperamenten*, Berlin: Springer 1921 and *Geniale Menschen*, Berlin: Springer 1929.

ought to be understood as having suffered from a form of manic-depressive psychosis. Moreover, Helweg claimed that this biologically-based sickness could fully explain Kierkegaard's life-view and his authorship. Helweg's towering influence as well as the landmark nature of his study provided Björkhem with a clear target against which to direct his own argument. Although he ultimately rejected Helweg's position, Björkhem remained committed to Kretschmer's categories in the articulation of his own view.

The overall task Björkhem sets for himself is both critical and constructive in nature. Regarding the former, Björkhem accuses Helweg of misdiagnosing Kierkegaard, pointing out that he not only misinterprets the textual and biographical evidence, but also that he relies upon *ad hoc* postulations in order to square his reading. This critical argument is the focus of Chapter 3. Concerning the latter, Björkhem looks again to Kretschmer's account and argues that a proper characterization of Kierkegaard would be to place him within the schizothymic constitution (as opposed to the cyclothymic).[3] In this manner, Björkhem suggests that although Kierkegaard may certainly be considered a psychological outlier, we need not think of him as mentally sick. This constructive argument comprises Chapter 4.

The three remaining chapters are largely biographical and methodological in aim. In Chapter 1 Björkhem touches upon the complex development of Kierkegaard's personality in its Copenhagen context and in Chapter 4 he outlines Kierkegaard's family background, concluding from these chapters that neither Kierkegaard's reclusiveness nor his familial history proves that he suffered from mental sickness. For Chapter 2, Björkhem makes several methodological remarks intended to bolster his project. As he claims here, despite the challenge of offering a psychological analysis of a deceased individual who cannot be investigated in a clinical setting, focusing on Kierkegaard's writings, even if such material is necessarily incomplete, provides an adequate means for allowing Kierkegaard's personality, life, and work to "stand out in a clearer light."[4] Although the discussion in these three chapters is important for Björkhem's overall argument, it is clear that the critical and constructive chapters comprise the heart of the text. As such, we may briefly consider the content of these two in greater depth.

In critiquing Helweg, Björkhem argues two central points. First, Helweg makes an elementary mistake in misclassifying Kierkegaard's somatotype, and because of this mistake his diagnosis proves deeply problematic. For Kretschmer, each individual human body can be generally characterized as one of two types, either the asthenic/leptosomic type (weak and slender), which corresponds with the schizothymic constitution, or the pycnic type (stocky and rotund), which corresponds with the cyclothymic constitution. From these brief descriptions, it seems obvious that Kierkegaard would fall under the former physique, and even Helweg admits as much.[5] Yet, despite this, Helweg nevertheless arrives at the opposite conclusion,

---

3 Whereas the schizothymic constitution can be characterized, for example, by introversion and an emphasis on one's own thoughts, the cyclothymic constitution can be characterized by unstable mood swings.

4 John Björkhem, *Sören Kierkegaard i psykologisk belysning*, Upsala: Nybloms 1942, p. 18.

5 Ibid., p. 35.

which Björkhem understands to be the consequence of Helweg's presupposition that Kierkegaard was manic-depressive and therefore he *must* be identified as pycnic. To justify this reading, Helweg is thus forced to resort to "artificial means"[6] such as, for example, arguing that illness and Kierkegaard's delicate constitution may have been responsible for wiping out Kierkegaard's original pycnic traits.[7] In the end, argues Björkhem, Helweg's argument leads to a rather forced and inaccurate as well as "lifeless and schematic" picture of Kierkegaard.[8]

Second, Björkhem accuses Helweg of over-interpreting the written material with which he is working in order to make his theory appear more plausible. As Björkhem warns, one must be careful not to draw too grand and speculative of conclusions from Kierkegaard's form of expression in that it is oftentimes exaggerated so as to make a point or to bring attention to an idea. Furthermore, Kierkegaard's apparently psychotic comments (even those pertaining to suicide) need not be indicative of mental sickness, but rather we can understand them as displaying the full range of normal human emotions. In Björkhem's words, "A human being can experience both heaven and hell within herself without therefore being mentally sick."[9] Only if such emotional remarks were altogether *absent* from Kierkegaard's writings, suggests Björkhem, would we have good reason to call into question Kierkegaard's mental health.[10]

Given his identification of Kierkegaard with the asthenic/leptosomic body type, Björkhem therefore argues in favor of construing Kierkegaard's constitution as schizothymic. For Björkhem, one can find clear reasons in support of this view by simply tracing out Kierkegaard's life. Already in his early childhood Kierkegaard experienced the world more vividly through imagination and his thoughts than through externalities.[11] Later, throughout his school years Kierkegaard hid his real self and his melancholic nature from others, and in this fashion he set up a protective barrier around his inner life.[12] As an adult, Kierkegaard lived as a loner who was among people but yet remained as disconnected from them as possible.[13] It is precisely for this reason that Kierkegaard broke his engagement with Regine and fled to the security of his authorship and to the cover of his pseudonyms. In the act of writing, Kierkegaard was able to find within his own thought a unified meaning for the confusing and chaotic world around him, and this inward-looking task would accompany him to the end of his life. For Björkhem, all of these characteristics displayed by Kierkegaard point to the schizothymic constitution, and though

---

6 Ibid., p. 40.

7 Aage Henriksen, *Methods and Results of Kierkegaard Studies in Scandinavia: A Historical and Critical Survey*, Copenhagen: Ejnar Munksgaard 1951 (*Publications of the Kierkegaard Society*, vol. 1), p. 117.

8 Björkhem, *Sören Kierkegaard*, p. 40.

9 Ibid., pp. 47–8.

10 Ibid., p. 46.

11 Ibid., p. 72.

12 Ibid., pp. 77–8.

13 Ibid., p. 84.

Kierkegaard is certainly an extreme schizothyme due to his genius, we need not make him out to be, as does Helweg, a manic-depressive mentally sick genius.

In the first few years of its publication, *Sören Kierkegaard i psykologisk belysning* received a decent amount of attention in the press and in academic journals. Although a number of reviewers praised the work, it is likely that the interest in the text had little to do with the quality of Björkhem's exposition, but rather was a reflection of a long-standing fascination, and at times even an obsession among readers with the question of Kierkegaard's psychological profile. Regardless, despite its initial appeal Björkhem's text has had little lasting influence on Kierkegaard scholarship. With its narrow focus on Helweg's argument and its reliance upon the categories of Kretschmer that have since been discredited, the book comes across as rather antiquated. Moreover, it appears that Kierkegaard scholars of late have grown somewhat weary of psychological analyses of Kierkegaard's person. Thus, rather than attempting to resurrect Björkhem's argument for a contemporary audience, these same scholars are likely content simply to leave it to rest in peace in the tombs and the tomes of history.

Matthew T. Nowachek

Reviews and Critical Discussions

Alm, Ivar, review in *Svensk teologisk kvartalskrift*, vol. 18, no. 3, 1942, pp. 263–5.
Bergström, Carl Olof, "Människans konst: En översikt över Svensk litteraturforskning 1942," *Orbis Litterarum*, vol. 1, no. 1, 1943, pp. 208–28, especially pp. 218–20.
Brandt, Gustaf, review in *Religion och kultur*, vol. 13, no. 2, 1942, p. 110.
Dyssegaard, Poul, "Var Søren Kierkegaard sindssyg?" *Kristeligt Dagblad*, December 4, 1942.
Hejll, Richard, review in *Den enskilde: Tidskrift för de ensamma*, vol. 4, nos. 3–4, 1948, p. 108.
Henriksen, Aage, *Methods and Results of Kierkegaard Studies in Scandinavia: A Historical and Critical Survey*, Copenhagen: Ejnar Munksgaard 1951 (*Publications of the Kierkegaard Society, Copenhagen*, vol. 1), pp. 123–4.
Marc-Wogau, Konrad, review in *Nordisk tidskrift för vetenskap, konst och industri*, vol. 18, 1942 (*New Series*), p. 419.
Ostenfeld, Ib, review in *Nordisk medicin*, vol. 16, no. 40, 1942, p. 3023.
Sjöstrand, Lars, "Var Søren Kierkegaards tungsinne andligt eller psykiatriskt betingat?" *Läkartidningen*, vol. 104, no. 42, 2007, pp. 3131–3.

Torsten Bohlin,
Sören Kierkegaard. Drag ur hans levnad och personlighetsutveckling
[Sören Kierkegaard: His Life and Personality Development],

Stockholm: Svenska Kyrkans Diakonistyrelses Bokförlag 1918, 176 pp.

Torsten Bohlin's *Sören Kierkegaard. Drag ur hans levnad och personlighetsutveckling* was published shortly after his dissertation *Sören Kierkegaard's etiska åskådning* (Sören Kierkegaard's Ethical View) (1918). In a review in the national ecclesiastical press, *Svensk kyrkotidning*, the book was greeted as "a marvellous little book" (*en förträfflig liten bok*). It was also described as "popular in character" (*populärt hållen*) while at the same time "not shallow or simplifying" (*utan förkonstling eller förtunning*).[1] And indeed, the book is both popular and scholarly at the same time; it is written in an appealing, at times almost poetic, Swedish prose, but at the same time draws extensively on Kierkegaard's writings, containing, for example, an endnote apparatus comprising more than 450 references. The work was published in a German translation in 1925.[2]

The book is largely biographical although not exclusively so. Chapter 1 deals with Kierkegaard's family background, childhood, relation to his father, and student years. Chapter 2 narrates Kierkegaard's engagement to Regine Olsen and the painful breaking off of the engagement. Chapter 3 is the book's only non-biographical chapter and offers an analysis of Kierkegaard's ideas in his aesthetic-philosophical writings. Chapters 4 and 5 resume a predominately biographical character, and deal primarily with the *Corsair* affair of 1846 and with the final attack on the Danish State Church in 1854–55 respectively. Due to the largely biographical character of the book, one might regard it as the second major Swedish contribution to the study of Kierkegaard's life, following Waldemar Rudin's *Sören Kierkegaard's person och författarskap* (Sören Kierkegaard's Personality and Authorship) (1880).

A marked feature of Bohlin's study is its "psychological" approach. A central claim throughout chapters 1 and 2 is that Kierkegaard's literary output is

---

1 Fredrik Dahlbom, review in *Svensk kyrkotidning*, vol. 15, no. 3, 1919, p. 30.

2 Torsten Bohlin, *Sören Kierkegaards Leben und Werden. Kurze Darstellung auf Grund der ersten Quellen*, trans. by Peter Katz, Gütersloh: C. Bertelsmann 1925.

heavily influenced and conditioned by inner psychological events and experiences of his life leading up to and including the break up with Regine. In particular, Kierkegaard is said to have inherited from his father such things as a sharp intellect, a lively imagination, a strict religiosity, and above all "a bottomless melancholy" (*ett bottenlöst tungsinne*).[3] It is partly against the background of this melancholy that Kierkegaard's painful breaking off of the engagement to Regine is to be understood. This break up is in turn said to have occasioned "an almost superhuman creativity" (*nästan övermänskliga skaparekrafter*) which was a precondition of Kierkegaard's subsequent literary output.[4]

Chapters 4 and 5 take a similar psychological approach. With regard to the *Corsair* affair, it is maintained that the Danish church's lack of involvement in the feud deepened in Kierkegaard's mind a sense that true Christianity was not present in the established church or in official Christianity, which in turn was a sort of psychological precondition of the final onslaught on the Danish church in 1854–55.

Bohlin's psychological approach to Kierkegaard accords with a general psychologically oriented scholarship that was in vogue at the Theological Faculty of Uppsala University (where Bohlin did his research) during the first decades of the twentieth century. Bohlin's dissertation supervisor at Uppsala, Professor Einar Billing, had pioneered a Swedish Luther renaissance, and many Luther studies of the time took a strongly psychological approach to the Reformer.[5] In his book Bohlin does the same thing with regard to Kierkegaard. From the 1930s and onwards the psychological approach of the Uppsala theologians came under attack from theologians at Sweden's second theological faculty, in Lund, in particular from Professor Ragnar Bring.[6] One of Bring's pupils, Valter Lindström, emerged in the early 1940s as the second major Swedish Kierkegaard scholar (after Bohlin). Not surprisingly, one of Lindström's main criticisms of Bohlin's approach to Kierkegaard was its "psychological tendency" (*psykologiserande tendens*).[7] In view of this, it seems fair to describe Bohlin's book as rooted in a distinctively Uppsaliensian Swedish theological tradition.

In *Kierkegaard Studies in Scandinavia* (1951) Aage Henriksen observed that Bohlin's second Kierkegaard biography, that is, his *Sören Kierkegaard. Mannen och verket* (Søren Kierkegaard: The Man and His Work) from 1939, has "essentially the same disposition" as Copenhagen theologian Eduard Geismar's groundbreaking six-volume *Søren Kierkegaard. Hans livsudvikling og forfattervirksomhed* (Søren Kierkegaard: His Life Development and Authorship) (1926–28). First Kierkegaard's

3 Torsten Bohlin, *Sören Kierkegaard. Drag ur hans levnad och personlighetsutveckling*, Stockholm: Svenska kyrkans diakonistyrelses bokförlag 1918, p. 7.

4 Ibid., p. 51.

5 Cf. Ragnar Holte, *Luther och lutherbilden. En kritisk granskning*, Stockholm: Proprius förlag 1984, pp. 31–5. Björn Skogar goes so far as to describe Bohlin's work on Kierkegaard as a "defense of Uppsala theology"; see Björn Skogar, *Viva vox och den akademiska religionen*, Stockholm: Symposium Graduale 1993, p. 143.

6 Bohlin, *Sören Kierkegaard*, pp. 31–5.

7 Valter Lindström, "Torsten Bohlin: Sören Kierkegaard. Mannen och verket," *Svensk Teologisk Kvartalskrift*, vol. 17, 1941, p. 72.

life is narrated up to his break up with Regine in 1841, then Kierkegaard's ideas of the existential stages are surveyed, thereafter the biography is resumed through the *Corsair* affair, the Christian production of 1846–52, and finally the attack on the Danish State Church in 1854–55.[8] What Henriksen did not observe, however, is that the disposition of Bohlin's second Kierkegaard biography preserved the disposition of Bohlin's *first* Kierkegaard biography, which means that Geismar's disposition ultimately derives from the work under consideration here. This overlooked fact may provide some further evidence for Aage Kabell's claim in *Kierkegaardstudiet i Norden* (Kierkegaard Studies in the Northern Countries) (1948) that Geismar's seminal work is in effect a "continuation" (*Fortsættelse*) of Bohlin's work.[9] Herein, perhaps, lies the chief legacy of Bohlin's marvelous little book.

Anders Kraal

---

8 Aage Henriksen, *Kierkegaard Studies in Scandinavia: A Historical and Critical Survey*, Copenhagen: Ejnar Munksgaard 1951, p. 156.

9 Aage Kabell, *Kierkegaardstudiet i Norden*, Copenhagen: H. Hagerup 1948, p. 181. Geismar's high regard for Bohlin's work is also testified to by Geismar's claim in *Søren Kierkegaard. Hans livsudvikling og forfattervirksomhed*, vols. 1–6, Copenhagen: G.E.C. Gads forlag 1926–28 (vol. 3, p. 21), that Bohlin's *Kierkegaards dogmatiska åskådning* (1925) is "the first thorough investigation of Kierkegaard's basic ideas" (*den første omhyggelige Behandling af Kierkegaards Grundtanker*).

Reviews and Critical Discussions

Algård, Nils, "Andliga nutidsfrågor," *Svenska Dagbladet*, September 21, 1919, p. B2.

Henriksen, Aage, *Kierkegaard Studies in Scandinavia: A Historical and Critical Survey*, Copenhagen: Ejnar Munksgaard 1951 (*Publications of the Kierkegaard Society*, vol. 1), pp. 141–58.

Julén, J., "Sören Kierkegaard. En ny utkommen, intresseväckande levnadsteckning," *Svenska Morgonbladet*, December 24, 1918, p. 9.

Kabell, Aage, *Kierkegaardstudiet i Norden*, Copenhagen: H. Hagerup 1948, pp. 171–87.

Liedgren, Emil, review in *Vår lösen*, vol. 10, no. 5, 1919, pp. 77–8.

— "En svensk Kierkegaard," *Stockholms Dagblad*, June 3, 1919, p. A6.

Skogar, Björn, *Viva vox och den akademiska religionen*, Stockholm: Symposium Graduale 1993, pp. 136–44.

Warmuth, Kurt, review of the German translation in *Theologisches Literaturblatt*, vol. 47, no. 13, 1926, pp. 201–2.

Torsten Bohlin, *Sören Kierkegaards etiska åskådning. Med särskild hänsyn till begreppet "den enskilde"* [Søren Kierkegaard's Ethical View with Special Reference to the Concept of the Single Individual],

Stockholm: Svenska Kyrkans Diakonistyrelses Bokförlag 1918, vii + 314 pp.

Torsten Bohlin's *Sören Kierkegaards etiska åskådning* is his doctoral dissertation, defended at Uppsala University's Theological Faculty in May 1918. The work is the first in a long series of books and papers on Kierkegaard by Bohlin. It is also the first Swedish academic dissertation devoted entirely to Kierkegaard's thought, and the second more lengthy study of Kierkegaard produced by an Uppsala theologian, following Waldemar Rudin's *Sören Kierkegaard's person och författarskap* (Sören Kierkegaard's Personality and Authorship) from 1880.[1] To some extent Bohlin understands himself to be continuing a theological interpretation of Kierkegaard put forth by Rudin, where a particular emphasis is placed on Kierkegaard as a "Christian personality." Indeed, already in his Preface Bohlin singles out Rudin's book as "beyond comparison the best work on Kierkegaard as a Christian personality."[2] Bohlin sees himself as carrying on this approach.

Bohlin's dissertation consists of ten chapters. Chapter 1 surveys Kierkegaard's writings and discusses the relation between Kierkegaard and his pseudonyms. Chapter 2 situates Kierkegaard in his cultural-historical context, discussing, for example, his relation to Romanticism, Hegel, and the Danish State Church. Chapter 3 discusses Kierkegaard's relation to (Plato's) Socrates, and argues that Socrates is a very

---

1 Waldemar Rudin, *Sören Kierkegaard's person och författarskap. Ett Försök*, Uppsala: A Nielsen 1880.

2 Torsten Bohlin, *Sören Kierkegaards etiska åskådning. Med särskild hänsyn till begreppet "den enskilde,"* Stockholm: Svenska kyrkans diakonistyrelses bokförlag 1918, p. V: "*den utan jämförelse bästa, som finnes om Kierkegaard såsom kristen personlighet.*"

important influence on Kierkegaard's thought. Chapter 4 deals with Kierkegaard's literary method. Chapter 5 analyzes Kierkegaard's ideas about the existential stages, the "leap," and the question of the criterion by virtue of which different existential stages are differentiated from each other. Chapter 6 deals with irony and humor as intermediate stages between the existential stages. Chapters 7 and 8 discuss the aesthetic, ethical, and religious stages, and chapters 9 and 10 conclude with an analysis of the concept of "the single individual" (*den enskilde*) as a key concept in Kierkegaard's thought.

In presenting his theological interpretation of Kierkegaard, Bohlin engages in a critical discussion with a German book that advocates a conflicting interpretation, namely, Wilhelm Bauer's *Die Ethik Sören Kierkegaards* (1913).[3] Bohlin understands Bauer as advocating the view that Kierkegaard is concerned with developing an ethics of autonomy in the spirit of Immanuel Kant, but whose successive failures to develop such an ethics led him to incorporate certain religious elements in his ethics that did not really belong there, and which with some effort could be removed. Bohlin sets out to refute this interpretation, which he regards as fundamentally mistaken.

Bohlin's criticism of Bauer focuses on Bauer's views of Kierkegaard's ideas about the different existential stages. The main point of controversy concerns the question about how the existential stages are to be differentiated, that is, what the criterion is by virtue of which Kierkegaard classifies different stages into different categories. Bauer, as Bohlin understands him, understands Kierkegaard's criterion as deriving from a dynamic between the assumptions of the universality and the individuality of ethics. The dynamics between these opposing assumptions give rise to a dialectical tension out of which the different stage categories emerge.[4]

Bohlin regards Bauer's Kierkegaard interpretation as "peculiar" (*egendomlig*).[5] Kierkegaard's criterion, Bohlin says, has nothing to do with the two assumptions spoken of by Bauer, but derives instead from Kierkegaard's theological belief-system. Basic to this system is the valuation of a loving relationship to God as the goal of human existence, and the belief that God places an unconditional and infinite demand on human beings to love God and to annihilate human selfishness.[6] Due to human selfishness, God's unconditional and infinite demand cannot but lead to various sorts and degrees of human sufferings, however, and these different sorts and degrees of human sufferings in turn function as the criterion by virtue of which Kierkegaard classifies existential stages into different categories.[7] In the ultimate analysis the difference between the two Kierkegaard interpretations is, says Bohlin, that whereas Bauer takes Kierkegaard to be "a moral philosopher in Kant's vein, continuing Kant's work by striving to move from a legalistic to a personality-oriented complete ethical autonomy," Bohlin, by contrast, takes Kierkegaard to espouse a thoroughly

---

3 Wilhelm Bauer, *Die Ethik Sören Kierkegaards*, Jena: J. Beck 1913.

4 Bohlin, *Sören Kierkegaards etiska åskådning*, pp. 120–4.

5 Ibid., p. 120.

6 Ibid., pp. 119–20.

7 Ibid., pp. 113–19.

"religious ethics" where "an ever deepening relationship to God" functions as the ultimate and underlying criterion and norm.[8]

In spite of a deep appreciation of Kierkegaard, Bohlin did not consider all aspects of Kierkegaard's ethics to be genuinely religious or even Christian. On the contrary, Kierkegaard's ethics is regarded as including a line of thought that is more "metaphysical" than genuinely religious, and which is said to derive from (Plato's) "Socrates." This line of thought has as its main claim that there is "an absolute qualitative difference between God and human beings," a claim that reaches its peak in Kierkegaard's affirmation of the "absolute paradox" of Jesus Christ as both God and man.[9] This idea of an absolute qualitative difference between God and man is said by Bohlin to be rooted in the Platonic distinction between the "eternal" and the "temporal."[10] Kierkegaard's idea of "suffering" as a ground for distinguishing between different kinds of existential stages, is said by Bohlin to be rooted in this Platonic idea of an absolute qualitative difference between God and human beings.[11] On this point Bohlin criticizes Kierkegaard's thought as not genuinely religious and indeed in conflict with Christianity's "real content."[12]

In judging certain aspects of Kierkegaard's ethics as neither genuinely religious nor compatible with Christianity's real content, Bohlin is, of course, presupposing a specific understanding as to what constitutes genuine religion and real Christianity. What this specific understanding amounts to is never clearly articulated in Bohlin's dissertation, however. But one clearly senses that Bohlin sympathizes with German liberal theology, which, as is well-known, rejected "metaphysical" lines of thought as neither religious nor compatible with real Christianity. Some positive references to the eminent liberal theologian Wilhelm Herrmann in the footnotes reinforce this impression.[13]

Bohlin's negative evaluation of allegedly non-religious and non-Christian elements in Kierkegaard's thought did not initially cause much stir (perhaps because of the times),[14] but later on came under heavy criticism from the Swedish Kierkegaard scholar Valter Lindström, who criticized this aspect of Bohlin's evaluation as biased toward a particular theological idea as to what constitutes genuine religion and real Christianity.[15]

Anders Kraal

---

8 Ibid., p. 124.

9 Ibid., pp. 68–9.

10 Ibid..

11 Ibid., pp. 113–24.

12 Ibid., p. 68.

13 See, for example, ibid., p. 109 note 1; p. 111 note 1; p. 284 note 1.

14 F. Dahlbom, review in *Svensk kyrkotidning*, vol. 14, no. 37, 1918, p. 439.

15 See Valter Lindström, "Torsten Bohlin: Sören Kierkegaard. Mannen och verket. 322 sid. Svenska kyrkans diakonistyrelses bokförlag, Stockholm (tr. i Uppsala) 1939. Pris kr. 7:50, inb. Kr. 9:50," *Svensk Teologisk Kvartalskrift*, vol. 17, 1941, p. 71; *Stadiernas teologi. En Kierkegaardstudie*, Lund: C.W.K. Gleerup 1943, pp. 10–11; and *Efterföljelsens teologi hos Sören Kierkegaard*, Stockholm: Svenska kyrkans diakonistyrelses bokförlag 1956, p. 44. For an overview of the Bohlin–Lindström debate, see Aage Henriksen: *Kierkegaard Studies in Scandinavia: A Historical and Critical Survey*, Copenhagen: Ejnar Munksgaard 1951, pp. 141–58.

Reviews and Critical Discussions

Dahlbom, F., review in *Svensk kyrkotidning*, vol. 14, no. 37, 1918, p. 439.
Harris, Edward, *Man's Ontological Predicament: A Detailed Analysis of Søren Kierkegaard's Concept of Sin with Special Reference to "The Concept of Dread,"* Uppsala: Almqvist & Wiksell International 1984, pp. 102–3.
Hedqvist, V., review in *Sydsvenska Dagbladet*, August 29, 1918.
Henriksen, Aage, *Kierkegaard Studies in Scandinavia: A Historical and Critical Survey*, Copenhagen: Ejnar Munksgaard 1951 (*Publications of the Kierkegaard Society*, vol. 1), pp. 141–58.
Kabell, Aage, *Kierkegaardstudiet i Norden*, Copenhagen: H. Hagerup 1948, pp. 171–87.
Liedgren, Emil, review in *Vår lösen*, vol. 10, no. 5, pp. 77–8.
Lindström, Valter, *Stadiernas teologi. En Kierkegaardstudie*, Lund: C.W.K. Gleerup 1943, pp. 10–11.
— *Efterföljelsens teologi hos Sören Kierkegaard*, Stockholm: Svenska Kyrkans Diakonistyrelses Bokförlag 1956, pp. 13–14; pp. 42–4; pp. 73–4; pp. 77–9; p. 231; pp. 299–300.
L.-I., E., "En bok om Kierkegaard," *Aftonbladet*, October 3, 1919, p. 10.
Ording, Hans, review in *Norsk Teologisk Tidsskrift*, vol. 28, no. 1, 1927, pp. 78–80.
Tiedje, T., review in *Theologische Literaturzeitung*, vol. 47, no. 14, 1922, pp. 329–31.

Torsten Bohlin, *Sören Kierkegaard och nutida religiöst tänkande* [Kierkegaard and Contemporary Religious Thought],

Stockholm: Svenska Kyrkans Diakonistyrelses Bokförlag 1919, 131 pp.

In *Sören Kierkegaard och nutida religiöst tänkande*, Torsten Bohlin discusses two main themes from Kierkegaard and evaluates these themes from the point of view of what he terms "contemporary religious thought" (*nutida religiöst tänkande*). Bohlin uses the phrase "contemporary religious thought" in a predominantly positive sense; his assumption is for the most part that contemporary religious thought is a good thing and that Kierkegaard's thought, to the extent that it is incompatible with contemporary religious thought, is *ipso facto* problematic. As major representatives of contemporary religious thought, Bohlin takes such figures as the German liberal theologian Wilhelm Herrmann and the Swedish Uppsala-theologian Nathan Söderblom (who was himself strongly influenced by German liberal theology). This work was translated into German by an anonymous translator and published in 1923.[1]

The two themes from Kierkegaard that Bohlin brings into relation to contemporary religious thought are Kierkegaard's ideas on truth and subjectivity (for example, the idea that truth is subjectivity), and Kierkegaard's idea of the paradoxical and of Christianity as the "absolute paradox."

With regard to Kierkegaard's ideas on truth and subjectivity, Bohlin devotes much of his discussion to the question of the relation between what are termed the "how" and the "what" of faith. The "how" of faith is the way in which one believes or has faith; the "what" of faith is the content of religion, that is, what one believes or has faith in. Bohlin argues that Kierkegaard's thinking harmonizes with contemporary religious thought in that it lays the stress on the mode of believing rather than on the content of faith. However, Bohlin also draws attention to some points of discrepancy. One such point pertains to the content of faith, where it is said that Kierkegaard did not really think that the mode of believing was *more important* than the content of faith. Rather, Kierkegaard is said to have stressed the mode of believing over against the content of belief not because the mode is as such more important,

---

1 Torsten Bohlin, *Sören Kierkegaard und das religiöse Denken der Gegenwart. Eine Studie*, Munich and Leipzig: Rösl & Cie 1923 (*Philosophische Reihe*, vol. 78).

but because Kierkegaard believed that in his age, where Hegelianism and philosophical speculation held such sway, this was particularly needed. Kierkegaard's stress on the mode of believing over against the content of faith was thus not an integral or essential part of Kierkegaard's thought, but was the outcome of a specific and context dependent application of his thought. Bohlin takes this to contrast with modern religious thought, which in a much deeper sense perceives that the mode of believing is more essential and important in religion than the content of belief.[2]

With regard to Kierkegaard's doctrine of the paradoxical, Bohlin argues that Kierkegaard's idea of Christianity as the absolute paradox is very problematic from the point of view of modern religious thought. Christianity is taken by Kierkegaard to be the absolute paradox inasmuch as it requires belief in the doctrine that Jesus Christ is both God and man. But here—Bohlin notes—Kierkegaard is taking the Athanasian dogma of the two natures of Christ to be essential to Christianity. Modern religious thought, however, is taken to have arrived at the conclusion that this dogma is not only inessential to Christianity, but that it did not even originate from Christianity; it entered Christianity under the influence of Platonic, metaphysical speculation. A Christian or evangelical-Lutheran view of Christ sees the "ethical-religious meaning of his life and work" (*den etiskt-religiösa innebörden av hans liv och gärning*) as the essential and important thing, not the "theoretical-metaphysical identity of Christ's being."[3] Bohlin makes a similar point with regard to the role that the concept of human sinfulness plays in Kierkegaard's doctrine of the paradoxical. Kierkegaard's concept of sin, says Bohlin, coincides with the Augustinian doctrine of the total corruption of human nature.[4] This doctrine is likewise taken to be at odds with contemporary religious thought, which takes a much more positive view of human nature. In view of these presuppositions of Kierkegaard's doctrine of the paradoxical, Bohlin concludes his study by asserting that "Kierkegaard's doctrine of the paradoxical belongs to the past. It does not belong to evangelical Christianity either" (*Kierkegaards paradoxlära tillhör det förflutna. Den tillhör icke heller den evangeliska kristendomen*).[5] Although Kierkegaard is believed to have had the truth of Christianity "in his heart" (*i sitt hjärta*), on an intellectual level he is said to have been "far" (*långt borta*) from "an evangelical understanding of Christianity" (*en evangelisk uppfattning av kristendomen*).[6]

Bohlin's above conclusion has provoked criticism from Kierkegaard scholars more sympathetic to Kierkegaard's theological presuppositions. In his "Editor's Introduction" to Eduard Geismar's *Lectures on the Religious Thought of Sören Kierkegaard* (1937), David F. Swenson defends Kierkegaard's doctrine of the paradoxical over against Bohlin's criticisms by posing a dilemma for Bohlin: can he—sc. Bohlin—"understand how God can forgive *his* sins. If he answers 'yes,' he comes

[2] Torsten Bohlin, *Sören Kierkegaard och nutida religiöst tänkande*, Stockholm: Svenska kyrkans diakonistyrelses bokförlag 1919, pp. 31–4; pp. 59–62.

[3] Ibid., pp. 94–5.

[4] Ibid., p. 80.

[5] Ibid., p. 130.

[6] Ibid., p. 130.

into sharp conflict with the entire spirit and purport of the personally assimilated religion which was so characteristic of Luther....And if he answers 'no,' he has *ipso facto* established the paradoxical as a category with respect to the central theme of Christianity."[7] In other words, either Bohlin must reject his Lutheran Christian belief in God's power to forgive his sins (which he ought to regard as paradoxical), or else follow Kierkegaard in accepting the paradoxical nature of Christianity. Aage Kabell objects in *Kierkegaardstudiet i Norden* (Kierkegaard Studies in the Nordic Countries) (1948) that Bohlin "is not entitled" (*er ikke i sin Ret*) to conclude that Kierkegaard's doctrine of the paradoxical belongs to the past and is no part of evangelical Christianity, for "[t]his claim is not only stylistically repulsive, but disregards the element of paradox in evangelical Christianity" (*[d]enne Ytring er ikke blot stilistisk forkastelig, men den underkender ganske det Moment af Paradoks, der visseligen er i evangelisk Kristendom*).[8] In making these objections Swenson and Kabell seem to understand the term "evangelical Christianity" in a different sense than Bohlin, however. They seem to be taking the term in a doctrinal and historical sense, as denoting the body of doctrines endorsed by Luther and the historical Lutheran church. Bohlin, however, seems to understand the term in a more systematic theological and normative sense, as denoting modern religious thought as represented, for example, by Wilhelm Herrmann and Nathan Söderblom.

Anders Kraal

7 David F. Swenson, "Editor's Introduction," in Eduard Geismar, *Lectures on the Religious Thought of Sören Kierkegaard*, ed. by David F. Swenson, Minneapolis: Augsburg Publishing House 1937, p. xxvii.

8 Aage Kabell, *Kierkegaardstudiet i Norden*, Copenhagen: H. Hagerup 1948, p. 178.

Reviews and Critical Discussions

Kabell, Aage, *Kierkegaardstudiet i Norden*, Copenhagen: H. Hagerup 1948, pp. 171–87.
Lindfelt, Mikael, *Teologi och kristen humanism. Ett perspektiv på Torsten Bohlins teologiska tänkande*, Åbo: Åbo Akademis förlag 1996, pp. 81–6.
Montan, E., review in *Vår lösen*, vol. 11, nos. 15–16, 1920, p. 228.
Stenström, Thure, *Existentialismen i Sverige. Mottagande och inflytande 1900–1950*, Stockholm: Almqvist & Wiksell 1984, pp. 58–61.
Swenson, David F., "Editor's Introduction," in Eduard Geismar, *Lectures on the Religious Thought of Sören Kierkegaard*, ed. by David F. Swenson, Minneapolis: Augsburg Publishing House 1937, pp. xxvi–xxix.
Thorbjørnsen, Svein Olaf, *Autonomi, teonomi og heteronomi: En analyse av Torsten Bohlins teologiske etikk med vekt på den etiske autonomis betingelser*, Oslo: Det teologiske Menighetsfakultet 1999, pp. 118–23, pp. 164–73.

Torsten Bohlin,
Kierkegaards dogmatiska åskådning i dess historiska sammanhang
[Kierkegaard's Dogmatic View in its Historical Context],

Stockholm: Svenska Kyrkans Diakonistyrelses Bokförlag 1925, 494 pp.

Torsten Bohlin's landmark study *Kierkegaards dogmatiska åskådning i dess historiska sammanhang* was published in Swedish in 1925 with a German translation appearing shortly thereafter in 1927.[1] Although Bohlin produced several other works on Kierkegaard in the initial years following the 1918 publication of his docent thesis as well as during his tenure as bishop over the diocese of Härnösand, this book on Kierkegaard's dogmatic view undoubtedly represents a high point both in Bohlin's Kierkegaard research and in his academic career in general.[2] As the most careful and detailed study of its kind in a time when few academics in Sweden were writing on the Danish thinker, *Kierkegaards dogmatiska åskådning* helped to set the agenda for an entire generation of Swedish Kierkegaard interpretation. Despite its initial impact, however, the text has seen its influence wane over the years due in large part to various criticisms that have been leveled against it.

As Bohlin notes in the Introduction, although Kierkegaard takes upon himself the practical and ethical task of illuminating the individual's relation to Christianity in response to the existentially impotent theology of Christendom, he never entirely abandons orthodoxy. Rather, in articulating his specific account of Christian existence Kierkegaard develops a dogmatic view broadly based on the central Lutheran notions of sin and faith. It is upon this view that Bohlin focuses in his monograph,

Research for this project was made possible by generous support from the Smith Family Fellowship.

[1] Torsten Bohlin, *Kierkegaards dogmatiska åskådning i dess historiska sammanhang*, Svenska Kyrkans Diakonistyrelses Bokförlag 1925; German translation: *Kierkegaards dogmatische Anschauung in ihrem geschichtlichen Zusammenhange*, trans. by Ilse Meyer-Lüne, Gütersloh: C. Bertelsmann 1927.

[2] In addition to his employment as professor in systematic theology at Åbo Akademi from 1925 to 1930, Bohlin taught dogmatics and moral theology at Uppsala University during the years 1929–34 with a short stint at the University of Jena in 1932, after which he served as a bishop in the Swedish Church from 1935 until his death in 1950.

arguing that at the heart of Kierkegaard's theology one encounters a fundamental dualism that calls into question the coherence of the Kierkegaardian position. More specifically, Kierkegaard's account is comprised of two diverging lines, the line of religious experience and the line of paradox.[3] Kierkegaard's presentation of Christianity through the lens of the former, however, is ultimately undermined by his reliance upon the metaphysical and intellectualist categories he inherits from the Hegelian speculative tradition in his attack upon that same tradition. In the end, then, it is such anti-intellectualist intellectualism that prevents Kierkegaard from fully embracing Luther's own rich account of Christianity.

To develop this argument Bohlin divides his work into eight chapters. Following the Introduction in which he presents a general account of Kierkegaard's dogmatic view, Bohlin dedicates Chapters 2 and 3 to discussing the concept of sin through a comparison of the psychological works *The Concept of Anxiety* and *The Sickness unto Death*, on the one hand, and the philosophical works *Philosophical Fragments* and the *Concluding Unscientific Postscript*, on the other hand. For Chapters 4–5 Bohlin turns to the concept of faith and explores topics such as the psychological structure of faith as well as the manner by which faith is shaped through the believer's relation to Christ as the paradoxical object of faith and through contemporaneity with Christ as prototype and redeemer. In the three remaining chapters, Bohlin clarifies the various aspects of Kierkegaard's view of God, discusses both revelation and history in the Hegelian philosophy of religion as well as the influence this has upon Kierkegaard, and finally compares Kierkegaard's dogmatic view to that of Luther. Because the concepts of sin and faith play such a central role in Bohlin's argument, we touch upon each in turn.

On Bohlin's reading, Kierkegaard develops two accounts of sin in his writings that are at deep variance with one another. On the one hand, in his psychological works Kierkegaard writes of sin largely from the position of his own concrete religious experience as a phenomenon that is "voluntaristically determined."[4] Moreover, he describes sin in a dual sense as both "a perversion of the human will in relation to God" and "a mastering power over all of humanity,"[5] and he argues that overcoming such sin requires that one become conscious of it through revelation and thereby flee to Christ as the savior who meets the sinner with grace.[6] On the other hand, in his philosophical works Kierkegaard describes sin as "intellectualistically determined" in the sense that it emerges not from religious experience but rather as a consequence of the teaching about Christ as the absolute paradox.[7] In this respect, overcoming such sin requires an abandonment of one's understanding in order to leap into absurdity where one can be radically transformed by God into a new creation.

With respect to Kierkegaard's understanding of faith, Bohlin likewise sees a deeply-rooted duplicity at play that parallels the duplicity uncovered in the concept

---

3 Bohlin, *Kierkegaards dogmatiska åskådning*, p. 217.
4 Ibid., p. 218.
5 Ibid., p. 198.
6 Ibid., p. 63; pp. 217–18.
7 Ibid., pp. 218–19.

of sin. As Bohlin argues, an analysis of the principal determinations of faith in Kierkegaard reveals that there are "two different expressions that are fundamentally opposed to one another, of which one is theocentric and the other is in a specific sense Christocentrically determined."[8] The theocentric expression of faith extends from Kierkegaard's religious experience of a personal God in which faith is construed as a relationship to the divine characterized by "life-communion" (*livsgemenskap*) and "unity of will" (*viljeenhet*) with God.[9] In contrast, the Christocentric expression of faith operates fundamentally as a response to Kierkegaard's speculative theological context and is based upon Christ as the absolute paradox that challenges the pantheism of the speculative tradition by asserting the radical qualitative difference between God and humanity.[10] What this means for Bohlin is that such faith is not merely informed by paradox, but rather it can be seen as paradoxical at its very essence.[11] As with Kierkegaard's notion of sin, Bohlin finds it difficult, in the end, to reconcile in a coherent fashion such divergent accounts of faith.

For Bohlin, the dualisms and contradictions at the core of Kierkegaard's dogmatic view can ultimately be traced back to the Danish thinker's ambivalent relation to the Hegelian philosophy of religion. Although Kierkegaard appeals to paradox in order to attack Hegel for his account of revelation and history as well as for undermining the qualitative difference between God and human beings, he nevertheless does so not by rejecting the Hegelian metaphysical and intellectualist categories,[12] but rather by retaining these categories and pushing them to their extreme. As Bohlin argues, this move entails that "regardless of how forcefully Kierkegaard asserts Christianity's irrational character in contrast to Hegel's understanding of religion, his irrationalism nevertheless still contains a pronounced intellectualistic element."[13] To conclude, Bohlin suggests that the end result of Kierkegaard harboring such an intellectualist strain is that he is held back from wholly embracing the rich and personal content of Luther's Reformation faith with its robust emphasis on spiritual freedom, grace, hope, peace, and joy.[14]

With respect to reception, *Kierkegaards dogmatiska åskådning* initially garnered a good deal of praise from Bohlin's academic contemporaries. For example, the Danish Kierkegaard scholar Eduard Geismar reportedly described the book in amiable terms as the first careful and detailed work on Kierkegaard's theology.[15] In addition, Lund professor Edvard Lehmann evaluated the work as groundbreaking, going so far as to claim that "all future research must either lean upon it or take a

8 Ibid., pp. 254–5.

9 Ibid., pp. 240–9.

10 See, for example, ibid., pp. 435–6.

11 Ibid., p. 258.

12 For example, dualities such as temporal/eternal, finite/infinite, and nature/spirit.

13 Bohlin, *Kierkegaards dogmatiska åskådning*, p. 435.

14 Ibid., p. 479; p. 486; p. 487.

15 See Sigfrid von Engeström, "Det teologiska författarskapet," in *Torsten Bohlin: En minnes- och vänbok*, ed. by Gert Borgenstierna, Nils Karlström, and Gustaf Risberg, Stockholm: Svenska Kyrkans Diakonistyrelses Bokförlag 1950, p. 66.

stance in relation to it."[16] Lehmann's prediction proved prescient regarding the decades immediately following publication of Bohlin's work, for in these years several notable scholars including Valter Lindström and Per Lønning felt it necessary in their own projects to acknowledge and address Bohlin's argument.[17] More recent researchers have unfortunately not afforded Bohlin as careful of consideration, with many of them quite content merely to dismiss Bohlin's account as outdated, simplistic, or undialectical.

When all is said and done, one gets the impression that although recent interpreters are warranted in their broad critiques, they have nevertheless moved too quickly in brushing aside Bohlin's work. With nearly 500 pages of dense Kierkegaard exposition this voluminous text contains innumerable buried gems that can still be of immense value for Kierkegaard research—that is, of course, so long as readers have the will and determination to continue to dig for them.

Matthew T. Nowachek

16 Edvard Lehmann, review in *Svensk teologisk kvartalskrift*, vol. 1, no. 4, 1925, p. 400.

17 See, for example, Valter Lindström, *Stadiernas teologi. En Kierkegaardstudie*, Lund: Gleerup 1943; Per Lønning, *"Samtidighedens situation". En studie i Søren Kierkegaards kristendomsforståelse*, Oslo: Forlaget Land og Kirke 1954.

Reviews and Critical Discussions

Aalders, W.J., review of the German translation in *Nieuwe Theologische Studies*, no. 10, 1927, pp. 313–14.
Bejerholm, Lars, "Bohlin," in *The Legacy and Interpretation of Kierkegaard*, ed. by Niels Thulstrup and Marie Mikulová Thulstrup, Copenhagen: C.A. Reitzel 1981 (*Bibliotheca Kierkegaardiana*, vol. 8), pp. 222–3.
von Engström, Sigfrid, "Det teologiska författarskapet," in *Torsten Bohlin: En minnes- och vänbok*, ed. by Gert Borgenstierna, Nils Karlström, and Gustaf Risberg, Stockholm: Svenska Kyrkans Diakonistyrelses Bokförlag 1950, pp. 61–86.
Geismar, Eduard, review in *Theologische Literaturzeitung*, vol. 51, no. 14, 1926, pp. 374–5.
Henriksen, Aage, *Methods and Results of Kierkegaard Studies in Scandinavia: A Historical and Critical Survey*, Copenhagen: Ejnar Munksgaard 1951 (*Publications of the Kierkegaard Society, Copenhagen*, vol. 1), pp. 141–6.
Lehmann, Edvard, review in *Svensk teologisk kvartalskrift*, vol. 1, no. 4, 1925, pp. 396–401.
— "En svensk bog om Søren Kierkegaard," in *Gads danske Magasin*, vol. 20, 1926, pp. 117–22.
Liedgren, Emil, "Torsten Bohlins senaste Kierkegaardsbok," *Vår lösen*, vol. 16, no. 12, 1925, pp. 277–8.
Ording, Hans, review in *Norsk teologisk tidsskrift*, vol. 28, no. 1, 1927, pp. 78–80.
Rodemann, W., review in *Kirchliche Zeitschrift*, vol. 50, 1926, pp. 799–805.
Rodhe, Edvard, "En blick på de trenne sista decenniernas svenska teologi," *Svensk teologisk kvartalskrift*, vol. 3, no. 4, 1927, pp. 305–35, especially pp. 327–8.
Sandelin, Kalle, review in *Finsk tidskrift*, no. 1, 1926, pp. 124–33.

Torsten Bohlin,
Sören Kierkegaard. Mannen och verket [Sören Kierkegaard: The Man and His Work],

Stockholm: Svenska Kyrkans Diakonistyrelses Bokförlag 1939, 322 pp.

Torsten Bohlin's *Sören Kierkegaard. Mannen och verket* is an updated version of his first Kierkegaard biography, *Sören Kierkegaard. Drag ur hans levnad och personlighetsutveckling* (Sören Kierkegaard: Life and Personality Development) (1918). Bohlin's first biography begins by narrating Kierkegaard's life up to his break up with Regine in 1841, then surveys Kierkegaard's ideas of the existential stages, thereafter resumes the biographical narrative through the *Corsair* affair, the Christian production of 1846–52, and finally the attack on the Danish State Church in 1854–55. Bohlin's second Kierkegaard biography preserves this same basic structure, but amplifies the account with about 120 pages of new material. Some of this new material draws on Kierkegaard research published in the intervening 21 years, whereas some of it consists more or less of restatements of analyses of Kierkegaard's thought published in Bohlin's previous books apart from his first Kierkegaard biography. The comprehensive endnote system of Bohlin's first Kierkegaard biography has been dropped in the second biography, and a few pages of recommended Kierkegaard studies are added in its place.

Bohlin's first Kierkegaard biography took a strongly psychological approach to Kierkegaard's life and work; Kierkegaard's literary output, for example, is to a large extent seen as impacted by a deep melancholy which Kierkegaard is said to have inherited from his father. The second Kierkegaard biography, under consideration here, expands on this theme, for example by discussing Danish psychologist Hjalmar Helweg's claim in *Sören Kierkegaard. En psykiatrisk-psykologisk studie* (Sören Kierkegaard: A Psychiatric-Psychological Study) (Swedish edition from 1933) that Kierkegaard suffered from manic depression. Bohlin considers this claim "very likely" (*[m]ycket möjligt*).[1] He notes, however, that Kierkegaard's manic depression never gained "the upper hand" (*herraväldet*) over his life, but was instead subjugated by Kierkegaard and used as a constructive force in his writing and thinking.[2] He also insists that the judgment that Kierkegaard suffered

---

1 Torsten Bohlin, *Sören Kierkegaard. Mannen och* verket, Stockholm: Svenska kyrkans diakonistyrelses bokförlag 1939, p. 264.

2 Ibid., pp. 264–5.

from manic depression is not a normative judgment, and that it in no way implies that Kierkegaard's thought lacks quality or value.[3]

Bohlin's first Kierkegaard biography did not contain much by way of critical analysis of Kierkegaard's thought, although this can be found in other books by Bohlin from roughly the same time, for example, *Sören Kierkegaard och nutida religiöst tänkande* (Kierkegaard and Contemporary Religious Thought) (1919) and *Kierkegaards dogmatiska åskådning i dess historiska sammanhang* (Kierkegaard's Dogmatic View in its Historical Context) (1924). In his second Kierkegaard biography Bohlin included some of these earlier critical analyses. For example, his earlier critical claim that Kierkegaard's thought includes, in addition to a genuinely religious and Christian line of thought, also a speculative and metaphysical line of thought at odds with genuine religion and Christianity, was brought up for renewed discussion and was again considered correct. This line of thought was taken to culminate in the idea of "an absolute distinction between time and eternity, between God and man" (*en absolut motsättning mellan tid och evighet, mellan människa och Gud*).[4] Bohlin once again judges this absolute distinction to run counter to genuine religious and/or Christian experience. Some references to popular theologians influenced by Kierkegaard are also found in the biography. Foremost among these is Karl Barth. Barth's theology is said to be heavily influenced by Kierkegaard's idea of an absolute qualitative difference between God and man—an idea Bohlin had objected to in various previous publications as a non-religious and non-Christian element in Kierkegaard's thought. Bohlin criticizes Barth's Kierkegaard interpretation as one-sided, saying that it draws on the "abstract metaphysical" (*abstrakt metafysiskt*) elements in Kierkegaard's thought but neglects Kierkegaard's "purely religious foundation" (*rent religiös[a] grundsyn*).[5]

Upon publication Bohlin's book was reviewed both positively and negatively. In a review by Ruben Josefsson in the national ecclesiastical press, *Svensk kyrkotidning*, Bohlin is commended for having shown that certain "metaphysically oriented" (*metafysiskt orienterade*) aspects of Kierkegaard's thought are "incompatible with a clearly evangelical point of view" (*icke kunna förenas med en klart evangelisk grundsyn*) and hence should be "protested" (*nedlägga protest*) against.[6] Here Kierkegaard's idea of an absolute qualitative difference between God and human beings is mentioned, which is taken to conflict with an evangelical understanding of God as "the God of mankind" (*människans Gud*) and of mankind as "God's mankind" (*Guds människa*).[7] In view of this Bohlin is taken to have shown that "neither his [sc. Kierkegaard's] life nor his doctrine can be used as a model to emulate" (*kan hans liv lika litet som hans lära användas som en förebild att efterlikna*).[8]

3 Ibid., p. 265.

4 Ibid., p. 292.

5 Ibid., p. 293.

6 Ruben Josefsson, "Kierkegaards aktualitet," *Svensk kyrkotidning*, vol. 37, no. 22, 1940, p. 337.

7 Ibid., p. 337.

8 Ibid.

A much more negative review, by Valter Lindström, was published in Sweden's main theological journal *Svensk Teologisk Kvartalskrift*. Like Josefsson, Lindström's review was mostly concerned with Bohlin's negative assessment of certain aspects of Kierkegaard's thought, and in particular the idea of an absolute qualitative difference between God and mankind. Lindström objects to Bohlin's assumption that there is some sort of opposition between a "metaphysical" and a "religious" way of thinking: "a metaphysical way of thinking typically expresses a religious experience, for which reason the opposition between a religious viewpoint and an abstract metaphysical tendency is highly disputable" (*ett metafysiskt tänkande i regel ger uttryck åt en religiös erfarenhet, varför själva motsättningen mellan en rent religiös syn och en abstrakt metafysisk tendens blir synnerligen diskutabel*).[9] In making this point, it is clear that Lindström is presupposing a very different understanding of what genuine religion is than what is presupposed by Bohlin. For Lindström, genuine religion can comprise metaphysical elements, whereas for Bohlin religion (or at least "pure" religion) cannot comprise such elements.

In spite of the sort of criticism put forth by Lindström, Bohlin's second Kierkegaard biography was by and large well received, and by 1951 we find Aage Henriksen reporting that "Bohlin's sober and compactly written book has become the one recommended to an academic reader as an introduction to Søren Kierkegaard: it is also firm and authoritative as a textbook."[10]

Anders Kraal

9 Valter Lindström, review in *Svensk Teologisk Kvartalskrift*, vol. 17, 1941, p. 71.

10 Aage Henriksen, *Kierkegaard Studies in Scandinavia: A Historical and Critical Survey*, Copenhagen: Ejnar Munksgaard 1951, p. 156.

Reviews and Critical Discussions

Hejll, Richard, review in *Den enskilde: Tidskrift för de ensamma*, vol. 4, nos. 3–4, 1948, pp. 106–7.

Henriksen, Aage, *Kierkegaard Studies in Scandinavia: A Historical and Critical Survey*, Copenhagen: Ejnar Munksgaard 1951, p. 156.

Hultgren, Gunnar, review in *Vår lösen*, vol. 31, no. 8, 1940, p. 317.

Isakson, Karl-Gustaf, review in *Frikyrklig ungdom*, no. 4, 1940, pp. 58–9.

Josefsson, Ruben, "Kierkegaards aktualitet," *Svensk kyrkotidning*, vol. 37, no. 22, 1940, p. 337.

— review in *Årsbok för kristen humanism*, vol. 2, 1940, pp. 89–90.

Lindström, Valter, review in *Svensk Teologisk Kvartalskrift*, vol. 17, no. 1, 1941, pp. 69–73.

Plum, N.M., review in *Kristeligt Dagblad*, February 13, 1940.

Sorainen, Kalle, "Introduktion till Kierkegaard," *Nya Argus*, vol. 33, no. 13, 1940, p. 128.

Zetterberg, Åke, "Kierkegaard, aktuell kristendomstolkare," *Folklig kultur*, vol. 5, no. 2, 1940, pp. 62–5.

Torsten Bohlin, *Kierkegaards tro och andra Kierkegaardstudier* [Kierkegaard's Faith and Other Kierkegaard Studies],

Stockholm: Svenska Kyrkans Diakonistyrelses Bokförlag 1944, 219 pp.

Kierkegaards tro och andra Kierkegaardstudier, published in 1944, was the final monograph on Kierkegaard written by priest and liberal theologian Torsten Bohlin prior to his death in 1950. As Bohlin points out in the opening paragraph, this work represents the fruits of more than a quarter-century of engagement with the Danish thinker extending back to the publication of his first book on Kierkegaard in 1918 and including the release of five additional monographs on various aspects of Kierkegaard's thought. Though few scholars in Sweden were writing on Kierkegaard when Bohlin began his research, the subsequent years witnessed a burgeoning of interest in the Dane with important Swedish academics such as Valter Lindström making a significant contribution to Kierkegaard scholarship. As such, Bohlin's text not only serves as something of a summary of his most important views on Kierkegaard, but it is also an attempt to engage in a critical fashion with a growing body of Swedish secondary literature.

Although Bohlin acknowledges with a deep sense of gratitude that his thought has been significantly enriched by his career-long study of Kierkegaard, he makes it clear in the Preface that in this work he assumes a critical stance. As he writes, "One can never follow [Kierkegaard] without reservation," for once one digs down into his thought one is met by a "misrepresentation of Christian faith and Christian ethos" that must be exposed.[1] Armed with this hermeneutic of suspicion, Bohlin proceeds to analyze several important themes in Kierkegaard's religious thought including the nature of faith, the nature of God, and the nature of Christian community, in relation to which he argues Kierkegaard's view is unsatisfactory not only in that it is shot through with inconsistencies, but also in that it affords inadequate attention to the God relationship, to human communion, and to religious experience.[2] In developing

Research for this project was made possible by generous support from the Smith Family Fellowship.

1 Torsten Bohlin, *Kierkegaards tro och andra Kierkegaardstudier*, Stockholm: Svenska Kyrkans Diakonistyrelses Bokförlag 1944, p. 6.

2 These critical points suggest the significant extent to which Bohlin was influenced by theological liberalism and particularly the thought of Friedrich Schleiermacher.

this argument, Bohlin undertakes five distinct studies in five chapters, to which we may now turn.

For the first two chapters, Bohlin covers Kierkegaard's unhappy engagement, particularly as this relates to his literary breakthrough, and the question of Kierkegaard as an apologist. Regarding the former, Bohlin claims that the broken engagement serves as the interpretive key for understanding Kierkegaard's entire development not only in that it manifests the depth of his melancholy and releases his poetic nature to produce *Either/Or*, but also in that it sharpens his view concerning the incommensurability of social life and the isolated existence of the Christian individual.[3] With respect to apologetics, Bohlin argues that although Kierkegaard is interested in elucidating authentic Christian faith and challenging his contemporaries to pursue such faith, he certainly cannot be understood to be an apologist in the typical sense of the word. Moreover, Kierkegaard's position, which Bohlin describes as "anti-intellectualistic intellectualism,"[4] is so radically wedded to the concept of the revealed paradox of faith in opposition to human understanding that any attempt to defend Christianity proves utterly meaningless.[5] Thus, if apologetics is to play any role for Kierkegaard, it is merely that of defying human attempts to grasp faith so as to help people arrive at a place where they are left on their own to leap unconditionally into the arms of God.

In Chapters 3 and 4, Bohlin turns his attention to analyzing Kierkegaard's account of faith and revealing some of the specific problems in this account. Much of the content of these chapters had been explored in far greater depth by Bohlin in earlier works,[6] and as such the claims made here are not altogether novel. With respect to faith, Bohlin notes that for Kierkegaard faith means breaking free from the impersonal collective in order to become a single individual before God, and such a process plays out in relation to Christ as prototype and redeemer but also to Christ as the absolute paradox. Because this account of faith stems from Romanic and Pietistic roots, but at the same time emerges as an attack upon nineteenth-century speculative thought, Bohlin argues that Kierkegaard is left with a deeply-conflicted description of faith as, on the one hand, a "child-like trusting faith in God" and, on the other hand, an "abstract metaphysical idea of the absolute."[7] In addition, Kierkegaard's view of sin is plagued by a similar duplicity between sin as a personal religious experience of guilt and sin as a consequence of the metaphysical teaching of paradox. For Bohlin, such irreconcilable elements in Kierkegaard's thought entail that one must abandon any attempt to understand such thought in a unified manner.[8]

---

3 Bohlin, *Kierkegaards tro*, p. 13.

4 Ibid., p. 32.

5 Ibid., p. 24; p. 32; p. 35.

6 Particularly, Torsten Bohlin, *Sören Kierkegaards etiska åskådning med särskild hänsyn till begreppet "den enskilde,"* Stockholm: Svenska Kyrkans Diakonistyrelses Bokförlag 1918 and Torsten Bohlin, *Kierkegaards dogmatiska åskådning i dess historiska sammanhang*, Stockholm: Svenska Kyrkans Diakonistyrelses Bokförlag 1925.

7 Bohlin, *Kierkegaards tro*, p. 78.

8 Ibid., p. 107.

Moreover, Bohlin suggests that given the problems in Kierkegaard's view, the best course of action for evangelical theology is simply to steer clear of it.[9]

In the final chapter, Bohlin engages with the topic of Kierkegaard and community. To begin, he frames the discussion in relation to two divergent interpretations, one which reads Kierkegaard as advocating a radical individualism that leaves no place for community,[10] and one which sees the concept of community as built into the very nature of Kierkegaard's account of faith.[11] It becomes immediately apparent, however, that Bohlin's primary interest here lies in criticizing the latter. In short, Bohlin argues that the attempt to relate absolutely to the absolute as a single individual, which is the characteristic religious movement for Kierkegaard, pushes the human person in the direction of radical inwardness with the consequence that "the human being is condemned to spiritual isolation."[12] Such an anti-community strain in Kierkegaard's thought can be seen in his opposition to marriage and in his rejection of the fellowship of the Danish state church for the individualistic pursuit of Christian imitation (*Efterfølgelse*),[13] but it is revealed most clearly in Kierkegaard's claim that becoming an individual through dying to oneself and to the world is inherent to the nature of the human being as a creature that exists before God. To conclude, then, Bohlin remarks that the latter of the divergent views mentioned above ultimately proves a failure in that it "builds upon a far too limited, one-sided selectively chosen part of Kierkegaard's tension-filled authorship."[14] In contrast, the former view, although undoubtedly an exaggeration, still points in the right direction.

Kierkegaards tro och andra Kierkegaardstudier received a good amount of academic attention in the years immediately following its publication, and even a few more recent Kierkegaard scholars have engaged with the work. The most significant impact the book has had on Kierkegaard studies, however, is the role that it played in fueling interesting debate within the Swedish context concerning both the methodological question of how to approach Kierkegaard's thought and writings and the interpretive question of how to understand Kierkegaard in relation to the concepts of the individual and the community. With his monograph *Efterföljelsens teologi hos Sören Kierkegaard*, Valter Lindström weighed in on both questions, reasserting his unified interpretation of Kierkegaard in response to Bohlin's criticisms and what he saw as Bohlin's fragmented reading as well as developing an account of the concept of imitation to counteract Bohlin's charge that Kierkegaard's use of the same concept leads strictly to denial of self, community, and life in general.[15] Moreover, regarding the question of Kierkegaard and community, several others scholars took

---

9 Ibid., p. 109.

10 See Johannes Hohlenberg, *Sören Kierkegaard*, trans. by Karin and Sven Stolpe, Stockholm: Bonnier 1943.

11 See Valter Lindström, *Stadiernas teologi. En Kierkegaardstudie*, Lund: Gleerup 1943.

12 Bohlin, *Kierkegaards tro*, p. 121.

13 Ibid., p. 134; pp. 142–3.

14 Ibid., p. 160.

15 Valter Lindström, *Efterföljelsens teologi hos Sören Kierkegaard*, Stockholm: Svenska Kyrkans Diakonistyrelses Bokförlag 1956.

up the discussion initiated by Bohlin, and in this fashion they helped to carry on the debate for nearly two decades.[16]

In conclusion, we may say that even though Bohlin's book offers little by way of novel content, it may nevertheless still be counted as making an important contribution to Kierkegaard studies. In his own time, Bohlin's clear, accessible, and challenging presentation of traditional Kierkegaardian concepts was able to help forward valuable discussion and debate, and should similar questions as those raised by Bohlin be resurrected in the contemporary context, *Kierkegaards tro och andra Kierkegaardstudier* would certainly be a good resource to consult.

Matthew T. Nowachek

---

16 See, for example, Per Wagndal, *Gemenskapsproblemet hos Sören Kierkegaard*, Lund: Gleerup 1954 and Berndt Gustafsson, *I den natt...Studier i Kierkegaards förfallsteori*, Stockholm: Svenska Kyrkans Dionkonistyrelses Bokförlag 1962.

Reviews and Critical Discussions

Briem, Efraim, "Ur religionens värld," *Sydsvenska Dagbladet*, December 13, 1944, p. 15.

Dymling, Carl, "Sören Kierkegaard i nyaste forskningars ljus," *Religion och kultur*, vol. 15, no. 3, 1944, pp. 142–7.

— "Sören Kierkegaard," *Göteborgs-posten*, August 17, 1944, p. 2.

Dyssegaard, Poul, review in *Kristeligt Dagblad*, April 25, 1945.

Gjesing-Pedersen, K., review in *Nationaltidende*, August 13, 1944.

Hejll, Richard, review in *Den enskilde: Tidskrift för de ensamma*, vol. 4, nos. 3–4, 1948, p. 109.

Henriksen, Aage, *Methods and Results of Kierkegaard Studies in Scandinavia: A Historical and Critical Survey*, Copenhagen: Ejnar Munksgaard 1951 (*Publications of the Kierkegaard Society*, vol. 1), pp. 151–2.

Hjertström Lappalainen, Jonna and Lars-Erik Hjertström Lappalainen, "Sweden: Kierkegaard's Reception in Swedish Philosophy, Theology, and Contemporary Literary Theory," in *Kierkegaard's International Reception*, Tome I, *Northern Europe and Western Europe*, ed. by Jon Stewart, Aldershot: Ashgate 2009 (*Kierkegaard Research: Sources, Reception and Resources*, vol. 8), pp. 178–80.

Holm, Sören, review in *Berlingske Tidende*, July 30, 1944, p. 4.

Isakson, K.G., review in *Frikyrklig ungdom*, no. 10, 1944, p. 15.

Lindroth, Hjalmar, review in *Ny kyrklig tidskrift*, vol. 13, nos. 5–6, 1944, pp. 184–5.

Rodhe, Sven Edvard, review in *Svensk teologisk kvartalskrift*, vol. 20, no. 4, 1944, pp. 321–3.

Schousboe, J., review in *Nationaltidende*, June 4, 1945.

Allan Green, *Kierkegaard bland samtida. Personhistoriska skisser* [Kierkegaard among His Contemporaries: Outlines of Personal Histories],

Eslöv: Gondolin 1995, 157 pp.

Already in the 1970s, the Swedish priest, theologian, and historian Allan Green was compiling research and notes with the intention of writing a historical work on Kierkegaard.[1] Green's efforts finally came to fruition in 1995 with the posthumous publication of the book *Kierkegaard bland samtida. Personhistoriska skisser*.[2] Shortly before his death two years earlier, Green was preparing to release his manuscript with a different publisher, but he put the project on hold because he felt that the text still needed to undergo several significant revisions. With his passing, the work was shelved to the lament of Green's contemporaries,[3] but it was later picked up by the author's widow Carin with the assistance of her daughter Marianne.[4] Carin Green followed her husband's work closely and therefore she was entirely qualified to carry out his editorial wishes, which resulted in the publication of the revised manuscript in its present form.

As Green notes in the Preface, his primary purpose in the book is not to discuss Kierkegaard's existential philosophy, but rather to provide a historical survey of individuals who are more or less connected to Kierkegaard and of whom a careful study promises to supply the reader with a richer picture of the great

Research for this project was made possible by generous support from the Smith Family Fellowship.

1 Bodil Brandoné, "Han ägnar pensionen åt prästforskning," *Sydsvenska Dagbladet*, September 3, 1977, p. 21. Although Green wore many hats, he was first and foremost a man of the church, serving as a priest in the congregations of Bjällerup and Stora Råby from 1939 to 1955 and later in Lund's Cathedral from 1955 until his retirement in 1977.

2 Allan Green, *Kierkegaard bland samtida. Personhistoriska skisser*, Eslöv: Gondolin 1995.

3 See, for example, Olle Nivenius and Tord Rydén, "Präst med litterär verksamhet," *Sydsvenska Dagbladet*, December 31, 1993, p. B9; Olle Nivenius and Tord Rydén, "Allan Green," *Svenska Dagbladet*, January 10, 1994, p. 16.

4 Sten Hidal, "Kierkegaards umgänge," *Signum*, no. 2, 1996, n.p.

Danish thinker.[5] Towards this end, Green not only dedicates a significant portion of his study to sketching accounts of major Danish figures in Kierkegaard's milieu such as Kierkegaard's parents and siblings, Regine Olsen as well as the church leaders Jakob Peter Mynster and Hans Lassen Martensen, but he also affords a fair amount of attention to individuals typically less-discussed in Kierkegaard studies such as the Danish King Christian VIII, the theologian Jacob Christian Lindberg, and the priest L.J.M. Gude. In addition, Green makes an interesting contribution to Kierkegaard scholarship with his brief survey of Kierkegaard's influence on several Swedish contemporaries such as Oscar Patrik Sturzen-Becker, Fredrika Bremer, and Albert Lysander as well as later Swedish intellectuals including Waldemar Rudin, Harriet Löwenhielm, and Klara Johanson. Such bridgework between Kierkegaard and Sweden is a much-welcomed contribution to a largely neglected research area, and Green's efforts thereby serve as a good example for future scholars of how to tie together in a fruitful manner Kierkegaard and the broader Scandinavian context.

As indicated by the descriptor "outlines" in the subtitle of his book, Green's presentation of the figures he covers is intended to be both brief and introductory, and therefore scholars interested in more developed and nuanced historical accounts would be better served by consulting other works.[6] However, as a single-volume general overview of the human context surrounding Kierkegaard, Green's approachable and easily-read sketches prove valuable for researchers to enrich their understanding of Kierkegaard as a historical figure or simply to gain a basic familiarity with some of the more interesting individuals of nineteenth-century northern Europe.

Despite Green's stated intention to focus his project on the figures connected to Kierkegaard, he nevertheless allows himself in a few places to depart from this task in order to discuss certain of Kierkegaard's aesthetic writings and philosophical themes. For example, in a chapter on Kierkegaard's pseudonymous work *Either/Or*, Green offers a nine-page summary of the various sections of the two-volume work paired with brief attempts to see Kierkegaard personally reflected in the work such as in identifying him *qua* poet with "Den Ulykkeligste" or by tying him to Judge William's existentialist-sounding admonition to choose.[7] Earlier, in the chapter "I Berlin" Green briefly discusses Kierkegaard's pseudonymous work *Gjentagelsen* and its associated concept of repetition, which Green admits "is among the most difficult of Kierkegaard's concepts to understand."[8] Nevertheless, Green argues that repetition is a religious and transcendent notion for Kierkegaard, which is shown in the fact that although Kierkegaard is unable to reunite with his former fiancé Regine after she becomes engaged to Fritz Schlegel, he nevertheless still believes in the possibility of some sort of repetition in the life to come.[9]

---

5 Green, *Kierkegaard bland samtida*, p. 7.

6 For example, *Kierkegaard and his Danish Contemporaries*, Tomes I–III, ed. by Jon Stewart, Aldershot: Ashgate 2009 (*Kierkegaard Research: Sources, Reception and Resources*, vol. 7).

7 Green, *Kierkegaard bland samtida*, p. 48; p. 53.

8 Ibid., p. 41.

9 Ibid., p. 42.

Perhaps the greatest strength of Green's work is its ecclesiastical focus. In previous writings, Green has proven himself a competent scholar of Swedish church history (and particularly that of the diocese of Lund) leading up to and including Kierkegaard's own era,[10] and this competence comes clearly to the fore in his ability to follow the various ecclesiastical threads within the Danish Lutheran church that are interwoven throughout Kierkegaard's life and thought. Not only does Green provide concise historical accounts of both Mynster and Martensen in which he emphasizes the various ways in which their paths as church leaders cross that of Kierkegaard, but his chapter on priests, "Präster," which incidentally is the longest chapter in the book, also includes insightful accounts of the Bornholm priest Adolph Peter Adler, the warm and friendly correspondence between the priest Hans Peter Kofoed-Hansen and Kierkegaard, Kierkegaard's respect for the priest Peter Johannes Spang, and the friendship between Kierkegaard and the priest Emil Boesen. The nuanced picture Green paints in this chapter is significant in that it resists the tendency to view Kierkegaard simply as an anti-clerical polemicist with spite for all Danish priests, and instead it nicely brings to light the multifaceted relations Kierkegaard had to the clergy with whom he was engaged in his writings and daily dealings.

From the handful of reviews of *Kierkegaard bland samtida*, it appears that the book did not make any massive waves in Kierkegaard studies, but it was still generally well received. For example, Bernt Eklundh remarks: "The book does not really provide so much that is new about Kierkegaard, but it is nevertheless interesting in that it describes both the greater and lesser known writers and artists in Copenhagen during the Golden Age of Denmark."[11] Similarly, as Bengt Hägglund notes, the familiarity with Kierkegaard's acquaintances provided by Green's work plays an important role in helping to overcome the entrenched view of Kierkegaard as a recluse while at the same time offering "a richer and more nuanced picture of Kierkegaard himself."[12] Despite such generally positive responses from Swedish readers, Green's text has yet to be translated, and as such it remains a largely untapped resource for international researchers.

In the end, Green's book is a good introduction to Kierkegaard's contemporaries from which even the most seasoned Kierkegaard scholar is certain to derive some benefit—if not new knowledge about Kierkegaard or those with whom Kierkegaard was engaged during his lifetime, perhaps simply the benefit of the enjoyment of reading through the numerous and oftentimes witty anecdotes with which Green sprinkles his text. As Green writes in the Preface: "It is out of thanks for what Kierkegaard has meant for me that I publish who book,"[13] and it is clear that Green's writing functions as a service of gratitude to an author who played a crucial role in his own intellectual and spiritual development. Ultimately, this service for Green is

---

10 See, for example, Allan Green, *Biskopar i Lunds stift 1060–1637 och händelser kring dem*, Lund: Gleerup 1973; Allan Green, *Biskopar i Lunds stift 1638–1865 och händelser kring dem*, Malmö: Liber 1986.

11 Bernt Eklundh, "Danmarks egen Sokrates," *Göteborgs-posten*, February 5, 1996, p. 38.

12 Bengt Hägglund, "Enstöring med förbehåll," *Sydsvenska Dagbladet*, April 1, 1996, p. A4.

13 Green, *Kierkegaard bland samtida*, p. 7.

an attempt to assign Kierkegaard the recognition that Green believes is deserved. Thus, to conclude his book Green notes in the addendum, "Søren Kierkegaard's misfortune was to be far too gifted, 'A genius in a market town.' If he never won real recognition during his lifetime but rather stood entirely in the shadow of mediocre people, great recognition has come to him in part."[14] With these words from the last few lines of his life's final work, Green suggests that the relevance of his study need not end with him and his own generation, but that it can also extend to a future generation of Kierkegaard scholars who are charged with the task of acquainting themselves with Kierkegaard's acquaintances and in this manner joining Green in helping to keep alive the memory of the great Danish thinker.

Matthew T. Nowachek

---

14 Ibid., pp. 153–4.

Reviews and Critical Discussions

Eklundh, Bernt, "Danmarks egen Sokrates," *Göteborgs-posten*, February 5, 1996, p. 38.
Fredriksson, Gunnar, "Läsvärt om den gåtfulle mannen i Köpenhamn," *Aftonbladet*, March 5, 1996, pp. 4–5.
Hägglund, Bengt, "Enstöring med förbehåll," *Sydsvenska Dagbladet*, April 1, 1996, p. A4.
Hidal, Sten, "Kierkegaards umgänge," *Signum*, no. 2, 1996, n.p.
Hultsberg, Peter, "Lättläst om Kierkegaard," *Skånska Dagbladet*, April 4, 1996, p. 20.
Lundberg, Bengt, "Från danska guldåldern," *Östgöta Correspondenten*, February 14, 1996, p. A4.
Rosdahl, Björn, "Folket kring Kierkegaard," *Helsingborgs Dagbladet*, June 12, 1996, p. 18.
Stenström, Thure, "Charmfullt om Kierkegaards nära och kära," *Svenska Dagbladet*, March 27, 1996, p. 28.

Edward A. Harris, *Gör ditt val. En introduktion till Kierkegaards subjektivitetsteori* [Make Your Choice: An Introduction to Kierkegaard's Theory of Subjectivity],

Stockholm: Spiritual Future 2003, 93 pp.

The relatively short text *Gör ditt val*,[1] issued in 2003 by a relatively small publisher, is one in a string of publications on Kierkegaard that Edward "Ted" Harris has produced in the years since completing his dissertation on Kierkegaard in 1984.[2] Due to his role as a priest and educator in the Swedish church as well as to his extensive cultural experience,[3] Harris has long been interested in the intersection of Christianity and culture—an interest clearly reflected in the argument and structure of his text. The subtitle of the book, however, is something of a misnomer in that the lengthy discussion Harris affords to what he identifies as the shift in the West towards "a materialistic mechanistic view of reality"[4] largely overshadows his development of Kierkegaard's view, which, apart from somewhat truncated treatments in Chapters 1 and 2, receives fewer than seventeen pages in the final chapter. Despite this rather limited engagement with Kierkegaard, Harris still manages to articulate an account of Kierkegaard's theory of subjectivity that, though not developed nearly to the extent that it could be, is nevertheless developed enough to be provocative.

The general aim Harris sets out for his book is to formulate a response to what he understands to be the long-looming crisis of existence that has overtaken modern Western culture. As Harris notes in the Introduction, both Kierkegaard's time and

Research for this project was made possible by generous support from the Smith Family Fellowship.

1 Edward A. Harris, *Gör ditt val. En introduktion till Kierkegaards subjektivitetsteori*, Stockholm: Spiritual Future 2003.

2 Edward A. Harris, *Man's Ontological Predicament: A Detailed Analysis of Sören Kierkegaard's Concept of Sin with Special Reference to The Concept of Dread*, Uppsala: Acta Univeritatis Upsaliensis 1984.

3 Born in Barbados and having resided for a decade in London before moving to Copenhagen and finally Stockholm, Harris began as a priest in Adolf Fredrik's Church in 1987 where he has also been involved with pilgrimages to countries including Egypt and Italy.

4 Harris, *Gör ditt val*, p. 31.

our own time are marked by a scientific-technological rationality that has resulted in an overall loss of interest in existential questions, which has in turn left the modern human person both self-less and soul-less.[5] Within such a nihilistic setting, Kierkegaard's theory of subjectivity has an important role to play in reminding the individual of her existential creativity, freedom, possibility, and responsibility, and in this fashion setting her on a trajectory towards what Kierkegaard identifies as the greatest good, *Salighed* (happiness/salvation).[6]

In order to set up Kierkegaard's view in response to the spiritual sickness of the West, Harris spends the greater part of his first two chapters sketching an elaborate philosophical story of the decline of Western culture. Central to Chapter 1 is Harris' outline of four different views of reality, which he identifies as material-realism (e.g., Democritus), idea-realism (e.g., Plato), concept-realism (e.g., Husserl), and concept-subjectivism (e.g., Kant). The general movement of Western culture away from realism, especially in the nominalist rejection of Aristotelian metaphysics, has allowed empiricism and materialism along with humanistic value subjectivism and scientific reductionism to become the dominant ideologies of the eighteenth and nineteenth centuries.[7] The problem Harris sees with this shift, however, is that since "the existential questions about reality's utmost structure, the foundational structures and characteristics of human consciousness, and the utmost value and meaning of existence lie beyond the reach of scientific-technological rationality, modern European intellectual life has lost a sense of the metaphysical and existential needs of the human being."[8] In Chapter Two, Harris outlines three broad attempts to attain *Salighed* in the midst of this crisis, namely, the materialistic, the humanistic, and the religious forms of life, and he associates Kierkegaard in part with the second and entirely with the third. In this fashion, in the first two chapters Harris both sketches a picture of the slide of Western culture into nihilism and suggests how Kierkegaard's religious view can serve as a promising alternative.

At times in his argument, Harris moves far too quickly, and it often feels as if his analysis goes a mile wide, but only an inch deep. As such, the reader is left with the impression that in painting with such broad brushstrokes Harris has in part sacrificed nuance for the sake of expository continuity. For example, Harris engages very little, if at all, with views anomalous to his own account (and which would thereby challenge its rather neat categories) such as non-atheistic versions of empiricism,[9] non-reductionist views of materialism,[10] and non-nihilistic accounts of ethical naturalism.[11] This presentation of the Western intellectual tradition, if not a serious

---

5 Ibid., p. 10.

6 Ibid. For a good discussion of this word, see Abrahim H. Khan, *Salighed as Happiness? Kierkegaard on the Concept Salighed*, Waterloo, Ontario: Wilfrid Laurier University Press 1985.

7 Harris, *Gör ditt val*, p. 21.

8 Ibid., p. 34.

9 See, for example, the view of George Berkeley.

10 See, for example, the position of Peter van Inwagen, who is himself a Christian materialist.

11 See, for example, virtue ethics and care ethics.

misrepresentation, at the very least runs the risk of over-simplifying what is, in essence, a richly complicated history.[12] In addition, just as with the subtitle of the book, the title of Chapter 1, "Kierkegaard's Age," is also something of a misnomer in that it develops a broad picture of the general underlying currents of eighteenth- and nineteenth-century European intellectual culture, but it largely glosses over the concrete figures and ideas in Kierkegaard's Copenhagen that significantly influenced Kierkegaard's life and thought. As such, it is not entirely clear that the extensive setup to Kierkegaard's theory of subjectivity actually fulfills the goal Harris envisions for it.

In Chapter 3, Harris finally turns to a more robust discussion of Kierkegaard's theory of subjectivity, and he does so in dialogue primarily with the *Philosophical Fragments* and the *Concluding Unscientific Postscript*. With subjectivity, claims Harris, Kierkegaard makes a definitive turn away from the dominant scientific-technological categories of his culture and towards the passionate inward life of the single individual, a life comprised of freedom, possibility, the impulse to will, and anxiety. In developing this point, Harris articulates four theses: first, *Salighed* is not written into the general structure of existence as an innate ability or pre-existing state; second, the individual cannot build *Salighed* on mere empirical knowledge; third, human striving to attain *Salighed* is not guided solely by universal or rational laws; and fourth, subjectivity is a necessary condition for attaining *Salighed*.[13] All four of these points converge in support of Harris' overall thesis and apologetic purpose. Thus, in wrapping up his argument, Harris writes: "It is only the single individual that can activate her own creative energy. It is only the single individual that can create a form of life. Kierkegaard sought the return of the theory of subjectivity in Western culture. Without the subjectivity of the single individual, Western culture will be influenced to an even greater extent by mechanization and technologizing."[14]

To conclude, we may note that Harris' book has some specific strengths, but that it also suffers from some serious shortcomings. On the one hand, with respect to the thinkers it covers, the book can certainly serve as a decent introduction to the history of Western philosophy, and, more specifically, for students engaging Kierkegaard for the first time, it offers an adequate enough starting point for future investigations. As such, the text would be entirely appropriate as a companion piece to Kierkegaard's writings that could be used in courses such as those Harris teaches at Adolf Fredrik's Church. On the other hand, the more competent Kierkegaard scholar will likely not find the text overly helpful in illuminating the finer details of Kierkegaard's theory of subjectivity. In other words, for such a scholar, Harris' introduction is simply far too introductory. One major reason for this shortcoming is that in making the primary focus of his text his apologetic attack on a certain more or less accurately described world-view, Harris unfortunately assigns Kierkegaard a relatively minor

---

12 In a January 11, 2009 radio program entitled "Kierkegaard och existentialismen," Harris notes that his task with Ann Lagerström has been "to simplify" (*att förenkla*) Kierkegaard's thought. There is nothing inherently wrong with this practice, but it is important that in the task of simplification one's exposition does not thereby become simplistic.

13 Harris, *Gör ditt val*, pp. 70–1.

14 Ibid., p. 83.

role and characterizes the Danish thinker in a manner that proves rather one-dimensional. Kierkegaard, of course, was himself a radical critic of his own age, and as such he would by no means be averse to carrying out contemporary cultural criticism; however, as is apparent, for example, in the distance he took from the free church movement in general and the Grundtvigians in particular, Kierkegaard was adamantly opposed to becoming the mouthpiece for either the popular or unpopular causes of his day. In the end, then, the question of whether Harris unfairly conscripts Kierkegaard into service within the current cultural wars or whether Harris justifiably appeals to Kierkegaard as an ally in the good fight remains an important one not only for Harris but also for his future readers who carry on the valuable, yet formidable task of articulating Kierkegaard's place in Western culture.

Matthew T. Nowachek

Review and Critical Discussion

Lappalainen, Jonna Hjertström and Lars-Erik Hjertström Lappalainen, "Sweden: Kierkegaard's Reception in Swedish Philosophy, Theology, and Contemporary Literary Theory," in *Kierkegaard's International Reception*, Tome I, *Northern Europe and Western Europe*, ed. by Jon Stewart, Aldershot: Ashgate 2009 (*Kierkegaard Research: Sources, Reception and Resources*, vol. 8), pp. 173–96; see pp. 182–3.

Ted Harris and Ann Lagerström, *Konsten att leva innerligt. Existentialism för den moderna människan* [The Art of Living Inwardly: Existentialism for the Modern Human Being],

Stockholm: LevNu/Wahlström and Widstrand 2008, 183 pp.

Konsten att leva innerligt. Existentialism för den moderna människan is a joint effort by priest Ted Harris and journalist Ann Lagerström to strike out in search of the meaning of life with Søren Kierkegaard as their interlocutor and with their readers as fellow seekers.[1] More specifically, the work is a result of several conversations in which Harris presented an interpretation of Kierkegaard's thought to Lagerström, who then reworked these conversations into their present form.[2] The book was a major success in Sweden and soon appeared in German, Danish, and Norwegian translations.[3]

The book is by no means scholarly, and neither is it intended to be so. As Lagerström states in the preface, her purpose is simply to make Kierkegaard's philosophy "concrete and useful for us who live today,"[4] and to this end she introduces the Dane's thought as something of a nine-step existential process that plays out through the three stages of sensuality, inwardness, and spirituality. The desire of the authors to address what they see as the general existential malaise characteristic of twenty-first century human beings is certainly commendable, but beyond this there is unfortunately little of merit that can be said for the text. From a research perspective, the most troubling aspect of the work is its rather problematic interpretations and appropriations of Kierkegaard, and as such I suggest an appropriate

---

Research for this project was made possible by generous support from the Smith Family Fellowship.

1 Ted Harris and Ann Lagerström, *Konsten att leva innerligt. Existentialism för den moderna människan*, Stockholm: LevNu/Wahlström and Widstrand 2008.

2 I refer primarily to Lagerström hereafter in that she is responsible for the written text.

3 Ted Harris and Ann Lagerström, *Die Kunst, innerlich zu leben. Existenzialismus für moderne Menschen*, trans. by Susanne Dahmann, Gütersloh: Gütersloher Verlagshaus 2009. *Kunsten at leve inderligt. Eksistentialisme for det moderne menneske*, trans. by Bodil Lodberg, Frederiksberg: Unitas Forlag 2010. *Kunsten å leve inderlig. Eksistensialisme for det moderne mennesket*, trans. by Karin Elisabeth Ellefsen, Oslo: Cappelen Damm 2009.

4 Lagerström, *Konsten att leva innerligt*, p. 11.

manner by which to exposit the work is simply to do so by tracing out a few of its more serious shortcomings.

One problem with the book is Lagerström's often undisciplined treatment of Kierkegaard's writings, which, to draw on a phrase from Roger Poole, represents a textbook case of blunt reading. Apart from a few passing remarks about Kierkegaard's pseudonyms,[5] Lagerström ignores altogether Kierkegaard's method of indirection communication, and she thereby indiscriminately decorates her text with pseudonymous quotations of which almost all are explicitly or implicitly attributed to Kierkegaard.[6] Overall, this practice results in a good deal of confusion. For example, by associating quotations from *Either/Or* that should be attributed to the aesthete A with Kierkegaard's voice, Lagerström gives the improper impression that Kierkegaard advocates unreservedly for embracing the aesthetic world-view. Kierkegaard, of course, is not opposed to the sensual or to aesthetic enjoyment, but he is clear at numerous places in his authorship that the aesthetic life is not an end in itself, and any attempt to make it such leads ultimately to despair.[7] Unfortunately, with such lack of nuance in presenting Kierkegaard's writings, Lagerström not only fails to do justice to Kierkegaard's authorial conventions, but she also leads her readers astray.[8]

A second problem is that Lagerström's simplistic presentation of the Climacean "truth is subjectivity" thesis leaves the reader with the sense that Kierkegaard recommends something of a self-fixated relativism. For example, in her description of Kierkegaard's thought Lagerström makes repeated use of egotistical-sounding phrases such as "discovering oneself," "finding one's own truth," "being true to oneself"or "listening only to one's inner voice," which lend themselves all too easily to misinterpretation in the direction of superficial self-affirmation. Furthermore, she attributes to Kierkegaard claims such as "nothing you do is wrong if the longing comes from within, if you live in tune with your own genuine needs,"[9] and "it is only you who can find out what is missing, it is only you who can know what is right, it is only you who can know what is true for you…[I]n order to come out of the emptiness you need to seek your own interpretation of reality, your own truth."[10] Although it is correct to say that for Climacus the individual must necessarily consider the question of truth from where she stands as an existing being, it is also important to remember that Climacus qualifies this account with the significant point that though human claims to truth are approximate, truth is nevertheless still objective for God.[11] Moreover, Climacus is also clear that because the individual is in a state of untruth, what he identifies as sin,[12] proper subjectivity is not merely self-referential, but

---

5 See, for example, ibid., p. 55; p. 56; p. 87.

6 See, for example, ibid., p. 7; p. 49; p. 107.

7 See, for example, Anti-Climacus' discussion in *SKS* 11, 157–62 / *SUD*, 42–7.

8 This latter point becomes particularly evident when one reads through some of the reviews of the book.

9 Lagerström, *Konsten att leva innerligt*, p. 50.

10 Ibid., p. 71.

11 *SKS* 7, 174 / *CUP1*, 190.

12 *SKS* 7, 189–91 / *CUP1*, 207–8.

rather it is that which plays out in relation to the paradoxical God-man.[13] Despite Harris' denial that his and Lagerström's account leads to egoism or narcissism,[14] it is difficult to see how such a one-dimensional reading of subjectivity avoids pointing its readers in this direction.

A third problem concerns Lagerström's presentation of Kierkegaard's view of love that he develops in *Works of Love*. As part of the second to last step in her third stage, spirituality, Lagerström points to the importance of loving unconditionally. Although there is nothing awry in this claim, Lagerström veers off course with her attempt to provide a more concrete description of this love. In her reading, love can be "love for things, for ideas, for my husband, the kids, for relatives and friends—I almost forgot, love for myself,"[15] and, crucially, love revolves around recognizing the value of other human beings and thereby loving them just as they are. Moreover, in support of this latter claim Lagerström appeals to Martin Buber's *I and Thou*. What is strikingly absent from this discussion is any recognition of the fundamental role in his love ethics that Kierkegaard affords to God as the ground of love, as the giver of the love commandment, and as the creator who imprints the other with the divine watermark that undergirds the demand to love.[16] The confusion here is made especially acute by Lagerström's use of Buber. In his own critique of Kierkegaard, Buber is concerned that Kierkegaard emphasizes the God–human relationship to such an extent and in such a fashion that radically devalues human–human relationships,[17] and thus it is incredible not only that Lagerström implies Buber and Kierkegaard share the same view, but that she leaves out God altogether in discussing Kierkegaard's account. Ultimately, then, Lagerström transforms Kierkegaard's love ethics into a rather generic humanism, and in so doing she removes from these ethics precisely what makes them so unique, powerful, and challenging.

Finally, although the interpretations highlighted above are themselves highly problematic, even more problematic is what does not show up in the text. Missing is any substantive discussion of central Kierkegaardian notions such as restlessness, paradox, offense, suffering, renunciation, dying to self, the imitation of Christ, and revelation. Apart from a few superficial references to Jesus,[18] Lagerström makes no mention of the God-man and the essential role he plays for Kierkegaard in both challenging human self-sufficiency[19] and in guiding his followers through the dual process of humbling and redemption.[20] Perhaps most telling is that the book contains not

---

13 *SKS* 7, 193 / *CUP1*, 210.

14 Mia Sjöström, "Livets mening i nio steg," *Svenska Dagbladet*, October 27, 2008, p. 18.

15 Lagerström, *Konsten att leva innerligt*, p. 150.

16 In addition, Lagerström overlooks Kierkegaard's claim that love for God (as referenced in the first commandment of Matthew 22:37–8) is the most fundamental form of love. See *SKS* 9, 27 / *WL*, 19.

17 Martin Buber, "Das Problem des Menschen," in his *Dialogisches Leben*, Zurich: Gregor Müller 1974, pp. 387–420.

18 Lagerström, *Konsten att leva innerligt*, p. 80, p. 135; p. 164; p. 167.

19 See, for example, Climacus' discussion in *SKS* 4, 222–8, 242–57 / *PF*, 13–20, 37–54.

20 See *SKS* 16, 197–257 / *JFY*, 145–213.

a single reference to sin.[21] Kierkegaard, however, is clear in his writings that without the notion of sin one cannot talk about grace, and without grace there is no possibility for real happiness (*Salighed*). In this respect, although Harris and Lagerström may have succeeded in articulating something of a pop-spirituality that can be gladly embraced by a modern culture both addicted to affirmation and allergic to criticism, their omissions entail that their project fails to offer a view of the meaning of life that is, in the end, recognizably Kierkegaardian.

In conclusion, we may say that *Konsten att leva innerligt* proves a rather regrettable exercise in Kierkegaard interpretation, and therefore it cannot be recommended in good faith either to scholars or to laypersons. Yet even more regrettable is that this text, which has been a commercial success with over 30,000 copies sold in Sweden alone,[22] is the only engagement that many Swedish readers, who would otherwise be rather uninterested in philosophy, will likely have with Kierkegaard's thought. Despite this, we may nevertheless hold on to a glimmer of hope that the curiosity of a few readers will be piqued just enough for them to put aside Harris' and Lagerström's book and instead to turn to Kierkegaard's own writings in order to begin again with the crucial question of the meaning of life.

Matthew T. Nowachek

---

21 This is incredible given that Harris has written a dissertation on the concept of sin in Kierkegaard's thought. See Edward A. Harris, *Man's Ontological Predicament: A Detailed Analysis of Sören Kierkegaard's Concept of Sin with Special Reference to The Concept of Dread*, Uppsala: Acta Univeritatis Upsaliensis 1984. Lagerström does refer to despair and anxiety a few times, but only in passing. See, for example, *Konsten att leva innerligt*, p. 52; p. 56; p. 65; p. 66; p. 75; p. 79; p. 98.

22 Lagerström reports this number (which does not include copies sold in Germany, Denmark, or Norway) on her personal website, www.lagerstrom.nu.

Reviews and Critical Discussions

Antonson, Marlene W., "Ted skissar ditt liv—På vilken våning bor du?," *Dagen*, October 14, 2008, pp. 12–13.

Berghagen, Malin, "Att leva innerligt," *Amelia*, July 25, 2013.

Brisson, Benedikte, "Fra sanselighed til inderlighed og derfra til åndelighed" [review of the Danish translation] in *Katolsk orientering*, June 27, 2010.

Chagas, Åsa, "Möt prästen och Kierkegaardforskaren som har fått nog av vår materiella jakt: Investera i ditt inre liv," *Impuls*, no. 8, 2008, pp. 24–7.

Fleischer, Christoph, review of the German translation in *Tà katoptrizómena*, vol. 11, no. 62, 2009 (on-line journal).

Gotfredsen, Sørine, "Falsk brug af Kierkegaard" [review of the Danish translation] in *Kristeligt Dagblad*, May 15, 2010, p. 13.

Gunne, Monica, "Du bestämmer själv meningen med livet," *Aftonbladet*, September 18, 2008, p. 44.

Hagström, Ingela, "Jag önskar att fler blir nyfikna på sin inre värld," *Dagen*, September 26, 2008, pp. 38–9.

Haizmann, Albrecht, "Kierkegaards *Einübung im Christentum* als evangelisches Exerzitium," in *Kierkegaard Studies Yearbook*, 2010, pp. 175–99, especially p. 183, note 23.

Hammar, K.G., "Vägen till en bättre existens," *Dagens Nyheter*, October 2, 2008, p. 69.

Hellström, Olle, "Kierkegaard light även för läkare," *Läkartidningen*, vol. 106, no. 17, 2009, p. 1206.

Herholz, Ylva, "Jakten på livets mening," *Fokus*, no. 3, January 16, 2009, p. 40.

Leonardz, Jenny, "Bara du kan svara dig själv," *Svenska Dagbladet*, September 27, 2008, p. 7.

Lerner, Thomas, "Lyckan får vi söka i oss själva," *Dagens Nyheter*, October 7, 2008, p. 22.

Lindgren, Ingrid, review in *Veteranen*, February 21, 2008.

Nilsson, Björn, review in *Hela Jorden*, nos. 5–6, 2008, p. 26.

Nyström Rönnås, Tina, review in *Allmänmedicin*, no. 6, 2008, p. 31.

Sanner, Eva, "Slarva inte bort ditt liv! Hitta känslan som leder dig rätt," *Hälsa*, no. 9, 2008, pp. 32–5.

Sjöström, Mia, "Livets mening i nio steg," *Svenska Dagbladet*, October 27, 2008, p. 18.

Skatvik, Frida, review of the Norwegian translation in *Salongen*, November 26, 2009.

Jonna Hjertström Lappalainen, *Den enskilde. En studie av trons profana möjlighet i Sören Kierkegaards tidiga författarskap* [The Single Individual: A Study of Faith's Profane Possibility in Søren Kierkegaard's Early Authorship],

Stockholm: Thales 2009, 196 pp.

Den enskilde. En studie av trons profana möjlighet i Sören Kierkegaards tidiga författarskap was published in 2009 by Thales Bokförlaget as the monograph form of Jonna Hjertström Lappalainen's doctoral dissertation from the University of Stockholm. A portion of the work for this project was carried out while Lappalainen was a guest researcher at the Søren Kierkegaard Research Centre in Copenhagen, and, as she notes, the text greatly benefited from her interaction with the students and faculty there.[1] Overall, the book is thorough and well-researched with good sensitivity to the complexity of Kierkegaard's thought and writings.

Lappalainen's central aim is to provide an interpretation of Kierkegaard's concept of the single individual (*den Enkelte*),[2] which she characterizes generally as an existential category and specifically as "a depiction of how the human being makes herself receptive to the new as absolutely new and the unknown as absolutely unknown."[3] Moreover, Lappalainen claims that even though his Christian faith is what leads Kierkegaard to develop this concept, we may nevertheless think of it as operating outside of the framework of Christianity as a condition for faith. It is in this sense

Research for this project was made possible by generous support from the Smith Family Fellowship.

1 Jonna Hjertström Lappalainen, *Den enskilde. En studie av trons profana möljighet i Sören Kierkegaards tidiga författarskap*, Stockholm: Thales 2009, p. 10.

2 I employ hereafter Kierkegaard's term rather than "the single individual" or the Swedish "den enskilde."

3 Lappalainen, *Den enskilde*, p. 11.

that *den Enkelte* can be understood in terms of a *profane* possibility.[4] To support this argument, Lappalainen begins with a reading of *The Point of View* after which she narrows her scope to Kierkegaard's early authorship from 1843 to 1846 and particularly the works *Fear and Trembling*, *Repetition*, and *The Concept of Anxiety*, as well as the upbuilding discourse "The Thorn in the Flesh" and the pseudonymous diary entry from *Stages on Life's Way* entitled "'Guilty?'/'Not Guilty'?" As Lappalainen suggests, it is in these writings that Kierkegaard most thoroughly develops the notion of *den Enkelte*, and he does so not by means of strict theoretical discourse, but rather by pointing to how it is concretely manifested in various religious and literary figures. Thus, for her own exposition Lappalainen focuses on the biblical characters of Abraham, Job, Adam, and Paul as well as Kierkegaard's character Quidam.

In Chapter 1, Lappalainen sketches a general account of *den Enkelte* that she fills out in greater detail in the subsequent chapters. With reference to Kierkegaard's description of the concept in *The Point of View*, Lappalainen argues that it means more than simply particularity in that it functions also as an expression of the individual's freedom and as a form of receptivity that precedes faith.[5] In contrast to scholars such as Gregor Malantschuk and Torsten Bohlin who conflate becoming *den Enkelte* with achievement of the Christian life,[6] Lappalainen emphasizes the distinction between the two by making the crucial point that although becoming *den Enkelte* is seen from the Christian perspective as a step on the path to faith, this notion as an existential category ought nevertheless to be understood as a non-religious end in itself.

For Chapters 2 and 3, Lappalainen turns her attention to the figures of Abraham and Job, respectively. Although these figures are similar in the sense that both display the horrible responsibility faced by *den Enkelte* when he enters into a direct relationship with a personal god,[7] they differ in that for Abraham such particularity plays out in his struggle with the ethical universal, and for Job it plays out in relation to repetition and guilt. As Lappalainen argues, in suspending the ethics of his society for a higher *telos*, Abraham freely adopts a silent loneliness characterized by pain and difficulty whereby he places himself in a new relationship to the unknown, that is "the single individual's receptivity before faith."[8] This new relationship, however, is not simply passive, but is also an active embracing of possibility—what Lappalainen describes as "a form of creativity that bursts forth from human existence."[9]

---

4 Ibid., p. 30; p. 137. Lappalainen intends here something along the lines of the original meaning of "profane" as used to describe that which stood outside of the temple and thereby outside of the holy. See p. 150, note 24.

5 Ibid., pp. 30–1.

6 See, for example, Gregor Malantschuk, *Frihedens Problem i Kierkegaards Begrebet Angest*, Copenhagen: C.A. Reitzel 1995 and Torsten Bohlin, *Sören Kierkegaards etiska åskådning med särskild hänsyn till begreppet "den enskilde,"* Uppsala: Svenska kyrkans diakonistyrelses bokförlag 1918.

7 Lappalainen, *Den enskilde*, p. 65.

8 Ibid., p. 53. On this point, see also Lappalainen's earlier essay, "Den osägbare: Den enskildes betydelse i *Fruktan och Bävan*," in *Tänkarens mångfald. Nutida perspektiv på Søren Kierkegaard*, ed. by Lone Koldtoft, Jon Stewart, and Jan Holmgaard, Gothenburg and Stockholm: Makadam 2005, pp. 12–25.

9 Lappalainen, *Den enskilde*, p. 57.

For Job, his particularity finds expression through the inward movement of repetition he undergoes in the process of renewing and regaining his love for life and for God, following the crushing loss of family, health, and wealth he endured at the hand of the accuser.[10] In addition, by refusing to believe the ethical condemnations of his friends and rather by remaining firm in the conviction that his guilt is determined by God alone, Job displays precisely what it means to exist in a "living relation to God"[11] in a manner characteristic of *den Enkelte*.

In Chapters 4 and 5 Lappalainen focuses on *The Concept of Anxiety* and the figure of Adam with the aim of describing the relationship between freedom and *den Enkelte*. In Lappalainen's reading, the fall of Adam into sin can be understood through three stages: first, Adam's anxiety unveils the possibility of possibility; second, within such anxiety a possibility is exteriorized; and third, this possibility is then realized in the committing of sin. Anxiety thus reveals Adam's freedom as the ability to choose, and for Adam this is experienced as something entirely new. Furthermore, Lappalainen points to the importance of the moment (*Øieblikket*) for Adam's freedom (and freedom in general) as "*den Enkelte*'s access to eternity in time,"[12] where the utterly new is revealed and in relation to which *den Enkelte* is afforded the opportunity to open himself to otherness. Such "naked receptivity"[13] tied to subjectivity in the moment is precisely what allows for freedom's repetition as the possibility of faith.

For the final chapter Lappalainen engages with the characters Quidam and Paul in relation to the issue of suffering. Suffering, for Lappalainen, serves as the path to freedom, and as such it should not be avoided, but rather harnessed in the service of developing one's receptivity. The figure Quidam from *Stages on Life's Way* certainly suffers in that he breaks his engagement with his beloved even though he still loves her. Quidam, however, does not embrace his suffering in the present, but rather he chooses to distance himself from it by turning his reflection to the past and future. As Lappalainen argues, "his inability to become *den Enkelte*...is his inability to endure suffering."[14] In contrast, Paul endures the greatest suffering of all, namely that of the abandoned spirit as a response to alienation in the world and to the self's own inadequacy and deficiency,[15] but unlike Quidam he embraces this suffering with joy in the here and now as a way of making himself receptive to the new and to the absolutely unknown.[16] In the end, suggests Lappalainen, this state of joyful suffering provides one of the richest pictures of what it means to exist as *den Enkelte*.

Even with its novel and interesting analysis of what is without question a central Kierkegaardian concept, Lappalainen's book has received far less attention than it

---

10 Job 1:6–12.

11 Lappalainen, *Den enskilde*, p. 66.

12 Ibid., p. 104.

13 Ibid., p. 107.

14 Ibid., p. 121. As Lappalainen also puts it, Quidam's failure can be described as the inability "to be out over 70,000 fathoms and [yet nevertheless] be joyful" (ibid., p. 122).

15 Ibid., p. 124.

16 Ibid., p. 131.

deserves. This is certainly due to the fact that the text remains untranslated and thereby inaccessible for many Kierkegaard scholars, but it is likely also a reflection of the relative lack of interest in Kierkegaard within Swedish academic circles. What is most unfortunate about such meager reception is that Lappalainen's project carries the potential to make a significant contribution to Kierkegaard studies. Despite its heavy emphasis on exposition, the text nevertheless has a polemical edge to it that could prove quite powerful, were the book to be placed in dialogue with certain current readings of Kierkegaard, particularly those from the non-European context.[17] Such dialogue, however, will regrettably need to wait until the monograph is translated into a world language or at least until Lappalainen explores other avenues for disseminating her argument to an international audience.

Matthew T. Nowachek

---

17 For example, Lappalainen's reading of Abraham as representing *den Enkelte* in relation to faith, but in a manner that one need not talk about faith in terms of a new generality, could potentially present an interesting challenge to the divine command theory reading developed by American scholars Philip L. Quinn and C. Stephen Evans.

Reviews and Critical Discussions

Ahlskog, Jonas, "Kierkegaard och lidandets mening," *Ny Tid*, March 30, 2012, p. 5.

Bornemark, Jonna, "Den enskilde och de båda: Om Jonna Hjertström Lappalainens avhandling *Den enskilde. En studie av trons profana möjlighet i Sören Kierkegaards tidiga författarskap*," *Lacuna*, no. 2, 2010 (on-line journal).

Eriksson, Johan, "Kierkegaard gick sin egen väg till Gud," *Svenska Dagbladet*, April 24, 2009, p. C12.

Lennart Koskinen, *Tid och evighet hos Sören Kierkegaard. En studie i Kierkegaards livsåskådning* [Time and Eternity in Søren Kierkegaard: A Study in Kierkegaard's Philosophy of Life],

Lund: Doxa 1980, 185 pp.

Over a two-year period leading up to the completion of his degree of doctor of theology at the University of Uppsala, Lennart Koskinen undertook a massive research program whereby he reportedly read through each and every one of Kierkegaard's published works.[1] The fruits of this intense study was the dissertation *Tid och evighet hos Sören Kierkegaard: En studie i Kierkegaards livsåskådning*, which was published in 1980 by Doxa Press as the second number in the *Philosophy of Life Research* (*Livsåskådningsforskning*) series edited by Anders Jeffener and Hampus Lyttkens.[2] Fourteen years later, the book was released by Nya Doxa under a new title and with a few minor changes.[3] Koskinen, himself a Finnish-born Swedish-educated Danish-proficient scholar who, at the time of writing, was already firmly rooted in the Swedish church,[4] brings an interesting perspective to the study of Kierkegaard. It is, nevertheless, Koskinen's religious angle that most clearly comes to the fore, particularly in his emphasis on Kierkegaard's faith as the basis by which to interpret Kierkegaard's view of time and eternity.

Research for this project was made possible by generous support from the Smith Family Fellowship.

1 Lennart Koskinen, "Kierkegaardska tankestråk hos Strindberg," a lecture in Adolf Fredrik's Church, Stockholm, September 19, 2013.

2 Lennart Koskinen, *Tid och evighet hos Sören Kierkegaard. En studie i Kierkegaards livsåskådning*, Lund: Doxa 1980.

3 Lennart Koskinen, *Søren Kierkegaard och existentialismen. Om tiden, varat och evigheten* [Søren Kierkegaard and Existentialism: On Time, Being, and Eternity], Nora: Nya Doxa 1994. Because the second version of the text is nearly identical to the first, I focus here on the original work.

4 Koskinen was welcomed into the priesthood in 1975, after which he worked with the Swedish church in Stockholm and Uppsala in the years between 1980 and 2003. From 2003 until his retirement in 2011, Koskinen served as bishop of the diocese of Visby.

Koskinen's overall aim in the book is to respond to what he perceives as a need within Kierkegaard research for a study that ties together in a single volume Kierkegaard's various reflections on the concepts of time and eternity, and particularly a study that draws out the significance of these concepts for philosophy of life research.[5] With this aim, Koskinen explicitly assumes that Kierkegaard expresses a unified life-view within his collected works from which it is possible to discern a unified account of time and eternity, and that this life-view is based fundamentally on Kierkegaard's Christian faith.[6] The general thesis Koskinen puts forward is fairly modest. As he remarks in the Introduction, "the concept of time plays a decisive role for [Kierkegaard's] ontological understanding of reality, his anthropology, and [his] view of history."[7] In developing this thesis, Koskinen therefore divides his book into three main parts that address the three topics of reality, the human being, and history.

In Part One, Koskinen carries out significant definitional and conceptual work in relation to the notions of reality, time, eternity, and the moment (*Øieblikket*). Kierkegaard views reality, in Koskinen's reading, as a synthesis of Jewish and Greek (Platonic) elements that is fundamentally dualistic in the sense of being divided between two distinct spheres characterized by five dialectical pairs: the creator/the creation, the holy/the profane, the infinite/the finite, being/non-being, and eternity/temporality.[8] With respect to the fifth pair, Koskinen argues the crucial point that eternity is not merely extended temporality, but rather it is of "an entirely different quality."[9] Because God with his eternal nature is qualitatively distinct from human beings, any meeting between the divine and the human necessitates that God must bridge the two spheres by revealing himself as the paradoxical God-man. For Kierkegaard, all of this occurs in the reality of the moment—a notion Koskinen views not only as "a *terminus technicus* running through the entire [Kierkegaardian] authorship," but also as one of the most crucial concepts for Kierkegaard as a Christian thinker.[10]

In Part Two, Koskinen focuses on a couple of central connections Kierkegaard draws between time and the human being: first, the manner by which the various stages of existence reflect various understandings of time, and second, how time plays into Kierkegaard's philosophical anthropology that he develops, most fully, in *The Sickness unto Death*. With respect to the latter, Koskinen follows a similar line of exposition that he began in Part One regarding Kierkegaard's dualistic view of reality, and he points to how the human being, as a dynamic synthesis of polar opposites, finds herself in a paradoxical relation to time. Although Koskinen provides a nice schematization of Kierkegaard's account in terms of four different dialectical aspects of the human person, his account does not offer too much that improves upon existing secondary literature on Kierkegaard's anthropology.

5 Koskinen, *Tid och evighet*, p. 13.
6 See, for example, ibid., pp. 13–14; p. 25; and p. 43.
7 Ibid., p. 12.
8 Ibid., p. 29.
9 Ibid., p. 59.
10 Ibid., p. 49.

In contrast, with respect to the former Koskinen does make several novel and interesting contributions. As he argues, Kierkegaard's writings can be understood as presenting four different existential stages,[11] each of which is related to time in a different manner. In the stage of immediacy, a person lives within time but not in a conscious manner that would foster existential development. The person in the aesthetic stage lives in the present and the past, but it is the past that ultimately dictates the meaning of her life. As Koskinen writes, "What is important for [the aesthete] is not what [s]he does, but what [s]he has done."[12] In the ethical stage, a person exists in relation to the full range of temporality—past, present, and future, and in her openness to the eternal, which comes in the form of "infinite demands of moral principles and values," she chooses her future and her self.[13] Despite this, however, she still remains thoroughly tied to temporality. The person in the religious stage is the only one who exists in relation to both time and eternity—a relationship made possible solely by divine revelation to the individual within the moment.

In order to substantiate his insightful theoretical analysis of the stages of existence and their relation to time, Koskinen turns to Kierkegaard's pseudonymous work *Stages on Life's Way* and its concrete characters. As he points out, the characters within the narrative illustrate various existential stages: the young man and the fashion designer are tied to the stage of immediacy; Constantin Constantius, Johannes the seducer, and Victor Eremita are connected to the aesthetic stage; and William Afham and Judge William are placed within the ethical stage. By engaging with their existential positions, argues Koskinen, it is therefore possible to gain a richer insight into time—not least of all because of Kierkegaard's impressive literary talents.

In Part Three, Koskinen turns to the issue of history as a crucial piece of any philosophy of life. For Koskinen, Kierkegaard is largely in agreement with Hegel with respect to what Kierkegaard calls profane history or world history in that he understands this history to develop through various stages including the pagan, the Greek, the Jewish, and the Christian.[14] Where Kierkegaard departs from Hegel, however, is in his view of how history relates to the single individual. Here Koskinen refers back to an earlier discussion concerning the importance of God breaking into time in the moment as the God-man, and he stresses that it is this historical movement, what he calls "holy history,"[15] that allows the individual the freedom to cooperate with God in shaping her own history.

Despite its overall value, Koskinen's book still suffers from a slight shortcoming. As Koskinen claims in the Introduction, one of his main goals is to display the broader relevance of Kierkegaard for philosophy of life research. The discussion

---

11 Koskinen further divides these four stages into a total of twelve sub-stages, each of which entails a slightly different relation to time. For a good schematization of this account, see ibid., pp. 88–9.

12 Ibid., p. 172.

13 Ibid.

14 Ibid., p. 133.

15 Ibid., pp. 137–8.

in Chapter 8, in which Koskinen turns his attention to Heidegger, appears to be an attempt in this direction. Unfortunately, however, this chapter moves rather quickly and thereby comes across as somewhat underdeveloped. As such, it is not clear that Koskinen actually achieves what he initially had envisioned for his work. In the republication of the book, Koskinen tries to make the connection between Kierkegaard and the broader intellectual context more obvious, most notably in the choice of the new title, which is undoubtedly meant as an allusion to Heidegger and his text *Being and Time*. The change of title, however, does not carry over into the content of the final chapter, which remains nearly untouched in the new edition. Reviewers of Koskinen's work were generally positive, but it was this issue concerning Koskinen's overall lack of engagement with other thinkers that drew some mild criticism.[16]

In the final assessment, Koskinen's book provides a clear and substantive discussion of Kierkegaard's various remarks on time and eternity, which makes it a valuable read for Kierkegaard scholars. Researchers interested in how Kierkegaard relates to the broader philosophy of life debate and to other thinkers with their own unique philosophies of life will be better off, however, looking to other works.

Matthew T. Nowachek

[16] Sven G. Strömberg, "Klart och lättfattligt om Tid och Evighet," *Nerikes allehanda*, September 26, 1980, p. 2.

Reviews and Critical Discussions

Benktson, Benkt-Erik, review in *Svensk Teologisk Kvartalskrift*, vol. 59, no. 1, 1983, pp. 40–2.

Hultsberg, Peter, "Tiden, varat, evigheten: Lennart Koskinen gör en djupdykning i Søren Kierkegaards tankevärld," *Barometern*, January 17, 1995, p. 14.

Lübcke, Poul, review in *Kierkegaardiana*, vol. 13, 1984, pp. 164–5.

Strömberg, Sven G., "Klart och lättfattligt om Tid of Evighet," *Nerikes allehanda*, September 26, 1980, p. 2.

Söderberg, Boel, "Kierkegaards ångest som en frisk fläkt," *Nerikes allehanda*, May 27, 1995, p. 4.

Lis Lind, *Søren Kierkegaard själv. Psykoanalytiska läsningar* [Søren Kierkegaard Himself: Psychoanalytic Readings],

Stockholm: Carlsson Bokförlag 2000, 206 pp.

Søren Kierkegaard själv. Psykoanalytiska läsningar was issued in 2000 by the fairly decent-sized publisher Carlsson Bokförlag. The author, Lis Lind, was born in Denmark in 1939 and educated in Stockholm, where she later became a psychoanalyst and specialist in general psychiatry with close ties to the Swedish Psychoanalytic Association. This work thus serves as a natural extension of Lind's Danish background, training, research interests, and professional involvement. Beyond the moderate amount of attention the text initially received, much of which was critical, Lind's book appears to have had little lasting influence on Kierkegaard studies.

Generally speaking, Lind's project represents yet another contribution to what has become a long line of studies in the archaeology of Kierkegaard's person, but what differentiates her particular approach from many of those that have come before is that she employs the tools of psychoanalysis to carry out her digging. In the Preface, Lind states straightforwardly that her subject "is Kierkegaard's personality, not his work,"[1] and as such she is concerned less with what Kierkegaard writes and more with what she believes can be read "between the lines."[2] To frame her analysis Lind nevertheless focuses on Kierkegaard's *Nachlaß* through which she weaves her way with both skepticism and suspicion in the hunt for unconscious motives and conflicts that reveal Kierkegaard as "human, all too human."[3] Ultimately, the results of this method are rather mixed: at times Lind's analysis leads to some illuminating psychological insights, but at other times it slides into absurdity with its wildly speculative and implausible conjectures. Navigating these two poles therefore requires of the reader a great deal of patience and diligence.

Research for this project was made possible by generous support from the Smith Family Fellowship.

1 Lis Lind, *Søren Kierkegaard själv. Psykoanalytiska läsningar*, Stockholm: Carlsson Bokförlag 2000, p. 8.

2 Ibid., p. 10.

3 Ibid., p. 9.

The book is divided into six chapters of varying length and quality. In Chapter 1, Lind provides a brief biographical sketch of Kierkegaard's life, family, and personal relationships, and there is nothing here that is out of the ordinary. Following this chapter, however, Lind makes an abrupt shift to a highly polemical (and often shocking) psychoanalytic approach with which she frames her investigation in Chapters 2–6 and by which she narrows in on themes such as sexual repression, deception, envy, manipulation, and sadomasochism. Lind's general conclusion from these five chapters is that Kierkegaard is both a deeply troubled and a deeply troubling individual, and she comes to this conclusion in part by focusing on what she understands to be several particular sexual and psychological pathologies at play in Kierkegaard's personality. With the aim of providing a sense of how Lind's psychoanalytic readings look in practice, we can touch upon what Lind sees as two of the more significant of these pathologies.

First, Lind claims that from his early years up until his death Kierkegaard wrestled with the turbulent force of an unruly libido. In true Freudian fashion, Lind begins her analysis with Kierkegaard's relation to his father, which she notes is characterized by masochism and latent homosexuality, and through which Kierkegaard "indirectly strengthened his feminine identification" by assuming the role of the passive recipient of punishment delivered from the hand of an authority figure.[4] This power relationship in turn bleeds into Kierkegaard's heterosexual investment of his libido in Regine Olsen, where he sets himself up as the sadistic master claiming the right of ownership over his female inferior.[5] Moreover, in Lind's reading Kierkegaard's libido even latches on to what would seem to be rather peripheral characters in the Kierkegaardian narrative such as Regine's father. Thus, in pointing to the 1848 journal entry where Kierkegaard describes his meeting with Terkild Olsen in Fredensborg,[6] Lind suggests not only that Kierkegaard assumes the role of seducer, but that his homosexual longings are also reciprocated by the seduced. As she remarks, "Councilor Olsen's exaggerated reaction to Kierkegaard's encroachment awakens suspicion that even the older man harbored an unconscious homosexual inclination for the younger, whose *liaison* with his daughter he had so passionately engaged himself in."[7] In Lind's assessment, 1849 marks a crucial year for Kierkegaard in which, following the breaking of contact with Regine, his "heterosexual libido was put out for good."[8] Consequently, Kierkegaard now turns the full force of his homosexual libido towards Mynster, to whom Kierkegaard assigns the role of the authoritative father-figure, who punishes his son and through whom Kierkegaard finds an avenue to live out his sadomasochistic fantasies.[9] Following Mynster's death, Kierkegaard no longer has a clear object for his love-hate, and therefore during his final attack on the

---

4 Ibid., p. 22.
5 Ibid., p. 27.
6 *SKS* 21, 80–1, NB7:10 / *KJN* 5, 83–4.
7 Lind, *Søren Kierkegaard själv*, p. 36.
8 Ibid, p. 43.
9 Ibid., p. 50; p. 126.

church he directs his libido entirely inward, resulting in what Lind understands to be a radical expression of narcissism.

Second, Lind attempts to bring to light what she sees as the pathology in Kierkegaard's perpetual ploy of hiding and deception, which she also ties to his obsessive need for control. In Lind's view, Kierkegaard is something of a master deceiver who has taken great efforts in his writings, and particularly in his *Nachlaß*, to remain hidden from the world. As Lind makes clear, such a tactic can once again be traced back to Kierkegaard's struggles with repressed homosexuality as well as to his masochistic feminine identification. For example, in discussing a journal entry from 1837 describing a scene in which Kierkegaard rushes off to his room after having received correction (or perhaps even scolding) from his father,[10] Lind remarks that "the father's surprising authoritative outburst was experienced as equivalent to a sexual violation, such that the young Kierkegaard was forced immediately to get out of sight in order to hide his arousal and shame."[11] In Lind's analysis, Kierkegaard's horror at becoming vulnerable before others is tied to a "deep-rooted fear of intimacy"[12] that drives Kierkegaard into hiding behind protective layers of irony and elaborate literary constructions, all of which are intended to serve the task of manipulating the picture that others have of him.[13] Furthermore, his fear leads him to distance himself from others so that from a safe vantage point he can thereby voyeuristically claim complete power over all of those who fall under his preying gaze.[14] For Lind, it is precisely Kierkegaard's ability to "hypnotize the reader with his passion and irony" as well as his "manipulative presence"[15] that makes him so dangerous and that therefore necessitates the method of skeptical and suspicious psychoanalysis as the most appropriate manner for engaging with the elusive Dane.

As regards reception, Lind's book attracted some initial attention in Scandinavia with assessments of its value dividing largely along disciplinary lines. Thus, for example, whereas one reviewer from within the psychoanalytic tradition praises the work as interesting, penetrating, and admirable,[16] scholars from other academic traditions have described Lind's project as "primitive psychological reductionism" and "strangely hostile and unnecessarily solipsistically oriented"[17] or, more bitingly, as "nonsense presented with enormous pretension" that provokes fits of laughter.[18] As becomes clear from a survey of the reviews, underlying this disagreement is a deeper

---

10 *SKS* 17, 135, BB:42 / *KJN* 1, 128, 130.

11 Lind, *Søren Kierkegaard själv*, pp. 73–4.

12 Ibid., p. 135.

13 Ibid., p. 143.

14 Ibid., p. 146.

15 Ibid., p. 7.

16 Eija Repo, review in *The Scandinavian Psychoanalytic Review*, vol. 24, 2001, pp. 131–3.

17 Kirsten Klercke, review in *Kierkegaardiana*, vol. 22, 2002, p. 266; p. 269.

18 Thure Stenström, "Nonsense om Kierkegaard locker till skrattkrevader," *Svenska Dagbladet*, January 30, 2001, p. 54.

debate over the validity of the psychoanalytic method itself and whether or not such a method can be appropriately employed in the service of biography in general.[19]

To conclude, we may return to the Preface and to one remark in particular that stands out from the others. As Lind writes, "One who has already become familiar with Kierkegaard and who has formed an opinion of him might have a difficult time recognizing him from my sketches...."[20] Of all the claims Lind makes over the course of her psychoanalytic project, this is undoubtedly the one to which the reader can assent with the fewest reservations. In the end, however, this same reader will likely be left with the suspicion that any failure of recognition ultimately has little to do with the discrepancy between who the reader may believe Kierkegaard to be and who Lind so confidently asserts him to be, but instead has more to do with the rather questionable use of what proves to be a far from unproblematic hermeneutical method that has been pushed well beyond the limits of what most scholars outside of the psychoanalytic tradition would understand as reasonable.

Matthew T. Nowachek

---

19 See, for example, Klercke, review in *Kierkegaardiana*, vol. 22, 2002, p. 266. Some scholars have even questioned the practice of treating Kierkegaard's journals and papers as straightforwardly autobiographical, which would also call into question Lind's psychoanalytical analysis. See, for example, Henning Fenger, *Kierkegaard: The Myths and their Origins*, trans. by George C. Schoolfield, New Haven and London: Yale University Press 1980.

20 Lind, *Søren Kierkegaard själv*, p. 9.

Reviews and Critical Discussions

Bergil, Christina, "Kierkegaard och Freud," *Sydsvenskan*, August 20, 2000, p. A4.
Bolinder, Jean, "Kierkegaard in på livet," *Skånska Dagbladet*, November 8, 2000, p. 13.
Ejvegård, Rolf, "Kierkegaard skrev ihjäl sig vid 42 års ålder," *Östgöta Correspondenten*, August 14, 2000, p. A14.
Klercke, Kirsten, review in *Kierkegaardiana*, vol. 22, 2002, pp. 265–9.
Repo, Eija, review in *The Scandinavian Psychoanalytic Review*, vol. 24, no. 2, 2001, pp. 131–3.
Rosdahl, Björn, "Vems perversioner driver förtattaren?" *Helsingborgs Dagblad*, October 16, 2000, p. 26.
Sjöstrand, Lars, "Var Søren Kierkegaards tungsinne andligt eller psykiatriskt betingat?" *Läkartidningen*, vol. 104, no. 42, 2007, pp. 3131–3.
Stenström, Thure, "Nonsens om Kierkegaard lockar till skrattkrevader," *Svenska Dagbladet*, January 30, 2001, p. 54.

Arnold Ljungdal, *Problemet Kierkegaard* [The Problem Kierkegaard],

Stockholm: P.A. Norstedt & Söners Förlag 1964, 120 pp.

Arnold Ljungdal's *The Problem Kierkegaard* was published in Swedish in 1964, with a Danish translation following the year after.[1] Although the overall aim of the book is polemical, Ljungdal articulates a deep ambivalence towards Kierkegaard throughout the text as he repeatedly vacillates between veneration and vitriol. This two-pronged engagement is not strange given Ljungdal's intellectual leanings both as a poet with an interest in Scandinavian literature and as a psychologically-attuned Marxist scholar and political activist with a virulent distaste for Christianity. Ultimately, the aggressive, confrontational, and sweeping nature of Ljungdal's project has been something of a double-edged sword: on the one hand, it initially sparked a lively debate in the Swedish press, but, on the other hand, it is undoubtedly one of the central reasons that Ljungdal's book has been overlooked by a later generation of scholars seeking a more charitable and nuanced account of Kierkegaard's life and thought.

In the Introduction, Ljungdal describes his task and motivation for writing by drawing on dramatic military imagery. As he understands it, the "Kierkegaard fever" that has long been raging on the European continent and in the Anglo-Saxon countries is now beginning to invade Sweden, and therefore the proper response is "to prepare one's arsenal and to ready the canons!"[2] For Ljungdal, Kierkegaard's religious message represents a "sick, twisted, and perverse" form of life-denying asceticism, and as such, he takes upon himself the charge of helping his Swedish contemporaries to distance themselves from it.[3] Despite these scathing words, Ljungdal nevertheless has difficulty discarding Kierkegaard altogether, for he not only finds certain aspects of Kierkegaard's authorship aesthetically and philosophically intriguing, but he

Research for this project was made possible by generous support from the Smith Family Fellowship.

1 Arnold Ljungdal, *Problemet Kierkegaard*, Stockholm: P.A. Norstedt & Söners Förlag 1964. (Danish translation: *Problemet Søren Kierkegaard*, trans. by Ina Rohde, Copenhagen: Stig Vendelkærs Forlag 1965.) This text develops some of Ljungdal's earlier ideas from his essay "Existentialisten Kierkegaard," *Zenit*, vol. 6, 1962, pp. 11–13; p. 16. The author's name occurs occasionally in the secondary literature as Ljungdahl.

2 Ljungdal, *Problemet Kierkegaard*, p. 5.

3 Ibid., p. 6.

also sees in Kierkegaard a potentially useful ally in the fight against the thriving logical empiricism fashionable in the Swedish academic circles of his time. For the remainder of the book, Ljungdal divides his work into two major parts, which we may briefly touch upon in turn.

Ljungdal's purpose in the first part is to challenge both Kierkegaard's presentation of himself as a Christian thinker and Kierkegaard's view of faith in general. As he argues, despite Kierkegaard's apparent claim to the contrary,[4] there is nothing in the authorship that supports Kierkegaard ever having an authentic meeting with a religious reality. Rather, everything from beginning to end is merely intellectual word-chopping that lacks in all genuine inwardness. For Kierkegaard, God is utterly qualitatively distinct, which makes personal contact impossible and necessitates that one undertake an irrational leap in order to enter into faith. Moreover, Kierkegaard insists that the path to faith must necessarily wind through the torturous terrain of guilt-ridden asceticism where one is forced to put to death all desire and love one has for life.

This view of Christianity, claims Ljungdal, is a reflection of Kierkegaard's psychological sickness that can be traced back to his upbringing and specifically to his tormented love-hate relationship with his father, as well as to his failed engagement to Regine with its accompanying sexual inhibition, anxiety, and guilt. In wrestling with these psychological problems, Kierkegaard turns not only to masochistic self-torment, but he also directs his neurosis outward against the community through his attack on the *Corsair* and the Danish State Church. Kierkegaard's battle with the latter was especially bitter in that Kierkegaard focuses much of his vitriol on the bishop J.P. Mynster, who, Ljungdal suggests, played the role of surrogate father in the absence of any healthy relation between Kierkegaard and his own father. Only at the end of this attack, argues Ljungdal, does Kierkegaard find relief from his derangement in that he finally was able "to give expression to the whole intertwined ambiguity and ambivalence of his feelings—to his unquenchable love-hate relationship with the religion that had been his life's comfort and his life's misery."[5]

In the second part, Ljungdal focuses on Kierkegaard as a philosopher and a writer as well as the Danish thinker's posthumous relevance. Ljungdal is far more positive here, arguing that instead of dismissing Kierkegaard as do the logical empiricists, we ought rather to read him through the lens of moral philosophy. With this claim, Ljungdal follows closely in the footsteps of Sartre before him in pointing to the moral significance of choice and responsibility as well as to the central importance of freedom as this plays out in the leap. Although there is little in this exposition that is novel, Ljungdal does nevertheless draw an interesting parallel between Kierkegaard and Marx with respect to the role that both play in the critique of speculative systems, even as he recognizes the clear difference between the thinkers in that the former is not concerned with political or social revolution, but rather with inward transformation.

---

4 See *SKS* 17, 254–5, DD:113 / *KJN* 1, 245–6.

5 Ljungdal, *Problemet Kierkegaard*, p. 52.

Perhaps Ljungdal's most significant contribution to Kierkegaard studies is his attempt to re-appropriate certain aspects of Kierkegaard's thought for secular purposes within his contemporary Swedish context. As Ljungdal sees it, his post-World War II era is marked by the overcoming of taboos and the decline of religious tradition, which has created a vacuum that neither science and technology nor logical empiricism can adequately fill. What is needed, he suggests, is a return to a minimalistic form of humanism, and Kierkegaard's moral account of existence can serve as precisely the vehicle to take us there. As such, Ljungdal rejects what he views as Kierkegaard's problematic Religiousness B, and instead he advocates for a version of a non-Christian and nearly content-less religiosity of Religiousness A that is built around human possibility. In the end, then, Ljungdal claims that this humanistic form of religion can play an important role as "an icebreaker which, in a time of darkness and freezing over, keeps a channel of water open towards a horizon beyond the present moment."[6]

With his lucid and sharp polemic, Ljungdal was able to draw a definite line in the sand regarding Kierkegaard, in relation to which scholars could conveniently position themselves. The most intense discussion of Ljungdal's text occurred in the Swedish press in the first few months after its publication, with a number of reviews praising the work and recommending that it be translated into Danish, on the one hand,[7] and with a proportionate number of reviews lambasting the work, on the other hand. Of the latter group, one of the most significant critics was the intellectual Lars Gyllensten, who, in his article "The Problem Kierkegaard Resolved," argues that Ljungdal utterly misunderstands Kierkegaard and thereby contributes nothing of value to the academic discussion.[8] This criticism was apparently significant enough to warrant a response from Ljungdal, in which he in turn accuses Gyllensten of utterly misunderstanding his own argument.[9] This dialogue, if one could call it that, represents little more than two ideologically divergent parties who have lined up on opposite sides of a battlefield only to spend their time shooting over the heads of one another. Unfortunately, this dynamic is largely representative of the entire newspaper debate.

Beyond the initial burst of interest, very little scholarly attention has been given to Ljungdal's book apart from attempts to locate it in the history of Scandinavian Kierkegaard reception.[10] In one sense, this silence is appropriate, for it is certainly the case that Ljungdal gives a myopic reading of Kierkegaard, especially in that he focuses so much attention on *Fear and Trembling*, while ignoring altogether texts such as the upbuilding discourses or *Works of Love* that provide a more detailed

---

6 Ibid., p. 115.

7 See, most notably, Henning Fenger, "Huvudet kallt, hjärtat varmt," *Kvällsposten*, October 4, 1964, p. 4.

8 Lars Gyllensten, "Problemet Kierkegaard upplöst," *Dagens Nyheter*, September 30, 1964, p. 4.

9 Arnold Ljungdal, "Gyllensten, Kierkegaard och mysticismen," *Aftonbladet*, October 13, 1964, p. 4.

10 See, for example, Bernard Delfgaauw, "De Kierkegaardstudie in Scandinavië," *Tijdschrift voor Filosofie*, vol. 38, no. 1, 1976, pp. 142–4.

picture of Kierkegaard's religious message. As such, his view of Kierkegaard is in large part a caricature. In another sense, this silence is not completely justified, for although caricatures are by nature exaggerated and distorted, they nevertheless still contain some small kernel of truth. Just as the caricatures of Kierkegaard published by the *Corsair*, though inappropriate in many ways, represent Kierkegaard in a manner that was not entirely incorrect, so also can we say that Ljungdal's presentation of Kierkegaard and his thought, although certainly lacking in charity and nuance at many points, is not entirely without value. Discerning exactly which aspects of Ljungdal's *Problemet Kierkegaard* meet the mark and which aspects fall short, however, is a task that will need to be left to future readers.

Matthew T. Nowachek

Reviews and Critical Discussions

Ahlberg, Alf, "Den gåtfulle Kierkegaard," *Dala-demokraten*, September 24, 1964, p. 2.

Aspelin, Kurt, "Den provokative Kierkegaard," *Aftonbladet*, September 28, 1964, p. 4.

Asplund, Johan, review in *Stockholms-tidningen*, September 23, 1964, p. 7.

— "Replik till Victor Svanberg," *Stockholms-tidningen*, September 29, 1964, p. 7.

Brandell, Gunnar, "Den orimlige Kierkegaard," *Svenska Dagbladet*, November 23, 1964, p. 4.

Delfgaauw, Bernard, "De Kierkegaardstudie in Scandinavië," *Tijdschrift voor Filosofie*, vol. 38, no. 1, 1976, pp. 136–58, especially pp. 142–4.

Eklundh, Bernt, "Konsten att missförstå Kierkegaard," *Göteborgs-tidningen*, September 21, 1964, p. 2.

Fenger, Henning, "Huvudet kallt, hjärtat varmt," *Kvällsposten*, October 4, 1964, p. 4.

Fält, Helmer, "Kritiskt om kristen kritiker," *Vestmanlands läns tidning*, September 29, 1964, p. 5.

Gyllensten, Lars, "Problemet Kierkegaard upplöst," *Dagens Nyheter*, September 30, 1964, p. 4.

Lappalainen, Jonna Hjertström and Lars-Erik Hjertström Lappalainen, "Sweden: Kierkegaard's Reception in Swedish Philosophy, Theology, and Contemporary Literary Theory," in *Kierkegaard's International Reception*, Tome I, *Northern Europe and Western Europe*, ed. by Jon Stewart, Aldershot: Ashgate 2009 (*Kierkegaard Research: Sources, Reception and Resources*, vol. 8), pp. 173–96, especially pp. 181–2.

Linder, Erik Hjalmar, review in *Göteborgs-posten*, November 9, 1964, p. 2.

Ljungdal, Arnold, "Gyllensten, Kierkegaard och mysticismen," *Aftonbladet*, October 13, 1964, p. 4.

Rydén, Joseph, "Personligt om Kierkegaard," *Jönköpingsposten*, October 5, 1964, p. 6.

Schwanbom, Per, "Personligt om Kierkegaard," *Arbetaren*, January 22, 1965, p. 4.

Strömberg, Sven, review in *Nerikes allehanda*, October 13, 1964, p. 4.

Svanberg, Victor, "Kierkegaard och en sociolog," *Stockholms-tidningen*, September 27, 1964, p. 7.

Waldemar Rudin, *Sören Kierkegaards person och författarskap. Ett försök* [Søren Kierkegaard's Personality and Writings: An Essay],

Stockholm: A. Nilsson 1880, 335 pp.

Sören Kierkegaards person och författarskap. Ett försök (1880)[1] was the first book on Kierkegaard written by a Swedish academic. Its author, Waldemar Rudin, was an influential professor at Uppsala University's Faculty of Theology. Rudin had in his earlier years been a prominent leader of a pietistic movement in the Church of Sweden. He had also taken a deep interest in Kierkegaard's life and writings for several decades (indeed, even while Kierkegaard was still alive).

Rudin's book was based on a lecture series given at Uppsala in 1877, delivered in response to a lecture series on Kierkegaard held by the influential Danish-Jewish literary critic Georg Brandes in Uppsala and Stockholm in 1876. Brandes' lectures were published in 1877 in both Swedish and Danish and can be said to have pioneered the field of "Kierkegaard Studies" in Scandinavia.[2]

Brandes was a freethinker of a rather anti-Christian sort, and his interpretation of Kierkegaard is colored by secularist ideals. He says, for example, that Kierkegaard did not put his talent "in the service of freedom but in the service of uncritical adoration (*Intet deraf blev stillet i Frihedens Tjeneste, Alt i den kritikløse Respekts*),"[3] and that Kierkegaard was "a Jesuit from birth, a Protestant Jesuit" (*en født Jesuit, en protestantisk Jesuit*).[4] Rudin, who was a moderately conservative theologian, quoted these sorts of accusations disapprovingly in his book.[5] Indeed, Rudin disliked Brandes' secularist approach to Kierkegaard intensely and intended his book to be corrective.

---

1 Waldemar Rudin, *Sören Kierkegaards person och författarskap. Ett försök*, Stockholm: A. Nilsson 1880.

2 The Swedish version was published under the title *Sören Kierkegaard*, Stockholm: Seligmann 1877, and the Danish version under the title *Søren Kierkegaard. En kritisk Fremstilling i Grundrids*, Copenhagen: Gyldendal 1877. The Danish version is reprinted in Georg Brandes, *Samlede Skrifter*, vols. 1–18, Copenhagen: Gyldendalske Boghandels Forlag 1899, vol. 2, pp. 249–418.

3 Brandes, *Samlede Skrifter*, vol. 2, p. 262.

4 Ibid., p. 260.

5 Rudin, *Sören Kierkegaards person och författarskap. Ett försök*, p. 4.

It was not only in Sweden that Brandes' secularist Kierkegaard evaluation provoked theologians. In Christiania/Oslo in Norway the theologian Fredrik Petersen—the author of the first systematic interpretation of Kierkegaard's "theology"[6]—delivered lectures in 1876 in opposition to Brandes,[7] and in Finland the theologian Herman Rådbergh wrote a review of Rudin's book in which he said that "after having read Brandes' book and become acquainted with his completely shallow and unfair understanding, one cannot but be grateful to Prof. Rudin for having dealt with the topic."[8]

Rudin's book consists of an Introduction followed by seven chapters. The Introduction is largely polemical and directed against Brandes. The ensuing seven chapters follow Kierkegaard's writings chronologically and consist in large part of long quotations from Kierkegaard's writings interspersed with Rudin's accounts of the various historical contexts of the writings and their various interrelations. Rudin intended his book to be the "First Part" of a two-volume work, and planned to publish a sequel that addressed three "chief questions" about Kierkegaard that Rudin believed needed to be answered in order to adequately understand Kierkegaard, namely: (1) "What he really was as a writer and person" (*[h]vad han egentligen var såsom författare och person*); (2) "What made him what he was" (*hvad som gjort honom till hvad han var*); and (3) "What the preconditions are for understanding and evaluating him" (*hvilka vilkoren äro för att förstå och bedöma honom*).[9] Rudin never published the sequel, however.

Nevertheless, in the Introduction Rudin indicates his answers to the above three questions in the context of accusing Brandes of having got Kierkegaard "completely wrong" (*hafva blifvit framstäld i en grundfalsk dager*).[10] Rudin mentions two specific mistakes in Brandes' Kierkegaard interpretation.

A first mistake is that Brandes "wants to make Kierkegaard a product of his circumstances" (*vill göra Kierkegaard till en ren naturprodukt af omständigheterna*).[11] He mentions, for example, that Brandes views Kierkegaard's religiosity as simply an inheritance from Kierkegaard's father.[12] In opposition to this, Rudin affirms "the workings of divine grace and providence and the free resolutions of the individual" (*den gudomliga nådens och skickelsens verk och den egna frihetens väldiga afgörelse*).[13] In other words, Rudin believes that a correct understanding of

---

6 Fredrik Petersen, *Dr. Søren Kierkegaards kristendomsforkyndelse*, Oslo: P.T. Mallings Boghandel 1877.

7 For more on this, see Thor Arvid Dyrerud, "Norway: You Have No Truth Onboard! Kierkegaard's Influences on Norway," in *Kierkegaard's International Reception,* Tome I, *Northern and Western Europe*, ed. by Jon Stewart, Aldershot: Ashgate 2009 (*Kierkegaard Research: Source, Reception and Resources*, vol. 8), p. 122.

8 Herman Rådbergh, "Sören Kierkegaards Person och författareskap [sic]; ett försök af W. Rudin," *Tidskrift för teologi och kyrka*, vol. 4, 1880, p. 233.

9 Rudin, *Sören Kierkegaards person och författarskap. Ett försök*, p. 13.

10 Ibid., p. 4.

11 Ibid., p. 5.

12 Ibid.

13 Ibid.

Kierkegaard involves appreciating that a work had been wrought in him by God's grace and also that Kierkegaard had contributed to who he was through his own volitional acts.

A further mistake that Rudin sees in Brandes' Kierkegaard interpretation is a failure to appreciate Kierkegaard's "religious viewpoint" (*religiösa ståndpunkt*).[14] According to Rudin, in saying, for example, that Kierkegaard did not put his talent "in the service of freedom but in the service of uncritical adoration," Brandes has missed "the very soul" (*själen*) in Kierkegaard's life and work.[15]

Rudin's book on Kierkegaard contributed to awakening and maintaining an interest in Kierkegaard in particular amongst Swedish theologians in the late nineteenth and early twentieth centuries.[16] In 1923 the most well-known theologian and ecclesiastical figure of the day, the Church of Sweden's Archbishop Nathan Söderblom, published an essay on Rudin in which he claimed that Rudin's book on Kierkegaard was "the most agreeable presentation we have of the greatest writer of the North and its most powerful disciple of Christ in modern times."[17] Around the same time Sweden got its first real Kierkegaard scholar in the form of the young Uppsala theologian Torsten Bohlin, who referred to Rudin's book as "beyond comparison the best work on Kierkegaard as a Christian personality."[18] Nevertheless, Bohlin did not examine or assess Rudin's approach to Kierkegaard in his own work and neither did subsequent Swedish Kierkegaard scholars. So while it is true that Rudin's Kierkegaard book functioned as the primary catalyst of Swedish Kierkegaard studies, it played no direct role in its subsequent development.

Anders Kraal

---

14 Ibid., p. 4.

15 Ibid.

16 An ecclesiastical commentator remarked in 1918 that Rudin's book is "[t]he presentation which more than any other seems to have guided the Swedish reading public into Kierkegaard's world of thought"; see Fredrik Dahlbom, "Torsten Bohlin: Sören Kierkegaards etiska åskådning; med särskild hänsyn till begreppet 'den enskilde,'" *Svensk kyrkotidning*, vol. 14, no. 37, 1918, p. 439.

17 Nathan Söderblom, *Waldemar Rudins inre liv*, Stockholm: Norstedt 1923, p. 78.

18 Torsten Bohlin, *Sören Kierkegaards etiska åskådning. Med särskild hänsyn till begreppet "den enskilde,"* Stockholm: Svenska kyrkans diakonistyrelses bokförlag 1918, p. v.

Reviews and Critical Discussions

Ahlenius, Holger, "Søren Kierkegaard. En dansk biografi och en svensk diskussion," *Vår lösen*, vol. 20, no. 4, 1929, pp. 82–7.
Anonymous, review in *Berlingske Tidende*, June 29, 1880.
Anonymous, review in *Aftonbladet*, July 24, 1880, p. 3.
Anonymous, review in *Allehanda*, August 21, 1880, p. 2.
Anonymous, review in *Stockholms Dagbladet*, November 16, 1880, p. 3.
Henriksen, Aage, *Kierkegaard Studies in Scandinavia: A Historical and Critical Survey*, Copenhagen: Ejnar Munksgaard 1951 (*Publications of the Kierkegaard Society*, vol. 1), pp. 39–42.
Hultgren, Gunnar, "Mysteriet Kierkegaard," *Vår lösen*, vol. 31, no. 8, 1940, pp. 320–1.
Rådbergh, Herman, review in *Tidskrift för teologi och kyrka*, vol. 4, 1880, pp. 231–4.
Skogar, Björn, *Viva vox och den akademiska religionen. Ett bidrag till tidiga 1900-talets svenska teologihistoria*, Stockholm: Symposion Graduale 1993, pp. 136–7.
Söderblom, Nathan, *Waldemar Rudins inre liv*, Stockholm: Norstedt 1923, pp. 77–9.
Sørensen, Axel, review in *Fædrelandet*, July 30, 1880.
Wirsén, Carl David af, review in *Post- och Inrikes Tidningar*, November 11, 1880, p. 3.

Ingmar Simonsson, *Kierkegaard i vår tid* [Kierkegaard in Our Time],

Stockholm: Themis 2002, 334 pp.

Kierkegaard i vår tid was written by poet, author, and playwright Ingmar Simonsson and published in 2002 by Themis Förlag. Since then, Themis has released several additional writings by Simonsson including a second work on Kierkegaard of length and scope comparable to the first.[1] Despite the relatively recent publication of *Kierkegaard i vår tid*, Simonsson's efforts to introduce the Danish thinker to the Swedish public extend back nearly three decades to his play *Kierkegaards Antingen-eller*, which was produced in Stockholm for Teater Aurora and which went on to enjoy a successful one-hundred show running over the course of the 1986–87 season.[2] The current book is therefore a product not only of Simonsson's long-standing interest in Kierkegaard but also of his long-developing relationship with the Dane's thought and writings.

As Simonsson notes in the Introduction, his primary aim is to articulate Kierkegaard's contemporary relevance through a presentation of the poet-philosopher's writings for the Swedish reader who is interested in Kierkegaard, but who may nevertheless be intimidated by the Dane's language and ideas.[3] The majority of the text is dedicated to Kierkegaard's pseudonymous authorship with one chapter each afforded to twelve different writings ranging from *Either/Or* to *Practice in Christianity*. In this fashion, Simonsson covers all of Kierkegaard's published pseudonymous works with the exception of Inter et Inter's article "A Cursory Observation Concerning a Detail in *Don Giovanni*." These chapters, however, are of dramatically varied lengths. For example, whereas *Either/Or* receives an impressive forty-six pages, other significant works such as *Fear and Trembling* and *Practice in Christianity* are

Research for this project was made possible by generous support from the Smith Family Fellowship.

1 Ingmar Simonsson, *Människans möjligheter—enligt Kierkegaard*, Stockholm: Themis 2013.

2 This play was later published in celebration of the bicentennial of Kierkegaard's birth. See Ingmar Simonsson, *Kierkegaards Antingen-eller*, Stockholm: Themis 2013.

3 Ingmar Simonsson, *Kierkegaard i vår tid*, Stockholm: Themis 2002, p. 7.

given a comparatively meager twelve pages and thirteen pages, respectively.[4] This exposition of the pseudonymous writings is framed by three chapters on the front end that provide a general overview of some of the major themes in Kierkegaard's writings, discuss both Kierkegaard's debut essay on H.C. Andersen and his dissertation *The Concept of Irony* as well as introduce the pseudonymous authorship, and by three chapters on the back end that survey the non-pseudonymous writings *Works of Love*, *The Point of View*, and *The Moment*.

Furthermore, in the service of his general aim Simonsson places Kierkegaard into dialogue with a host of more recent thinkers hailing from a variety of academic disciplines. For example, alongside Kierkegaard's voice are heard the voices of familiar figures such as Adorno, Bakhtin, Bauman, Bourdieu, Camus, Foucault, Freud, Habermas, Heidegger, Jung, Kafka, Lévinas, Marcuse, Nussbaum, and Sartre.[5] One consequence of incorporating such a broad line-up of intellectuals into his exposition of Kierkegaard's thought and writings is that Simonsson has a tendency at times to wander off course into what seems like rather secondary discussions, which on occasion gives the text the feel of a general introduction to contemporary intellectual history rather than an in-depth engagement with Kierkegaard. Fortunately, however, Simonsson is usually successful in directing his detoured reader back to Kierkegaard's text.

One of the more interesting and valuable aspects of the book is the discussion Simonsson affords to Kierkegaard's use of pseudonyms. For Simonsson, Kierkegaard's pseudonymous authorship can be thought of as "polyphonic poetry in completely different voices," and to miss this point is to miss a large part of Kierkegaard's thought behind his work.[6] What is of particular interest in this exposition is the perspective Simonsson brings to the topic as a dramaturge and the comparison he draws between Kierkegaard's pseudonymous project and the world of theater. As he argues, the pseudonyms function for Kierkegaard much like characters in plays function for the playwright, namely, as providing various roles and world-views from which one is able to explore and to test existential possibilities.[7] Moreover, just as following characters in a play as they struggle to overcome obstacles can prove existentially enlightening for an audience, putting oneself into the struggles of Kierkegaard's authors can likewise prove existentially valuable for Kierkegaard's readers as they navigate the complexities of their own lives.

In addition, Simonsson claims that Kierkegaard's method of pseudonymity carries particular significance with respect to the way in which Kierkegaard's authors challenge the reader to become a concrete existing individual in defiance

4 This is likely a reflection of Simonsson's own aesthetic interests as well as the fact that Simonsson, in his previous work on Kierkegaard, dedicated much of his attention to *Either/Or*.

5 Simonsson engages with a host of thinkers in addition to those named here, some of which are less well-known. Such broad engagement is reflected in the fact that the bibliography lists 77 secondary sources.

6 Simonsson, *Kierkegaard i vår tid*, p. 39.

7 Ibid., pp. 43–4.

of senseless conformity to "the crowd" (*Mængden*). It is on this issue, Simonsson suggests, that Kierkegaard is perhaps the most relevant for our time—a point demonstrated by the fact that Kierkegaard's critique of mass society and his effort to fight the oppression of the many has been shared or taken up by thinkers as significant as Heidegger, Jung, Fromm, Marcuse, Foucault, and Bauman.[8] As Simonsson nicely puts it, "Kierkegaard's reaction against 'the outer becoming the inner' receives another meaning today. We can see it as resistance against various powers that threaten our inner life and as an assertion of the significance of the self in defying this gigantic influence to which we are presently subjected. It is precisely our own existence that is on the line."[9]

With respect to reception, *Kierkegaard i vår tid* has not had nearly the same broad appeal and success as Simonsson's earlier dramaturgical project. Despite the scant number of reviews the book received, one of these was nevertheless written by the respected literary scholar Thure Stenström, who was fairly positive, but at times also ambivalent about the book. For example, Stenström describes the text as providing "a good number of interesting and useful observations," and he compliments Simonsson for his energetic presentation, depth of learning and patience, but he also points out in a more critical vein that Simonsson's engagement with Kierkegaard's writings is at places rather thin and that the work suffers from several stylistic shortcomings.[10] In the end, however, Stenström remarks that although Simonsson's task is without question a simplification and popularization of Kierkegaard's thought and writings, such a task can still be of value, especially when taken up with the dedication Simonsson displays—a dedication appropriate for a thinker with whom it is never quite possible to be finished.

In conclusion, we may note that *Kierkegaard i vår tid* is rather typical as a piece of Swedish Kierkegaard scholarship in the sense that it remains largely introductory and expository.[11] This, however, is not necessarily a bad thing, for accessible introductions to Kierkegaard's thought and writings are still needed and still prove helpful in the Swedish context where Kierkegaard continues to be seen as something of an enigma. What is potentially more problematic is that the book is also typical in the sense that it affords a great deal of attention to the pseudonymous writings to the exclusion of Kierkegaard's other works. Indeed, Simonsson himself even makes the explicit choice not to engage in any depth with the upbuilding

---

8 See ibid., pp. 52–7.

9 Ibid., pp. 58–9. Simonsson makes a similar connection between Kierkegaard and the contemporary critique of mass society in his chapter on *The Sickness unto Death*, pp. 241–60.

10 Thure Stenström, "Kierkegaard populariserad," *Svenska Dagbladet*, November 26, 2002, p. 52.

11 For a good description and survey of typical Swedish Kierkegaard scholarship, see Jonna Hjertström Lappalainen and Lars-Erik Hjertström Lappalainen, "Sweden: Kierkegaard's Reception in Swedish Philosophy, Theology, and Contemporary Literary Theory," in *Kierkegaard's International Reception*, Tome I, *Northern and Western Europe*, ed. by Jon Stewart, Aldershot: Ashgate 2009 (*Kierkegaard Research: Sources, Reception and Resources*, vol. 8), pp. 173–96.

discourses.[12] Such a relation to Kierkegaard's authorship is really no different from that which Kierkegaard described in 1848 when he wrote, "With my left hand I passed *Either/Or* out into the world, with my right hand *Two Upbuilding Discourses*; but they all or almost all took the left with their right."[13] Therefore, given how Simonsson frames his exposition and given the texts on which he focuses, it would perhaps have been more appropriate and accurate had the book instead been entitled *The Left-Handed Kierkegaard in Our Time*.

Matthew T. Nowachek

---

12 Simonsson, *Kierkegaard i vår tid*, p. 8. Simonsson does mention the upbuilding discourses at a few places in his exposition, but only in passing. See, for example, p. 50; p. 104; p. 131; p. 203; p. 300; and p. 308.

13 *SKS* 16, 21 / *PV*, 36.

Reviews and Critical Discussions

Eriksson, Johan, review in *Bonniers litterära magasin*, no. 1, 2003, p. 95.
Hoff, Jan, review in *Computer Sweden*, no. 14, 2003, p. 6.
Stenström, Thure, "Kierkegaard populariserad," *Svenska Dagbladet*, November 26, 2002, p. 52.